Ideology of the Hindi Film

Ideology of the Hindi Film

A Historical Construction

M. Madhava Prasad

DELHI
OXFORD UNIVERSITY PRESS
CALCUTTA CHENNAI MUMBAI
1998

Oxford University Press, Great Clarendon Street, Oxford OX2 6DP

Oxford   New York
Athens   Auckland   Bangkok   Calcutta
Cape Town   Chennai   Dar es Salaam   Delhi
Florence   Hong Kong   Istanbul   Karachi
Kuala Lumpur   Madrid   Melbourne   Mexico City
Mumbai   Nairobi   Paris   Singapore
Taipei   Tokyo   Toronto

and associates in

Berlin   Ibadan

ISBN 0 19 564218 X

Typeset by Eleven Arts, Keshav Puram, Delhi 11 0 035
Printed at Pauls Press, New Delhi 110 020
and published by Manzar Khan, Oxford University Press
YMCA Library Building, Jai Singh Road, New Delhi 110 001

For Jan

Preface

I ndian film studies began to acquire an identity as a separate discipline identity in the eighties. While academic interest in Indian cinema has a slightly longer history, the publication of the works of Ashish Rajadhyaksha, Ravi Vasudevan and others, marked the beginning of a focus on cinema, not merely as a site for occasional forays by anthropologists, sociologists, psychologists and Indologists, but as a field with an institutional specificity that could only be ignored at the risk of a serious misreading of its cultural significance.

The question is not simply one of establishing a new discipline, a new enclosure within the humanities for the production of expertise. For film studies, as it participates in the re-definition of culture as an object of study, the primary conceptual shift has to be towards a radical contemporaneity, 'a receptivity to the present' as a way of breaking out of 'a paralyzing historicism' (Dhareshwar 1995: 318). This present is marked by the fact that the distinctions between an indigenous past and an inauthentic alienating interregnum (the staple of post-colonialism) can no longer be taken for granted. The field of culture, uprooted and reconstructed by the democratic revolution, can no longer be located in an eternal, unchanging India. Nor, on the other hand, can any ready reckoner of free-market democracy provide the concepts for grasping the reality of the present or the future in store for us. For film studies, as for cultural studies in general, the challenge is to define its object without recourse to either of these established procedures. In that spirit, the present work examines Indian cinema as a modern cultural institution whose unique features can be related directly or indirectly to the specificity of the socio-political formation of the Indian nation-state.

I take this opportunity to thank the teachers, friends, institutions and strangers who have helped with criticism, materials and support, over the last few years to bring this work to completion.

viii • *Ideology of the Hindi Film*

I am indebted to Marcia Landy, who, as supervisor of my doctoral project, gave me in my moments of uncertainty, her fullest attention and encouragement. A true friend, philosopher and guide, she made it possible for a group of students at the University of Pittsburgh—Amy Villarejo, Mathew Tinkcom, Barbara White, Sally Meckling, Joy Fuqua and myself—to discuss and critically engage with a wide range of debates in aesthetic and political theory. All of them will no doubt agree with me that those couple of years were vital to our intellectual formation.

I thank Paul Bove and Colin MacCabe for the interest they showed and for their crucial interventions at important stages of the project; and Keya Ganguly whose engagement with the project was brief but constructive. T.G. Vaidyanathan and Donald Morton, practitioners of a critical pedagogy, were responsible for introducing me to film studies and for sharpening my critical skills. Thanks are also due to Lisa Armstrong, Abhijit Banerjee, Tuli Banerjee, Moinak Biswas, Satish Deshpande, Lucy Fischer, Mary John, Biju Mathew, Vijay Prashad, Gautam Premnath, Asok Sen, Ravi Vasudevan, Paul Willemen and the Oxford University Press's anonymous reader, who not only commented on the whole text or individual chapters, but also helped to locate films and other materials and discussed the project with me at various stages. A special acknowledgement in this regard is due to Vivek Dhareshwar, Tejaswini Niranjana and Ashish Rajadhyaksha whose encouragement, criticism and extended discussions over the years have been of immeasurable value. For the warm welcome and for making me feel at home during my initial lonely days in Calcutta, and not least for the feast of music, I thank all my friends, in particular Nandinee Bandyopadhyay, Vivek Dhareshwar, Moinak Biswas, Indira Chowdhury, Sibaji Bandyopadhyay, Rahul Bose, Kirstie Millward, Tuklu, Sushil Khana and Rajashri Dasgupta. The opportunity to teach and to discuss some new ideas at the Film Studies department of Jadavpur University helped in revising and expanding the text.

Chapter 2 was read at the Cultural Studies Seminar of the Centre for Studies in Social Sciences, Calcutta in February 1996. I thank my colleagues and other members of the audience for their valuable comments. A slightly different version was presented at the Seminar organized by the National Film Archives of India, Pune on the occasion of the centenary of cinema in 1995.

Chapter 9 was first presented at the Workshop on 'Making Meaning in Indian Cinema' at the Institute for Advanced Study, Shimla in 1995. It was subsequently published in the *Journal of Arts and Ideas* in January 1996.

A part of Chapter 4 was published in the *Journal of Arts and Ideas* (December 1993) with the title 'Cinema and the Desire for Modernity'.

Thanks are also due to the director and staff of the National Film Archives of India, Pune and to the *Screen* Documentation Centre, Bombay for use of the library and help with locating materials.

My debt to Janaki Nair, who has been my companion right through this long period, is too great to be acknowledged. She has been the first and most reliable critic of all that I have written and without her support and encouragement, this book would never have been completed.

Contents

1

Introduction: The Ideology of Formal Subsumption

[A] certain kind of cinema exists only
because a certain kind of state exists.

—*Saeed Mirza*

The Specificity of Indian Cinema

Until recently film theory functioned with the presupposition that there was some profound, ineluctable kinship between cinema and modern Euro-American culture. It had seemed to investigators of the cinematic institution that film technology had been invented to meet an already existing cultural need, that its advent in Europe at the end of the nineteenth century was, so to speak, no accident. The '*emblematic* quality of cinema' was attested to by a series of such 'no-accident' propositions as Judith Mayne (1993: 22) has described them. These situated cinema in a cultural context already inclined towards realist representation, in an era that saw the expansion of consumption supported by modern advertising. This was also the time of emergence of psychoanalysis, which would later provide the tools for analysing the cinematic institution but which in its turn, would appear to have been the manifestation of a historical necessity. (Mayne 22)

Classical Hollywood cinema seemed to exemplify this intimate cultural kinship. Accordingly, film theory occupied itself with the Hollywood film text, considering either particular films or an abstract, general form that stood in for all possible texts in the dominant mode.

It is true that some of the lasting achievements of film theory were made possible by this set of assumptions. But students of mainstream Indian cinema confront here a pre-emptive force that defines it in advance as a *not-yet-cinema*, a bastard institution in which the mere ghost of a technology is employed for purposes inimical to its historic essence.

This hegemonic alliance between advanced capitalism and the cinematic institution was approached by western film theory as a challenge to its efforts at building an alternative cinema committed to progressive social goals. The goal of the theoretical project was to disengage the spectator from his/her habitual, pre-designated location in the dominant cinematic apparatus through a process of critical unravelling of the apparatus, and thereby to produce a politically conscious audience for another cinema. For Indian film studies, the implications of the assumption underlying this have a special significance: if the technology of cinema could be disengaged from the naturalized hegemonic formation within which it served the dominant advanced capitalist ideology, by the same token it could be regarded as in itself empty of any cultural content and capable of entering into other combinations in which its potential could be realized in a completely different form.

Film technology, developed in the capitalist centre, arrived in India during colonial rule and captivated audiences here as it had done elsewhere. It was as part of a movement to promote indigenous enterprise that the idea of an 'Indian cinema' was conceived. If Phalke is considered the pioneer of Indian cinema, it is not only because he made the 'first' Indian film, but because he conceived of film-making as a nationalist, specifically 'swadeshi' enterprise, and produced Indian images to occupy the screens (Rajadhyaksha, *JAI* 1987: 47–8). Film technology thus did not arrive in a vacuum. There was a cultural, political, social field from within which some people, encountering a new technology of representation, devised ways of putting it to uses that accorded with the field. The technology did not bring with it, readymade, a set of cultural possibilities which would be automatically realized through the mere act of employing it. At the same time, the technology is not neutral, simply sliding into the role assigned to it by the cultural-political field it enters. It has its own unsettling, re-organizing effects on the field.

These effects could be of two kinds: (1) effects specific to the technology, deriving from the unprecedentedness of the naturalistic reproduction of the world, the use of a camera to capture reality in movement and replay it at a different site, etc., and (2) effects that can be traced to the western provenance of the technology, where the 'emblematic' features acquire prominence and in keeping with the logic of technical transfers in a colonial or postcolonial situation, assert themselves as the goal of film practice. One could define these as effects deriving, respectively, from film technology on the one hand and from the (western) cinematic apparatus on the other.

To separate the technology in this fashion from the apparatus which it seemed to inhabit so naturally, is to reopen the old question about the neutrality of technology. Today, few people would contest the proposition that technology is never neutral. Nevertheless, when we are talking about transfers of technology across cultures, we have to face the possibility that the established structures of the host culture will determine the way in which it functions there. Thus it has been shown by Rajadhyaksha (*Framework* 1987: 20–67) that still photography, when first introduced into Indian representational practices, did not automatically enforce a realist imperative on these practices. Instead, photographic reproductions were submitted to already existing principles and protocols and subsumed into an art practice governed by non-realist representational aims.[1] Film technology, similarly, enters into a combination of elements within which its reality-effects are employed in ways that conflict with established perceptions of its historic essence. It is equally clear that the introduction of this new element into the Indian context has far-reaching transformative effects. The (western) cinematic apparatus, on the other hand, is a globally effective ideological apparatus which presents a particular combination of elements (where the realism-cinema connection is asserted strongly) as the only realization of the specific genius of cinema. This apparatus also has its determining effects on film-making in a (post)colonial context, serving as a model for a modern aesthetic that every modern nation must aspire to (re)produce, according to the developmentalist logic that governs the rise and co-existence of nation-states.

Indian cinema has evolved under such atypical conditions. As a

---

[1]See Rajadhyaksha, 'Neo-traditionalism: Film as Popular Art in India':

'Portrait painters began using the [photographic] print only to get a good facial likeness, after which they would paint upon the photograph and reintroduce earlier decorative conventions, like planar surfaces, flattened walls and floors. What is more interesting . . . are the more "documentary" pictures taken by Indians. These inevitably use flat planes, emphasising surface, seldom using perspective to suggest a point of entry into the composition or a pathway for the look, jettisoning many of the standard principles of "balance" or symmetry that the Europeans observed (Rajadhyaksha, *Framework* 1987, p. 33). See also Geeta Kapur, 'Mythic Material in Indian Cinema' (*JAI* 14/15: 79–107).

national cinema[2] it is unlike those of the European countries which are (or were) sustained by state support, as part of an attempt to retain a sphere of national activity within a field dominated by Hollywood. When an effort to produce a cinema that would similarly represent the nation was launched in India, the adversary was not Hollywood but the indigenous popular cinema produced in Bombay and Madras. A vast cultural gap and government restrictions prevented Hollywood from expanding very far beyond a small urban élite market.[3] On the other hand, in post-independence India, the policy of independent growth adopted by the state also played a role in creating the conditions for the expansion and consolidation of a national audience, which was, in most parts of the country, either solely captive to the Bombay industry or divided in its loyalties between a regional product, and the Bombay or Hollywood films.[4]

[2] See Higson (1989) for a discussion of the idea of national cinema, with particular reference to Europe. In a European context, the so-called national cinemas are often weak, state-sponsored efforts to counter the Hollywood hegemony as the popular cinema for the majority of Europeans is Hollywood. In India, until now, Hollywood cinema has only enjoyed a restricted audience. Thus, there is a stronger case for identifying Indian cinema as a national cinema. The problem here is one of internal segmentation: raising Hindi cinema to the status of national cinema can only be at the cost of ignoring major regional film industries such as those of Bengal, Maharashtra, Tamil Nadu, etc.

[3] This needs to be qualified. There has been a *popular* audience for 'foreign films' right from the early days of Indian film history. In the colonial era, the government favoured measures to discourage Indian audiences from flocking to the American films which showed the ruling race in an unfavourable light. In this context British policy on cinema, inspired by fears of social disorder, was not unhappy with the trend towards mythologicals (See Baskaran nd). Although the mythologicals may have served their purpose, this did not destroy audience interest in the foreign product. (One wonders if the Nadia films were not designed with an eye on such divided aesthetic loyalties of audiences.) At present, in most cities, there are, apart from the front rows of the exclusively 'foreign film theatres', one or two halls which specialize in reruns of popular Hollywood films (mainly action films) as well as, increasingly, soft porn probably produced exclusively for Third World urban markets. There has also always been a large popular audience for Hollywood and non-Hollywood action films, with stars like Jean-Paul Belmondo, Terence Hill and Bud Spencer, Bruce Lee, Jackie Chan, and Schwarzenegger acquiring their own significant fan following. Hindi films sometimes try to assimilate the content of these films, though not always successfully.

[4] Strictly speaking, we should be speaking of Indian cinemas, rather than one cinema. There is some amount of film production in every major Indian language and there are at least six important non-Hindi film industries, although not all of them are thriving at the moment: Bengali, Kannada, Malayalam, Marathi, Tamil and Telugu. Nevertheless, Hindi cinema has functioned as a site of production and exploration of national identity and ideology, and depends on the talents and finances drawn into it from the other language cinemas. Hindi cinema has also assisted state policy by spreading knowledge of Hindi, the projected national language, across the country. As an industry with a national market, it also attracted talent from all parts of the country, especially from non-Hindi speaking regions like Calcutta and Madras, giving Bombay cinema an undeniable national character.

The cinemas of India, in spite of significant differences,[5] share a common ground, a set of aesthetic concerns, certain dominant tendencies, which show that far from simply remaining in a prolonged state of not-yet-ness, Indian cinema had evolved a particular, distinct combination of elements, putting the technology to a use that, whether consistent with the camera's ontology or not, was consistent enough over time to suggest ideological effectivity.

Even as we recognize the mainstream western cinematic institution as the manifestation of a particular combination of technological, economic, political, cultural and historical elements, and thereby open up a space for the investigation of other such combinations specific to other social formations, it is necessary to acknowledge the dialectical negation of this thesis which consists in recognizing that this particular combination is, indeed, *the* dominant one among all possible combinations, and that it is precisely this that accounts for the primacy it has been accorded in film theory. This dominance is evident not only in the global circulation of Hollywood cinema, but also in the way that realist cinema has proved to be indispensable, in the Indian case at any rate, as the site that enables discourse *about* Indian cinema, providing the tools for critical intervention, determining at an unconscious level, the reading practices we bring to bear on Indian film texts, as well as serving as an ideal for film-making to aspire to. In other words, over the decades, the effects of the apparatus have become more and more prominent, making it difficult to conceive of a culturally distinctive use of technology.

Further, the developmentalist trajectory of the modern Indian state has itself led to the advocacy of an evolutionist aesthetic programme for the cinema, not only by state functionaries but by film-makers (including many who make the song-and-dance films) and intellectuals as well. The industry has been constantly bombarded by journalists, politicians, bureaucrats and self-conscious film-makers with prescriptions for achieving an international-style realist cinema. The not-yet-ness of the Indian popular cinema is thus not just a

[5]Satyajit Ray, among others, has noted the 'artificiality' and inauthenticity of Bombay cinema, attributing this to its lack of a specific cultural base, as it has to cater to a multitude of culturally distinct audiences. From the viewpoint of a realist aesthetic, of which Ray was an untiring champion, this is no doubt true. But since we are speaking of an aesthetic that (as will become clear later) is distinctly and consistently non-realist, such an accusation is premature. Authenticity is a distinctly modern problem. Even in the regional cinemas, a substantial number of films are made in the 'Bombay' style. Thus it seems that what is acutely manifested in Hindi cinema is not exclusive to it, and that we must take into consideration not only the lack of linguistic specificity but also the problems of a transitional social formation.

biased opinion coming from western or westernized critics, but also a thesis at work within the industry as the instrument of a drive towards change. It is thus inadequate to simply explain away the mainstream western cinema as the result of a particular combination of elements, without accounting for the way in which it has produced a common ground for practice and reflection in other areas of the world as well.

This is not only inadequate but also problematic, in so far as this would reduce the specificity of Indian or any other distinct national cinema to a matter of pure cultural difference. Proclaiming the difference of Indian cinema as an obvious and absolute fact in itself would lead us into a specular enclosure within which this difference will be forever defined only by reference to the global dominant, requiring no attempt to investigate the specific structures and logics of the institution as it has evolved in India. This trap can only be avoided by locating the Indian cinematic institution simultaneously on two overlapping grounds: (1) the socio-political formation of the modern Indian state, with its internal structure as a determining factor in cultural production, and (2) the global capitalist structure within which this modern state and the cinema we are dealing with necessarily enter into relations of heteronomy, dependency, antagonism, etc.

The Ideology of Formal Subsumption

This book is partly an attempt to analyse Hindi cinema as an instance of what I propose to call the ideology of formal subsumption. At the centre of this ideology is an ideologeme whose conceptual expression most frequently takes the form of the co-existence of modernity and tradition. Fredric Jameson, who introduced the term ideologeme to critical discourse, defines it as the 'minimal unit' of organization of class discourse:

> The ideologeme is an amphibious formation, whose essential structural characteristic may be described as its possibility to manifest itself either as pseudoidea—a conceptual or belief system, an abstract value, an opinion or prejudice—or as a protonarrative, a kind of ultimate class fantasy about the 'collective characters' which are the classes in opposition (Jameson 1981: 87).

An adequate description of an ideologeme must demonstrate its susceptibility 'to both a conceptual description and a narrative manifestation all at once' (ibid.).

The binary modernity/tradition, whether it is employed to indicate conflict or complementarity, amounts to an explanation, 'a conceptual or belief system' which regulates thinking about the modern Indian social formation. This binary also figures centrally, both thematically and as an organizing device, in popular film narratives.[6] In a social formation characterized by an uneven combination of modes of production only formally subordinated to capital, where political power is shared by a coalition of bourgeoisie, rural rich and the bureaucratic élite, the explanatory scheme in question functions as a disavowal of modernity, an assurance of the permanence of the

[6]A.K. Ramanujan, the late poet and scholar, is reported to have remarked once: 'I do not believe in god; I believe in people who believe in god' (Karnad, Rujuvathu 1994: 40). Ramanujan was more sensitive than most people to the forms in which ideologies were effective in the national discourse. It is not surprising therefore that he should have formulated so well, in a proto-narrative form, a key ideologeme of modern India whose effectivity can be traced in a range of discursive sites where it may not always be so explicitly formulated.

This formulation has the distinct advantage of providing, in its very syntax, a glimpse in miniature of the articulating, structuring effect of this act of suspension of disbelief. The caesura that separates the two segments of the formulation is also the link that reveals the structured, hierarchical relationship between them. We notice here a syntactical relay across the gulf of the caesura, of a subjectivity that first posits and then suspends itself in order to make place for the concluding phrase, 'those who believe in god'.

Belief and unbelief alone are not in question here; they also stand in for a range of meanings associated with the two proposed segments, including the binary of tradition and modernity. The speaking subject here is clearly located in modernity and through the double-barrelled proposition, establishes a relation with the other term, a relation of compromise, a relation in and through which a certain crisis is sought to be resolved. In short, it proposes that the eroding power of modernity, of which the speaker's disbelief is a sign, shall be reined in, suspended, as a gesture of goodwill towards the community of believers, as a declaration of truce, a precondition for the constitution of a nation out of these two segments.

This strategic suspension or disavowal of modernity proposes a fictive contract that either supplements or takes the place of that other fictive social contract (Balibar 1992) which, since the French Revolution, has served as the blueprint of political modernity. What is proposed here is a contractual relationship between two segments of the population, rather than between all individuals, separately defined as Citizens, equal in 'all' respects. The individual, defined in modern political theory as a combination of a political function (citizen) and a pathological, feeling, suffering, experiencing subject is here replaced by two segments of the population, which separately embody these two elements, requiring the act of belief as the bond that will realize the nation. Thus, it is only as a corporate entity composed of these two segments, only in its totality, and not in respect to each individual, that the modern political entity is here realizable.

state of formal subsumption. Such an assurance can only be ideological in nature, operating on an unconscious plane as a guarantee of national identity. It runs counter to the drive, on another level, towards modernization and the establishment of bourgeois hegemony.[7]

Thus the disavowal of modernity on the ideological plane has co-existed with the contrary drive to modernization, the project of passive revolution that the state adopted at its birth. Barring moments in recent history when the state attempted to break the stalemate engendered by this co-existence (the most significant being the era of authoritarian populism culminating in the internal emergency of 1975), the synchronic dimension of modern Indian history has until recently been centrally defined by the state of uneasy equilibrium between these two dynamics.[8]

If some of these processes are becoming visible now it is perhaps because we are nearing the end of that prolonged stalemate and entering headlong into a full-scale transformation which has already rendered obsolete many of the discourses and institutions of the earlier era. The political spectrum has expanded outwards, with Hindu nationalism at one end appropriating the fragile national project in an attempt to re-establish political unity on a communal

---

[7]See Dhareshwar's reading of Ananthamurthy's story, 'Suryana Kudure', in 'Postcolonial in the Postmodern' (*EPW* 1995).

[8]In a note of 1958, entitled 'The Basic Approach', Nehru attempts to rethink some of his fundamental views on modern society. Written at a time when he was grappling with the crisis in Kerala following the setting up of the first elected Communist government there, this text has been described by his biographer S. Gopal as signifying 'a reversion to the earlier Nehru of the 1920s, the conventional Hindu untouched as yet by rationalist ideas and the unquestioning worshipper of Gandhi . . . . He was now a socialist but was seeking to mix his left-wing ideas with a sophisticated form of religious commitment' (Gopal 1984: 62). Present-day neo-Gandhians, who pit Gandhi against Nehru, fail to see this complementarity, and the fact that Nehru himself was the original neo-Gandhian. Rejecting communism because it sacrificed the interests of the individual in the name of society, Nehru proposed a paradoxical model in which 'opportunity is given to the individual to develop, provided the individual is not a selected group, but comprises the whole community'! 'In such a society,' moreover, 'the emphasis will be on duties, not on rights' (Nehru 1983: 285). The confusion and lack of conviction are rounded off at the end when, having introduced a Vedantic notion that supports the idea of society as an organic whole, the author concludes: 'But obviously it does not solve any of [life's] problems and, in a sense, we remain where we are' (ibid: 286). We will see how the ideology of formal subsumption served, in the context of passive revolution, to produce the reassurance that 'we remain where we are'.

foundation;[9] while on the other hand the process of globalization seems to be eroding the function of the state as a political constraint on a re-vitalized, rampaging capitalism.

It is against this background that the question of the state as a factor in cultural processes is examined here. I study cinema as an institution that is part of the continuing struggles within India over the form of the state. Unlike the situation in advanced capitalist countries, where an achieved hegemony manifests itself through the subordination of all internal conflicts to the overall dominance of the state formation, it is my argument that in a peripheral, modernizing state like India, the struggle continues to take the form of contestations *over* the state form. Cultural production too registers this reality through the recurring allegorical dimension of the dominant textual form in the popular cinema. The kernel of truth in Fredric Jameson's controversial assertion that Third World texts are 'necessarily allegorical' (Jameson 1987: 141) is revealed when we read it in this spirit. What the allegorical dimension of texts represents is the continuing necessity to conceive the state form which will serve as the ground for cultural signification. Through the allegorical scaffolding, texts register the instability of their ground of practice and signification, as well as the continuing possibility of struggles *over* the state, or struggles to reconstitute the state. Through such a re-foregrounding of the state as a political rather than a purely administrative entity this study asserts its continued relevance as a ground of transformative struggles.

This study is a critical reading of Indian cinema as a site of ideological production, understood in the spirit of the above remarks, as the (re)production of the state form. It attempts to identify the social bases of the coherence of cinematic ideology or, where relevant, the lack of such a coherence.

The concept of ideology is central to the practice of cultural critique. Marx and Engels themselves defined ideology in at least two different ways. The famous metaphor of the *camera obscura* was employed in *The German Ideology* (Marx 1987) to define ideology as the inverted representation of real social relations. A later definition of ideology described it as the universalization of the particular interests of a class.

[9]See in this connection reflections (in Balibar and Wallerstein 1991) on how when national unity cannot be founded on linguistic homogeneity, racist or other foundations will be sought. See also Deshpande's essay, 'Imagined Economies' (*JAI* 1993: 5–36) for an argument about the erosion of the idea of the nation as a 'community of producers'.

The second definition provides the link with Gramsci's concept of hegemony, which refers to the process of establishment and maintenance of an order that is acceptable to all classes while being under the control and serving the interests of the ruling classes. The 'deputies' of the dominant group exercise the function of 'social hegemony' which consists of

> The 'spontaneous' consent given by the great masses of the population to the general direction imposed on social life by the dominant fundamental group; this consent is 'historically' caused by the prestige (and consequent confidence) which the dominant group enjoys because of its position and function in the world of production (Gramasci 1971: 12).

The complement to social hegemony is the 'direct domination' effected by the use of state power.

Louis Althusser translated Gramsci's terms hegemony and domination as ideological and repressive functions, and borrowing from psychoanalysis, elaborated a systematic theory of ideology as a process of interpellation of individuals as subjects.[10] The constitution of the subject is effected by a process of socialization undertaken by the principal ideological apparatuses of the state: under capitalism these are the school and the family. The reproduction of social relations (the relations of production and power) hinges on this process of subjectification, without which there would only be a state of pure dominance enforced by the repressive apparatus. By responding to the call of the state to identify him/herself, the subject is interpellated or 'recruited' by the Symbolic. The definition of ideology as 'a representation of the imaginary relationship of subjects to their real conditions of existence' (Althusser 1971: 162) suggests that ideology involves a process of self-recognition by which the subject comes to acknowledge the truth or naturalness of its conditions of existence. Ideological processes are unconscious and inescapable: there is no position outside ideology.

Nevertheless, there is a distinction in Althusser between ideology in general as against particular ideologies which opens the way for a consideration of the ideological state apparatuses (ISAs) as sites of struggle. Ideologies are not 'born' in the ISAs, they are not generated by institutions. They arise 'from the social classes at grips in the

[10]In this context it is interesting to note Foucault's contention (Foucault 1982: 208–26) that the specificity of the modern state lies in the combination of two forms of power, which he calls the totalitarian and the pastoral (derived from the Church), one directed at the population as a whole, the other focused on the individual.

class struggle: from their conditions of existence, their practices, their experience of the struggle, etc' (Athusser 1971: 186). The ISAs are thus not monolithic, inescapable prisons in which all individuals are ensnared. It is not a relation between an institution and an individual but an individualized recruitment whose initiation is traceable to the classes in struggle in the social. The ISAs are 'the *form* in which the ideology of the ruling class must *necessarily* be realized, and the form in which the ideology of the ruled class must *necessarily* be measured and confronted' (ibid, 1971: 185–6). This is to say that the institutions or apparatuses which serve an ideological function are the means of production of a consensus about the naturalness of the existing order. These institutions are *state* apparatuses in the sense that the state itself is (apart from its repressive and administrative apparatuses) nothing but the embodiment of the prevailing consensus, and as such has to include the apparatuses through which ideologies are put into circulation. It may be asked how it is that schools and families, which are or can be 'private', are defined as *state* apparatuses. This objection would be justified if these institutions are understood to be agencies created by the state in pursuit of its goals, thereby implying that the state is separate from and pre-exists the ideological apparatuses. However, their role must be understood as consisting in producing and maintaining a representation of the 'resolvedness' of class conflict, the consensual world picture which is the materialization in ideology of the state.

Thus the ideology of (social) *forms* offers the most productive site of inquiry for cultural critique. The critique of 'ideological forms in which men become conscious of [social] conflict and fight it out' follows from the notion of the ideological apparatus as a site of (displaced) class conflict. These forms have a location, a space of elaboration and reproduction, without which they would be robbed of their consistency and durability (Johnson, 1986/87: 45).

It is through the combined effectivity of ideological forms that subjects are constituted and reproduced. In the practice of cultural critique in a Third World context we are made aware of the fact that these forms are neither of a fixed type and number, nor is their combined effectivity predictable according to some fixed model. The crux of the problem lies in the articulated and internally differentiated nature of the hegemonic formation that results from the combination of different modes of production. This is in sharp contrast to the tendency to homogenization that characterizes the hegemonic process in advanced capitalist countries. In other words, certain state forms may be defined by the co-existence of bourgeois and pre-capitalist ideologies, that is neither hegemonic in the advanced capitalist sense, nor constituting purely a case of what Ranajit Guha (1989) has called 'dominance without hegemony', a condition characteristic of the colonial state.

The problematic can be stated in terms of two concepts of the theory of capitalist social processes: one is Marx's distinction between formal and real subsumption, and the other is Gramsci's concept of the passive revolution. Gramsci used the term passive revolution to describe a situation in which a bourgeois state is established first, and then undertakes to create the conditions for its hegemony—the creation of civil society, the expansion of the market, etc. This concept has proved useful to political theory in thinking about the mode of functioning of the postcolonial state. Partha Chatterjee has argued, for instance, that ' "passive revolution" is the *general* form of the transition from colonial to post-colonial nation-states in the 20th century' (1986: 50), and that this mode of transition consists in the establishment of a national state which will undertake reform from above to gradually modernize the nation (ibid: 48).

Within the framework of this general thesis, the specific case of the Indian state requires further elaboration. Social theorists have argued that the Indian state *form* is bourgeois in so far as it is based on the parliamentary democratic form of government identified with bourgeois dominance and because it 'impos[es] on the economy a deliberate order of capitalist planning' (Kaviraj, *EPW* 1988: 2430–1). However, this is still not a bourgeois state in the classic sense because the capitalist class does not occupy a hegemonic position. The Indian state's control is not based on pure repression, but it is not based on the bourgeoisie's 'moral-cultural hegemony' either. Power is exercised by a ruling coalition in which the bourgeoisie is one of the partners, along with the landlords and the professional classes.

The coalitional nature of political power has certain important consequences. The coalition functions through protocols which reflect the pressures that each element of the coalition brings to bear on the other elements in the pursuit of its own interests. Thus, it could be said that two conflicting tendencies co-exist and give rise to a central contradiction of the Indian state: the trajectory of the passive revolution, which is an expression of the bourgeoisie's hegemonic aspirations, conflicts with and is complemented by, what can be termed the politico-ideological process of *reproduction of the conditions of formal subsumption,*[11] a necessity imposed by the coalitional nature of state power. Here the notion of formal subsumption is to be understood in a broad sense as encompassing more than just the economic arrangements. Marx employed the term to distinguish two phases of capitalism. Under conditions of formal subsumption, capital takes control of the production process without transforming it. Real subsumption begins when capital revolutionizes the production process and inaugurates the extraction of *relative* surplus value. But as Balibar has suggested, the distinction has a much broader significance:

> If one thinks about it carefully, the idea of this 'real' subsumption . . . goes a long way beyond the integration of the workers into the world of the contract, of money incomes, of law and official politics: it implies a transformation of human individuality, which extends from the education of the labour force to the constitution of a 'dominant ideology' capable of being adopted by the dominated themselves (Balibar and Wallerstein, 1991: 4).

It is the absence (until recently) of such a thorough-going process of all-round transformation that calls for recourse to 'reproduction of conditions of formal subsumption' as a general term for the synchronic structure consisting of ideological and political arrangements within which the project of passive revolution was put into operation.

It is my contention that the specific form taken by the political structure is of primary importance to the study of ideologies. In the absence of such a specification, cultural critique is condemned to vacillate between the two poles of tradition and modernity. On the other hand, there is a constant temptation to simply regard Indian culture as the 'other' of western culture, to contrast the homogenization of the one with the anarchic exuberance of the other. This mode of analysis is predicated on an erasure of the political difference and an overemphasis on cultural difference abstracted from the social formation as a whole. The attempt here, on the other hand, has been to place cultural production firmly within the

[11]The term formal subsumption is usually employed to refer only to capitalist relations of production. In that area, Jairus Banaji (1990) was one of the few to employ the distinction between formal and real subsumption in an essay on agrarian relations in colonial India that formed part of the famous 'mode of production' debate; see also Alavi (1990). I use the term in a far more general sense, to refer to a relation between capitalist and pre-capitalist domains not only in itself but *as it is represented and reproduced in ideology.*

political and economic framework of the Indian nation-state. It is in the light of such a conceptualization of modern Indian ideology that this study proposes to analyse the cultural work of the Hindi cinema as the exemplification of an aesthetic of formal subsumption. Such a broad characterization clearly cannot be expected to account for all of the products of the Bombay film industry, nor is it meant to provide an exhaustive explanation for all the elements even in films that might correspond to this label. The effort at theorization will have served its purpose if by means of it we are able to make sense of some of the dominant trends within this institution over the last fifty years.

This study proceeds in two directions: (1) it examines, at the most general level, the political, economic, historical and cultural determinants of popular Hindi cinema as a step towards the elaboration of a theoretical framework for Indian film studies; (2) it undertakes a historical construction of a conjuncture in recent Indian history when, in the midst of a major political crisis, the Bombay film industry underwent a significant transformation, affecting its overall structure as well as the formal properties of individual film texts.

Indian Film Studies

In histories of world cinema produced in the west, Indian cinema usually makes its appearance in 1956, the year in which Satyajit Ray burst on the international film scene with *Pather Panchali*.[12] Some narratives may attempt a brief recap of the decades preceding this (Cook: 1990), but in general the evolutionary thrust of film historiography does not allow for a consideration of early Indian cinema as one of the national cinemas of the silent era. Moreover, having begun in 1956, these narratives do not attempt to tell the whole story, however briefly, concentrating instead on those realist/ artistic products which correspond to a certain conception of true cinema. We have already encountered the spontaneous philosophy behind this approach, in the form of the developmentalist ideology which regards non-realist cinema as not-yet-cinema, as well as the emblematism that has dominated theoretical reflections on the field. The prevalence of this ideology has meant that serious writing on

[12]See for eg. David Cook (1990) and Eric Rhode (1978).

Indian cinema was for a long time restricted to a consideration of the works of masters like Ray, Ghatak, and others. The prestige of Indian cinema at home and abroad, was enhanced by such writings, especially by the influential western admirers of Ray, but these writers did not feel the need to situate this cinema in the Indian film historical context, a tendency that was encouraged by the perception that that context served, if at all, only as a backdrop of mediocrity against which the auteurs shone even brighter.

On the other hand, popular Indian cinema has attracted a considerable amount of attention as the site of an authentically folk culture, from anthropologists and Indologists or others employing the tools of these disciplines.[13] In this type of study the tendency is to read popular cinema as evidence of the unbroken continuity of Indian culture and its tenacity in the face of the assault of modernity. Other studies, employing the tools of ethnography, study film culture as a field of reception consisting of popular audiences conceived as a self-sufficient, closed group, ill-at-ease in the modern spaces they inhabit, but whose cultural *needs* are fully satisfied by the films they see.[14]

The first body of texts, while recovering some Indian films as works of art for a national or international high culture, at least do not lose sight of the political dimension, the context of Indian modernity which is a constant concern of the films and film-makers they concentrate on. The second approach, reserved for the popular cinema, however, tends to be largely indifferent to the political dimension, preferring to situate the cinematic institution in a continuous tradition of Indian myth-making and autonomous folk

[13]For instances of this approach, see Kakar (1980), O'Flaherty (1980) and Misra (1985, 1988/89).

[14]How firmly this approach is rooted in western practices of 'othering' is demonstrated by the difference between the goals of ethnographic popular culture studies in the west and in a country like India. In the west such studies (of reception) are engaged in re-affirming the freedom of the 'free individual' by demonstrating the automaticity and inevitability of audience resistance to ideological interpellation. The individual subject is free because she is so constructed as to never completely fit the position that the text offers her. On the contrary, non-western subjects are distinguished by being completely at home in their ideological environment, the films they see corresponding exactly to their needs. The very notion of cultural 'need', which figures prominently in this context, is an indication of the closed system of demand and supply (the perfect market) that is being assumed. Among those who have employed the idea of cultural need are S. Bahadur (1982, 1985), A. Nandy (1987–8), R. Thomas (1985, 1987). Reception studies/ ethnographies include S. Dickey (1993), Pfleiderer and Lutze, and a 'quickie' by Dissanayake and Sahai (1992).

culture. Thus, an effective division of labour is posited between these two kinds of cinema: one is modern, informed by the concerns and cares of the modern nation-state; while the other is the domain of 'tradition' or oral/folk culture (depending on whether the interest in cinema is of Indological or ethnographic provenance). Some even attribute to the latter a conscious purpose: of asserting its autonomy, difference and even hostility to the 'modern' sector (Nandy 1987–8: 1.1–1.3).

Such an approach, which reproduces the ideology of formal subsumption in critical discourse, does not take into account the fact that the relation between popular cinema and the cultural 'community' that converges around it as its privileged collective addressee is mediated by the market. It disregards the fact that the functioning of the capitalist industry which produces and markets these films is determined by a variety of factors, including the political structure and the hegemonic project of the modern state; that there can be no simple and unmediated reproduction of 'tradition', 'myth' or any other residual substance by a cultural institution that is based on modern technology and relies on the desires and interests of dispersed, anonymous audiences, some of them created by the industry itself. Nor does it take into account the unconscious processes that inform cultural production and reception, except in a transhistorical, Jungian form, where myths and archetypes propagate themselves through the unconscious agency of human beings.

In recent years, however, there has emerged a small but growing body of critical writing which situates the popular cinematic institution in a modern political-economic context, national as well as global.[15] Chidanand Das Gupta's *The Painted Face* (1991) and Sumita S. Chakravarthy's *National Identity in Indian Popular Cinema* (1993) are two book-length studies of recent origin which attempt a

[15]In what follows only a few texts from which this study derives a problematic are discussed. Apart from the texts discussed below, mention may be made of writings by P. Bandhu (1992), V. Dhareshwar and T. Niranjana (1996), A. Nandy (1987–8), M.S.S. Pandian (1992), S.V. Srinivas (1996), R. Thomas (1987), and P. Willemen (1993), which evince a shared concern for theoretical advances in the study of Indian cinema even as they differ vastly in their approaches. The writings of film-makers like Ritwik Ghatak, Dadasaheb Phalke, Satyajit Ray, Mrinal Sen, Kumar Shahani are also of theoretical interest.

More compilations of texts from the early decades of cinema history, such as Bandyopadhyay (1993) and Basu and Dasgupta (1992) are an urgent necessity. So is the project to make available to the national public the writings on cinema that exist in the regional languages, especially Bengali, Hindustani, Marathi, Telugu and Tamil.

comprehensive understanding of Indian popular cinema. Das Gupta describes his book as an exploration by a critic committed to art cinema of 'the mind behind the Indian popular film' (ix). The justification for such a compromising venture is the rise to power of the Telugu film star N.T. Rama Rao, which reveals, once again, the power of cinema over the masses. For the most part, Das Gupta conforms to the safe model of cinema-as-myth, and while recovering a few exceptions from the general mass, regards Hindi cinema as trash that is worth worrying about. While employing Sudhir Kakar's and Ashish Nandy's ideas about the Indian psyche, mythology, etc., he is more brazen than them in identifying popular Hindi cinema with a 'primitive' mass at the core of Indian society (1991: 26), while redeeming another segment that is capable of analytical thinking and appreciates realism. The masses' inability to distinguish myth from fact is Das Gupta's central thesis, and at the end of the long journey through popular cinema, he is relieved to be able to return to his realist haven.

Sumita S. Chakravarty deploys some of the metaphors and discourses used by Das Gupta while rejecting his simplistic judgement. Most importantly, Chakravarty relocates discussions of Indian cinema within the context of the modern nation-state emphasizing its 'eminently contemporary mode of expression' (1993: 8). Such a shift away from 'traditional accounts of this cinema' is of vital importance in a situation where the 'myth' and 'Indian psyche'-based interpretations dominate, with their eternalist proclamations, and while claiming to reveal the truth about Indian cinema, actually contribute to the maintenance of an Indological myth: the myth of the mythically minded Indian. To maintain, as Chakravarty does following Stephen Heath, that 'no film is not a document of itself and of its actual situation in respect of the cinematic institution' (ibid: 164) is not simply to opt for a better approach to Indian cinema; it is also to assert the radical contemporaneity of the time we live in, the determining effect of the synchronic structure of modern India on all our memories of the past.

Chakravarty's metaphor of 'imperso-nation' (although she calls it a concept, it is closer to the 'puncepts' of American deconstruction), however, echoing Das Gupta's metaphor of the 'painted face' and justified by the centrality of performance (as opposed to realist acting), seems an inadequate signifier for the diversity of the content she presents. It seems to indicate her desire to locate Indian cinema in an indeterminate, postmodern global culture. Of course, the world-wide circulation of Hindi cinema, among Indian migrants as well as other Third World audiences, may seem to justify such a move. But by doing so, the specificity of Non Resident Indian (NRI) nostalgia, the question of why Hindi cinema appeals to certain Third World audiences, and the entirely different question of the national context of production and distribution are lost sight of. The metaphor functions, most of the time, as a non-interfering linking device, making its appearance at the beginning of every analysis, only to be forgotten as the film text begins to reveal its complexities. It thus ends up functioning rather as a signifier of the absence of a theoretical framework. A dependence on thematic unities results in a blindness to generic differences, to the questions of form and address, and the history of audience segmentation, a weakness reflected, for instance, in the odd suggestion that new cinema was addressed to 'rural and/ or urban working class' audiences (1993: 246).

One of the early attempts at theorizing Indian aesthetic modernity and within that framework, exploring the specific modern character of cinema, was undertaken by a group associated with the *Journal of Arts and Ideas*. Under a broadly defined programme of investigation into Indian modernity, Geeta Kapur (1987), Anuradha Kapur (1993) and Ashish Rajadhyaksha (1987, 1993) have produced studies of the evolution of a modern aesthetic from the beginnings in colonial nineteenth-century India to the present, focussing on theatre, art and cinema. These studies have demonstrated the importance of the question of *frontality* as a mode of representation in popular culture:

> . . . frontality of the word, the image, the design, the formative act. This yields forms of direct address; flat, diagrammatic and simply profiled figures; a figure-ground pattern with only notational perspective; repetition of motifs in terms of 'ritual play'; and a decorative mise-en-scène' (G. Kapur 1987: 80).

In the context of indigenous attempts to master a new technology, the still camera, the 'aesthetic relation' (Rajadhyaksha, *Framework* 1987: 32) implied by frontality is plunged into 'a crisis regarding questions such as just how the frame may be entered, or the ethics of "directly" apprehending the "real" ' (ibid: 33). This description tends to somewhat overemphasize the role of technology in producing the crisis and only hints at the political constraints which are more explicitly stated in a reading of early Indian cinema through this thesis: 'Pulling towards the static, the gaze pulled towards [the] idealist, purely specular *frontal* aspect of the image' (*JAI* 1987: 67). The frame's ability to 'directly' apprehend the real was thus constrained by an idealization, offering the image as an anchor, a resting point for the gaze. It was thus a case of a technologically aided reproduction of a visual economy that is related to the institution of *darsana* (see Chapter 3). These critics also develop the points of contrast between this mode and the realist mode, with its different set of spectatorial protocols. Anuradha Kapur, writing on theatre, outlines the cultural implications of the two divergent types of image-spectator relations thus:

> Frontality of the performer *vis-à-vis* the spectator . . . enables among other things this relationship of erotic complicity. Now 'frontality' has several meanings in the open theatres of earlier times. But perhaps a set of altogether different meanings come about with the construction of proscenium theatres, which is where Parsi companies performed. In open theatres 'frontality' of the performer indicated a specific relationship between viewer and actor. Turning the body towards the spectator is a sign that there is in this relationship no dissembling between the two: the actor looks at the audience and the audience looks at the actor; both exist—as actor and audience—because of this candid contact. A reciprocally regarding theatre transaction of this kind is substantially different from one made in a theatre that takes an imaginary fourth wall, standing where the stage ends and the seating begins, as its governing convention. Parsi theatre companies perform in the proscenium but take as their governing convention an eye and body contact that comes from earlier open stages (A. Kapur 1993: 92).

This combination of codes, old and new, also signifies a combination of narrative movement, and spectacle as that which arrests the gaze. In the Parsi theatre, the narrative, confined to the frame of the stage, proceeds in linear fashion but the actors 'display themselves', thereby continually arresting the narrative flow. This is not however a serial alternating process but one in which both 'presentation' and linear progression occur simultaneously.

In the cinema, however, this unified 'spectacular narration' is over time broken up into its component parts and a serial recombination of the two codes is effected. This has been cogently argued by Ravi Vasudevan, who demonstrates, through an analysis of a segment from *Andaz* (1949), how this combination of codes takes place and how and what it signifies (Vasudevan, *JAI* 1993: 60–6). The serial combination includes three kinds of elements: segments of linear narrative, brief moments of iconic stasis, and the tableau, in which a static visual arrangement is infused with narrative value. Vasudevan relates this combination to the exigencies of Indian culture, defining it as 'a rhetorical strategy which makes the cinema both attractive as something new in the field of the visual, and culturally intelligible because it incorporates a familiar visual address' (ibid: 65). Here, Vasudevan seems to be interpreting the combination of codes in purely textual terms by suggesting that the icon and the tableaux simply facilitate access to the pleasures of the modern. He offers a stronger and more suggestive reading later, observing that 'there is a strong tendency to subordinate movement and vision toward a stable organization of meaning, in an iconic articulation. This has a parallel in the way in which the narrative reorganizes the family so as to secure a stable position for the middle class hero' (ibid: 72). This reading links the textual strategies to 'a certain normalizing discourse and hegemonic closure' (ibid: 72). It points in the direction of an active mobilization of the 'familiar' in the service of a hegemonic cultural project. Vasudevan rightly rejects any sociologically inspired allocation of the pleasures deriving from the use of these different codes to different segments of the audience and emphasizes the difficulty of separating traditional and modern modes of address (ibid: 72).

One of the aims of this book is to carry this project forward by foregrounding the political dimension of the problem of textual *form*. The aesthetics of frontality and its interface with realist conventions of narration have to be seen in the light of the individual subject's position within different political orders and the corresponding constraints and protocols of spectatorship. The realist barrier that the proscenium arch represents as well as the degree of integration and linearization of the narrative are both determined by a social competence related to the generalized figure of the citizen and the constraints and compulsions of cultural production and commodification in capitalist societies.

The difference between the aesthetics of frontality and the aesthetics of realism may be formulaically represented as follows: In the frontal spectacle, the performer is the bearer of a message from the Symbolic, and the performance a vehicle for its transmission to the spectator through the direct contractual link established in the theatre. In the realist narrative, the Symbolic, in its *contractual* aspect, is represented by the citizen-spectator, whose interpretive authority brooks no challenge from within the frame of representation. This requires some elaboration.[16]

The question is: what is the nature of the fictive contractual relation that sustains the film text as performance? The answer suggested by the above formula is that in performances governed by the frontal aesthetic relation, a message/meaning that derives from a transcendent source is transmitted to the spectator by the performance, whereas in the realist instance, no such transcendent source of a meaning/ message can be posited. Instead, the text is figured as *raw material* for the production of meaning, the latter task being the spectator's by right. Thus, in the first case, the performance as a whole (i.e., including the activity on stage and in the seats) is an apparatus for the *devolution of a message/meaning* that pre-exists any performative instance; whereas in the latter, the performance as a whole is an apparatus for the *production of meaning* through the combined activity of the artist/producer and the spectator on the text as raw material.

Consequently, in the first case textual integrity is provisional, and derives not from any internal articulation of its elements but solely from the control exerted by the transcendent point of emanation of the message;[17] whereas in the latter instance, such a transcendent point of devolution of meaning being absent, the text must achieve an internal articulation that guarantees its identity as a separate individual product.

The realist aesthetic is governed by the latter fiction. In it the spectator has the opportunity, the *right*, to repeat the production process—the processing of raw material to generate meaning—that has already been accomplished by the producer/artist. Even if all the spectators arrive at the *same* meaning, they must be assumed to have done so individually, through their own labour of interpretation.[18]

This is the philosophy that is expounded in Bazin's theory of realism, for instance. In Bazin's rendering of the problem, the threat of a direct, *interpreted*, communication comes from a political source: the politically committed director. Like God, whose messages are

[16]There is a third, intermediate possibility, emblematized in the didactic aesthetic of revolutionary art (Brecht, Eisenstein).

[17][E]very continuity is effected *via* the gaze [of the spectator]' : Rajadhyaksha, 'The Phalke Era, *JAI* 1987: 70).

[18]Recent film theory thus makes a virtue out of necessity when it claims as its own discovery the fact that spectators are active producers of meaning rather than passive recipients of it. This productive labour of the spectator is assumed by the realist text and does not constitute either a sign or a guarantee of resistance.

communicated directly through the mediation of the performer, the director too can present action in the form of an unambiguous message:

> While analytical montage only calls for him [the spectator] to follow his guide, to let his attention follow along smoothly with that of the director who will choose what he should see, here [in the cinema of 'depth'] he is called upon to exercise at least a minimum of personal choice. It is from his attention and his will that the meaning of the image in part derives (Bazin 1967: 36).

Bazin associates the freedom of choice provided by depth of focus to the 'liberal and democratic . . . consciousness of the American spectator' (Williams 1980: 44). But he is also clear that it is a question of a purely *formal* freedom of choice. What analytical montage presents, far from being false, is 'consistent with the laws of attention'. But in being pre-selected, 'it deprives us of the privilege, no less grounded in psychology, which we abandon without realising it, and which is, *at least virtually*, the freedom to modify our method of selection at every moment' (ibid: 42, emphasis added). The director's freedom to choose is thus in conflict with the spectator's and such a choice amounts to 'a clear standpoint on reality as such'. What is the danger that this represents? It is the danger of a *realized* individuality, as opposed to which a virtual one formally reiterates the availability of choice, and in order to be able to do so, must forever desist from actually making a choice. Individuality must always be provided for but never realized.

The freedom in question is thus not an 'objective' freedom, verifiable by reference to the diversity of choices made by subjects. It is a potential, given through and testifying to the privilege of citizenship. The director, in order to respect the individual's freedom must curb her/his own freedom, must in other words, merge his/her own identity into the invisible frame of the state, clearing the ground for the full unfolding of the reality of nation/civil society.

At the same time, Bazin argues that this freedom given to the individual spectator to make his/her own choice from a field of objects does not result in a diversity of choices, because there are 'laws of attention' which assert themselves, and in practice, ensure that more or less the same choice is made by all. Thus, not only the director but the citizen too is duty-bound to restrict his/her freedom to a virtual plane. While reality is 'by definition' diverse, the perception of this diversity, as an act of citizenship, must not lead to a diversification of perception. To admit that the eye's choice of objects from a field of perception could be arbitrary and unpredictable would be to jeopardize reality itself and would lead to anarchy.

Bazin's theory foregrounds the relationship between a political system and an ideology. In the case of the Indian popular cinema, we encounter a situation that seems to correspond to the non-realist model that Bazin criticizes. It is tempting at this point to take the sort of line that Noel Burch (1979) has elaborated in relation to Japanese cinema, and conclude that the distinction represented by frontality could be made the basis of a theory of the Indianness of Indian cinema. Such a conclusion would, however, pre-empt the exploration of the political dimension of cultural production. By ignoring the political dimension, we ignore the immense range of cultural possibilities that exist between the poles of 'western' realist or modernist practice and 'traditional' or non-western 'survivals'. We would thus end up reducing politics itself to a western cultural predilection.

The book is divided into two parts. Part I, consisting of Chapters 2,3 and 4 is an investigation of the conditions of possibility of the dominant textual form of popular cinema, commonly referred to as the 'social'. Chapter 2 is devoted to the economic conditions—the prevailing mode of production, the mode of manufacture adopted— and their role in the reproduction of the dominant textual form. Chapter 3 is a reading of this form as a symptom of the ideological resolution of conflicts within the social formation, of producing and representing the 'consensus-effect' that sustains that formation. Drawing on the theories of realism and melodrama, I propose that the dominant form is a compromise formation reflecting the coalitional nature of political power. The definition of the spectator's position within the cinematic apparatus is discussed here with reference to the notion of citizen and the continued and broadened effectivity of the temple-centred institution of *darsana*. In a discussion of women's melodrama, it is argued that the social, in its all-inclusive character, can also function as an instrument of active resistance to generic differentiation.

Chapter 4 reinforces the argument about the non-contingency of the emergence and effectivity of the dominant form by taking up a peculiar feature of Indian censorship, the prohibition of kissing. This is shown to be a displaced prohibition of representations of the 'private' in the bourgeois sense, which facilitates the perpetuation of an ideological community-effect. The minimal unit of the private domain is the nuclear family, whose rise to pre-eminence coincides with the dissolution of pre-capitalist patriarchal enclaves and the emergence of the modern state as the sole supervizing authority over the family as the site of biological reproduction and socialization.[19] From the point of view of the pre-capitalist elements of the coalition, such a re-organization of the social represents a curtailment of its scopic privileges. Thus, while the resolution of the popular film narrative involves the constitution of the nuclear couple, the couple is reinserted into the space of the clan or the family in its political form.

This general theoretical framework serves in Part II, as a point of departure for a conjunctural analysis, of the developments in the film industry during a brief period of political crisis from the late sixties to the mid-seventies. The project is to develop a historical construction showing the broad lines of transformation of the field of film culture. In Chapter 5, I characterize the crisis as a disaggregation of the social or a breakdown of the consensus established and maintained by the ruling coalition. The dominant textual form also came into crisis in this period under the twin pressures of state intervention in cultural production and social changes brought about by political upheavals. The industry responded to this crisis through a process of internal segmentation, which created two proto-genres, the new cinema and the middle-class cinema, while also leading to a transformation of the dominant textual form in the direction of a populist aesthetic of mobilization. The Film Finance Corporation, a state agency, entered feature film production as part of a strategy of cultural intervention, forcing the industry to respond in the manner described. This period thus marked the emergence of a developmentalist realism which produced a spectatorial point of view coinciding with the gaze of the state. It also led to the consolidation of a middle-class cinema, in which the private, as the space of middle-class identity, was elaborated. The popular cinema, on the other hand, went through a phase of uncertainty before regrouping around a figure of mobilization, a charismatic political-ideological entity embodied in the star-persona of Amitabh Bachchan. Aesthetically, these three segments represent

---

[19]The nuclear family's dominance must be understood as ideological. As Michele Barret and Mary Macintosh (1990) point out, in reality, this form is not statistically predominant even in the advanced capitalist countries.

statist realism, the realism of identification, and the melodrama of mobilization and counter-identification respectively.

Chapter 6 traces the process of construction of the star-figure of Amitabh Bachchan and the manner in which it was deployed in the evolution of an aesthetic of mobilization. Chapter 7 takes up the middle-class cinema of identification, whose generic specificity derives from the effects of ordinariness, familiarity, and realism. This cinema addresses the middle-class subject as a beleaguered entity, facing a threat to her/his identity from the encroachments of the rest of society, in particular the glamorous world of popular culture, and the politically awakened masses. These films also deal with the problem of private space and the related problem of the possibility of middle-class spectatorship. Chapter 8 concludes the study with an analysis of the first three films of Shyam Benegal as instances of an evolving developmental aesthetic employing a statist realism. Although the developmental narrative comes into its own only with *Manthan* (1976), both *Ankur* (1974) and *Nishant* (1975) contribute to its construction by employing strategies of distancing which produce the peasant/rural poor as an object of study and sympathy.

These three segments or genres arose in a moment of disaggregation which rendered the old integrated modular text of the feudal romance obsolete. However, this was by no means an irreversible process, nor were the three segments established on a permanent basis. The aim of my project is to demonstrate the manner in which segmentation functioned as a mode of resolution of the crisis at the level of the industry, and to identify the aesthetic possibilities it generated as well as the new strategies of containment that emerged as a result. As an analysis of developments in a conjuncture, it is not intended as an assertion of the absolute novelty of each of these 'aesthetic' practices. On the contrary, the argument foregrounds the way in which all three segments drew from previously existing practices of signification and narrative codes in their attempt to meet a demand for new narratives that was widely perceived to have arisen among the audiences.

Finally, as suggested above, this mapping of the field of popular cinema has become possible now in part because the social conditions described in the book are fast disappearing as global capitalism has been unleashed on the subcontinent with unprecedented haste. Having constructed a theoretical edifice for the study of popular cinema, we are thus also faced with the task of dismantling it, of witnessing its certitudes dissolve in the flux of contemporary events. In the final essay that forms the epilogue to the main text, a symptomatic reading of two recent films, *Damini* and *Roja*, is undertaken, to bring to light, in their formal structure, an allegory of real subsumption that points to the possible direction in which certain new players, functioning by new rules and employing new strategies, are attempting to move the film industry.

PART I

2

The Economics of Ideology: Popular Film Form and Mode of Production

There is a good deal of writing on the economics of the film industry, some of it by professional economists.[1] This constitutes a valuable body of information on the sources of finance, the roles of various agents (producers, distributors, exhibitors) in the industry, the relations of power and dependency that develop between these agents as a reflection of their relative financial position, the revenues accruing to the government from the industry, the avenues for legitimate and reliable finance, etc. When we place these details alongside the actual cultural content of the films, the ideologies they circulate, there are, however, some questions that arise that have so far remained unaddressed. These questions are neither strictly economic, like the ones just described, nor purely cultural, but belong to a border area between them, overlapping with both. This is the area with•which this chapter is concerned: the point at which political, economic and ideological instances intersect.

The film-maker Kumar Shahani has remarked: 'The biggest problem seems to be that we are working within a capitalist framework and we do not have a capitalist infrastructure. It is all run on highly speculative lines, on some systems of trading and circulation of money' (Rizvi and Amlad 1980: 13). Shahani's remark points to an extremely vital link between the mode of organization of the

[1]Panna Shah (1981), R.D. Jain (1960), M.A. Oommen and K.V. Joseph (1991), Manjunath Pendakur (1990), Someswar Bhowmik (1986); reports of the inquiry commissions appointed by government are also a good source of such information and analysis.

industry and the opportunities for experimentation afforded by that industry. Thus to focus on economic questions relating to the industry is not simply to 'flesh out' the background to cultural production but to uncover the nature of the nexus between economic, ideological and political forces that shape the conditions of possibility of cultural production in India.

In exploring this area, our point of departure will be the dominant textual form of the popular Hindi cinema, the form that has enjoyed pre-eminence in the Bombay film industry for nearly four decades. It is a form that would be familiar to anyone who has watched even a small number of the Bombay films. Even in other languages, especially in films from the south, the same textual form serves to organize the cinematic spectacle to a large extent. In the last few years, the industry has been undergoing changes which may lead to mutations of this form, or the introduction of new ones, but as yet the form associated with what I will call the feudal family romance has by no means exhausted itself.

Let us try to define this form. A definition of form, as opposed to a description of content, should be such as to account for, among other things, the narrative structure, the organization of elements within the structure, the means employed to carry the narrative forward from one stage to the next and those by which narrative closure is achieved.

The feudal family romance employs a narrative structure that goes back to the 'romances' that preceded the advent of modern realist fiction in the capitalist west.[2] The romance was typically a tale of love and adventure, in which a high-born figure, usually a prince, underwent trials that tested his courage and at the end of which he would return to inherit the father's position and to marry. This narrative structure occurs, not in its original form, but in the form that it acquired in popular theatre, where the entertainment programme would include the narrative interspersed with other elements like the comic routine, music and dance, etc. It was the Parsi theatre that first popularized this form in India. Indian cinema, however, did not adopt this form straightaway. It could not possibly do so in the silent era, but even after the introduction of sound, the adoption of this form was a gradual process. It stabilized roughly during the 1950s, and was to remain unchallenged until the beginning

[2]See McKeon (1987) for a detailed discussion of the romance form as precursor of the novel.

of the 1970s, when new elements were introduced, without, however, completely discarding the old form.

At its most stable, this form included a version of the romance narrative, a comedy track, an average of six songs per film, as well as a range of familiar character types. Narrative closure usually consisted in the restoration of a threatened moral/social order by the hero. This form was flexible enough to include a wide range of contingent elements, including references to topical issues, and propaganda for the government's social welfare measures (to please the censors). Thus, it should not be thought of as being necessarily and completely a bearer of feudal values, even though the overall narrative form derived from romances of the feudal era.

However, Bombay, as well as other centres of film-making have also witnessed campaigns against this form even during the period of its dominance, in favour of 'realism', a term which was defined in a variety of ways. For people in the industry who were dissatisfied with the dominant form, the model to emulate was Hollywood: in periodicals like *Screen* and *Filmfare*, film-makers would confess to a preference for films that were realistic and justify their own inability to make such films by blaming the poor taste of the audience. Whenever big-budget films failed, leading to a crisis, the press would repeat its advice: the audience has rejected the old *masala* film, it wants realistic, authentic stories, not songs and dances. Film-makers were urged to work with a ready script and adhere to short, tight schedules. Producers would try, every few years, to unite and impose order on the industry's functioning, to regulate the work schedules of stars, to co-operate in reducing the duplication of themes, etc.

In spite of this recurring effort, the so-called 'formula film' held on to its position of pre-eminence. The question that arises therefore is how and why this form was able to dominate the scene for so long. In this chapter, we will investigate this question primarily from the economic angle.

Before proceeding with the analysis, I will set down for convenience, the general conclusions the study arrives at:

(i) As regards the production sector, I will argue that the mode of production in the Hindi film industry is characterized by fragmentation of the production apparatus, subordination of the production process to a moment of the self-valorization of merchant capital, the consequent externality of capital to the production process, the resistance of the rentier class of exhibitors to the expansionist drive of the logic of the market, and the functional centrality of the distributor-financier to the entire process of film-making.

(ii) The Hindi film industry has adopted what Marx calls the 'heterogeneous form of manufacture' in which the whole is assembled from parts produced separately by specialists, rather than being centralized around the processing of a given material, as in serial or organic manufacture. This is of significance to the status of the 'story' in the Hindi film.

(iii) There is evidence of an ongoing struggle between two broadly defined tendencies within the industry, one committed to an ideological mission in keeping with the goals of the postcolonial state's controlled capitalist development and aspiring to the achievement of a homogenized national culture, the other moored in a pre-capitalist culture, employing a patchwork of consumerist and pre-capitalist ideologies and determined to maintain its hold over the production process from the outside. In this context the role of the state as the primary agent of capitalist development becomes crucial. The unfolding of the struggle between these two contending forces has involved appeals for particular forms of state intervention, a campaign for realism and melodrama, and concerted efforts to establish the production sector on an independent basis. It is a struggle, in other words, to effect an adequation of the political, economic and ideological instances.

In the run-up to independence, a section of the industry expected that the government of free India would recognize the potential that cinema held as a medium of mass education and would give it the same encouragement that was envisaged for other industries. It was felt that a modernizing nation would need a modern cultural institution to undertake the requisite ideological tasks. In 1945, five producers from Bombay, Calcutta, Lahore and Madras undertook an expedition to Europe and America to study the conditions of the film industries there. Their report (*Report of the Indian Film Industry's Mission to Europe and America,* nd) was full of admiration for western efficiency, and concluded with suggestions that would be repeated by industry spokespersons for decades to come. Government support was sought for establishing the industry on a 'stable and progressive foundation'. The state was urged to supply finance, to launch the indigenous manufacture of raw film and equipment, to start a film council and a film institute (which had been proposed before but had been squashed in the Legislative assembly just before the publication of the report); and lastly, a 'Central Film Academy and Research Institute' was proposed to 'combat . . . anti-Indian propaganda vehemently carried on abroad especially in the United States before and during the last war' (*Mission*: 59–60).

The report projected the industry as a partner in the about-to-be independent country's campaign to modernize and project a good image abroad. This was in conformity with the model of socio-economic progress that was emerging as the chosen path for India, and was embodied in Nehruvian socialism. Among others this consisted of a combination of measures to develop indigenous capital, to enable it by protection and other state-initiated economic measures to consolidate itself, while launching a social programme of progressive education, the gradual emancipation of the population into an awareness of the rights and responsibilities of social democracy. But the Nehruvian state did not do for the film industry what it was committed to doing for other industries. Nehru himself had remarked that the film industry was not a priority for the new nation,[3] causing considerable anxiety in industry circles. Despite attempts to portray the industry as sharing the government's (and in particular Nehru's) views about the role of cinema, and the assertion that it was the state's duty, in a capitalist society, to develop entertainment facilities, nothing concrete materialized.

The need to establish film-making as an industry was emphasized by Phalke[4] earlier in the century and continues to be a recurrent motif in debates on the future of Indian cinema. To gain 'industry status' is to acquire legitimacy in the eyes of the state, to be accorded the privileges of a successful native industrial venture. In practical terms such a recognition would translate into availability of institutional finance and a collaborative approach on the government's part.

It is not as if the state was unaware of the uses of cinema as a tool of mass education. Building on the existing infrastructure for, colonial propaganda film production, the Films Division expanded into a gigantic machine producing newsreels and documentaries for screening in commercial theatres and other places. This was also a

[3]*Filmfare*, 28 November 1952, p. 5

[4]See the translations of Phalke's writings published by the National Film Archives of which a selection has been reprinted in *Continuum* 2.1 (1988/89) 51–73. Especially significant is the fact that Phalke conceived of Indian cinema as part of the Swadeshi campaign to develop indigenous industry. For a further discussion of Phalke and swadeshi, see A. Rajadhyaksha, 'The Phalke Era', *JAI* (1987).

source of revenue, since a small fee was charged for each screening. Thus the state policy conformed with the imperative of reproduction of conditions of formal subsumption. The industry's demand was for initiatives that would enable a transformation of the prevailing film aesthetic. The state's response was to impose a parasitical propaganda element on every screening, which was meant to take care of education in modernity, leaving the form of the feature itself untouched.

Following the Film Enquiry Commission report, however, a Film Finance Corporation (FFC) was set up in 1960. With a budget that was too small to earn it a major role in the industry, the FFC gave out insufficient loans to producers who consequently ended up with incomplete films and unrepayable loans. Later, a revised policy of financing low-budget, non-commercial films was implemented, inaugurating the era of the 'new cinema,' which will be discussed later on. As far as the mainstream cinema was concerned, the FFC brought about no change in the existing state–industry relations. The institution that was expected to change this state of affairs was the Film Council, also recommended by the Film Enquiry Committee (FEC) report. Without the 'political' alliance between the state and the industry that the Film Council would have represented, the economic intervention via the FFC was ineffectual. However, though the industry as a whole clamoured for the economic assistance promised by the FFC, only a few producers were willing to enter into an institutional alliance with the state that would impose obligations on both parties.

Similar ideas for government–industry co-operation had been floated even before independence. Fazalbhoy's review reports for instance, that the Indian Motion Picture Congress of 1939 was envisaged as a permanent body that would function as a 'central organisation' of the industry as recommended previously by the 1927 ICC report (Fazalbhoy nd: 84–5). This central body was, in the eyes of it proponents, a symbol of the will to lead the film sector into the industrial era, of the industry's self-image as a national institution with developmental responsibilities (ibid: 96–7). The 1951 *Report of the Film Enquiry Committee* (FEC *Report*), reviving the idea, observed:

> On the organizational side we would recommend that early steps should be taken to set up a statutory Film Council of India as the central authority to superintend and regulate the film industry, to act as its guide, friend and philosopher, and to advise the Central and

State governments in regard to various matters connected with the production, distribution and exhibition of films. Such a Council, we envisage, will give the industry the necessary stimulus and inspiration to regulate its affairs on healthy and constructive lines, ensure that organizationally it functions in an efficient and business-like manner, ensure professional conduct and discipline in its various branches and enforce standards of quality which would make the film a cultural agent and an instrument of healthy entertainment (FEC *Report* 1951: 187–8).

The Council had to *regulate* the industry without *controlling* it. It was to have statutory powers and the authority to institute research projects, training institutions, a 'story bureau', a casting bureau, a production code administration on the lines of the one in America, etc. (ibid: 189–94).

This measure came up for consideration frequently and was blocked each time by the resistance of a large section who claimed that control rather than benign regulation was the government's real motive. Throughout the fifties, sixties and the early seventies, the idea of a Council was discussed in the film press, with a mounting sense of urgency as the Indira Gandhi regime unfolded its 'socialist' agenda. Support for the idea came from established film-makers like V. Shantaram, Raj Kapoor, Satyajit Ray, Mohan Segal, etc. and from the technicians' and cineworkers' unions which stood to gain from a well-organized industry. It is possible that some of those who openly supported the idea were motivated by a fear of displeasing the government. Opponents of the plan were people with a more traditional business approach like Sunderlal Nahata, Chandulal Shah and lastly, J. Om Prakash, who as elected head of the Film Federation of India, warned his membership that they would have to achieve internal unity in order to ward off the threat of a Film Council.[5]

Clearly, the long-term benefits that might accrue from a stable infrastructure were not very attractive to those whose interests were best served by preserving the anarchic backward capitalism that

[5]*Screen,* 12 July 1968, p. 1; 19 July 1968, p. 13; 14 February 1969, p. 1; 16 May 1969, p. 1; 23 May 1969, p. 8; 14 November 1969, p. 1; 14 August 1970, p. 1; 23 October 1970, p. 1.

Also *Filmfare,* 4 April 1952, p. 4; 27 May 1955; 6 January 1956, p. 5; 3 February 1956, p. 3; 17 February 1956, p. 3; 25 May 1956, p.19; 16 October 1964; 30 October 1964, p. 5; 17 January 1969, p. 7; 11 April 1969, p. 5; 4 July 1969, pp. 27, 29, 31; 1 August 1969, p. 23; 5 December 1969, p. 7; 16 January 1970, p. 7; 28 August 1970, p. 5; 11 September 1970, p. 5; 17 December 1971, p. 7; 2 May 1975, p. 9.

reigned in the industry. Behind the stated fear of government control was a real apprehension of having to forego the benefits of a substantial inflow of black money. It became clear in the course of this conflict between the supporters and opponents of the proposal, that the industry was not ready for a transformation of the prevailing relations of production and power. That the proposal came to nothing is not surprising: even its supporters were not ready to make a crusade of it. Their reluctance was reinforced by fears that the Indira Gandhi regime was contemplating radical measures like nationalization and licensing of producers. In 1980, the *Report of the Working Group on National Film Policy* (NFP *Report*) dismissed the Council idea as ill-advised and instead recommended 'indirect' measures to improve quality (*Report* 1980: 20).[6] Nevertheless, while it lasted, the idea of a Film Council served as a measure of the changing relations between government and industry. It became the focus of a discourse of industrial advancement tied to the project to develop a new, bourgeois aesthetic, a developmental vision of cultural production and state-backed capitalist growth.

The Organization of Production

The film texts that reach us as finished products are made possible, not only by 'cultural' factors, but also by the mode of production that prevails in the industry, and in the society in which that industry operates. Janet Staiger (1985), who has done an exhaustive study of the Hollywood mode of production, begins by asserting that the socio-economic 'base' does not enjoy any privileged role as determinant in the emergence of technology and ideological forms, as Jean-Louis Comolli (1993) had argued. Instead, following John Ellis (1992) and Geoffrey Nowell-Smith, she regards the conditions of film practice—ideological, economic, political and technological—as 'a series of histories' constituting 'the terrain of possibilities' (Staiger 1985: 87–8).

[6]B.K. Karanjia, as editor of *Filmfare* and the FFC chair, had championed the proposal, revived the idea in a 1987 article and harked back to the regulation vs. control debate. However, the advent of television, the liberalization measures of the Congress regimes, a new culture of vigorous middle-class consumerism and the industry's scramble to survive in a competitive environment had meanwhile so transformed the scene that the idea of state-supported capitalist growth seemed distinctly odd.

Staiger argues that we cannot simply assume that the 'group style' that dominated Hollywood film-making was made possible by historical conditions extraneous to it. It is equally possible that certain production practices were adopted *because* they were the best for the particular style of film-making that the industry desired (ibid: 88). Staiger is right in rejecting the economic determinism implied by the argument that the style is just a reflection of the adopted mode of production. However, she does not take up the same question in a larger context: that is to say, do the socio-economic conditions prevailing in the society as a whole have anything to do with the choice of style and form?

Staiger identifies a series of 'systems of production', i.e. the modes of combination of the 'factors of production' in the Hollywood film industry. She traces the ways in which the labour force, the means of production, and financing combine in different ways to constitute in different periods of film history, specific 'systems of production' organized around the central function of a particular skilled member of the firm: the 'cameraman' system of production, the director system, the 'director-unit' system and so on (ibid: 85–153, 309–64).

In order to determine what systems of production may be in operation in Bombay, it is necessary to first understand the relations between the different sectors of the film industry and the way production is organized within the network formed by these sectors.

The FEC report of 1951 notes that unlike the concentration of production in the hands of a few concerns in Hollywood, 'India is distinguished by a plethora of producers' (FEC *Report*: 64). The figures cited show the extent of fragmentation:

Table 1
A Plethora of Producers

Year	Films	Producers	Maximum films by a single producer
1939	167	94	9
1940	171	102	7
1946	200	151	–
1947	283	214	7
1948	264	211	6

Source: Report of the Film Enquiry Committee, 1951: 64, 323–4

The average number of films made per producer was highest in 1939 at less than two. By 1948 the average had dropped to just over one film per producer. Not only were there a large number of producers turning out one or two films a year, but a significant number of them were 'newcomer independents' afflicted by a high rate of 'infant mortality'.

The production sector of the industry can thus be divided into two broad segments consisting of a tiny group of 'established' producers and a large number of independents. This has been the general trend at least since 1939, that is to say, before India was drawn into the war effort. Y.A. Fazalbhoy's *Review* (nd) published soon after the 1939 Indian Motion Picture Congress that was held in Bombay, shows that under-capitalization was very much the norm even in the 'studio era', thus reducing the importance of the break that was attributed (by Barnouw and Krishnaswamy (1980), for instance) to an influx of black money that lured stars away from the studios during the Second World War years.

To begin with, Fazalbhoy traces the entry of independent producers to the early thirties when the arrival of sound suddenly freed the Indian language film from competition with imported films and led to its undisputed leadership and a vast expansion of its market. Thus,

> every qualified and unqualified man rushed into film production and over four hundred pictures were made in some of the earlier years. Very soon came a glut in the market and a number of studios and producing companies closed down because their products could not be sold profitably. The industry has not yet recovered from the depression that came in the train of these successive disasters (*Review,* nd).

He concludes with the now familiar prescription that organization 'on more scientific principles' and 'better facilities for finance' could alone prevent the high rate of failure of the production companies.

The Indian producer, according to Fazalbhoy,

> is usually satisfied if he can take one picture in hand at a time and follow it up to its end through many months of hard labor. The economies in overhead expenditure that come from producing a number of pictures at a time have necessarily to be sacrificed (ibid).

Establishing the industry on a firm capitalist basis, with high capital investment and mass production were seen to be crucial but the industry's 'internal organization' was too weak to achieve this and thus could not attract the support of the government and the public.

> If the extremely small units of the present day succeed in expanding
> sufficiently to ensure economic working or if they merge into larger
> units, they can not only get sufficient financial support, but also secure
> such an important voice in commercial matters that governmental
> authorities will scarcely be able to ignore them (ibid: 7).

Related to these symptoms of economic disorder and fragmentation
is the question of how the individual film itself is put together:
Studio facilities being limited, the lack of pre-planning adds to delays
and necessitates last minute improvisations (Fazalbhoy *Review*: 10–11).
Dialogue, role development and even the story's line of progression
were being decided during the production. The NFP report, published
in 1980, did not see any change in this regard (NFP *Report*: 17).
Thus, while a large number of films are produced every year, there
is no 'mass production' in the strict sense of the term. The importance
of this detail will make itself felt as we proceed.

The studios, an important cornerstone of the film industry, were
in a position of unquestioned dominance in the 1930s, when the
film world was 'beginning to have the look of an organized industry'
(Barnouw and Krishnaswamy 1980: 117). Why were they then unable
to hold on to their position of strength when it was challenged by
the independent newcomers? As it is usually understood, the strategy
of the newcomers was based on a shrewd calculation of the role of
the star in the success of a film. The stars, whose incomes in the
studios were moderate, were lured away with the offer of huge
sums, thus drawing the studios into a competition from which they
never recovered. The elevation of the stars to the status of
independent values, capable of a sort of self-valorization, upset the
control over the production process which had enabled the studios
to maintain their methods and (non)disciplines of work. This was
also the occasion for the entry of 'black money' into the industry.
The newcomers, backed by the tainted surpluses of blackmarketeers
(later they would be joined by smugglers), offered a part of the high
payment to the stars in the form of unaccounted money, which
would be 'tax-free'. During the last years of British rule, this practice
was even regarded as a patriotic act (ibid: 127).

But there is another reason for the loss of dominance: although
the studios were large well-organized production centres, they
functioned on what Barnouw and Krishnaswamy call the 'one-big-
family' principle. 'The big companies of the 1930s, like the Phalke

company before them, seemed to be extensions of the joint family system. Many of the companies had, in fact, clusters of relatives' (ibid: 117). Thus, these companies were functioning in a market economy, producing commodities for mass distribution, but the production relations were based on kinship loyalties.

From the trends noted above it would be reasonable to conclude that the transformation wrought by the influx of independent producers intensified rather than caused the dispersed mode of functioning of the industry. The independent producer was at best a small-scale capitalist entrepreneur who could depend on the availability of low-wage casual labour and freelance acting talent with enormous wage differences between the stars, the 'character actors' and the 'extras' and could rent all the requisite technical services and equipment. The star, who was previously only one of the more important units of congealed value (or 'symbolic capital') to go into the product, now became the primary source of value.

A separate distribution sector for the Indian film industry was a late development. In the silent era, when Indian films formed only a small segment of the total films exhibited in the country, only imports were put on the market by distributors. A distribution sector for Indian films only emerged with the birth of the talkies and an increase in Indian language film production. Distribution and exhibition are the two sectors of the entire process that are widely acknowledged to be the most profitable. The proliferation of small and short-lived production companies with no fixed capital and limited working capital has meant that the distributors' profits have emerged as one of the main sources of finance for film production.[7] The separate existence and the relation of dependence between the distribution and production sectors ensures that capital remains permanently dissociated from the production sector which it subordinated to its own self-valorization. Capitalist enterprise is still in its emergent form here and for all practical purposes remains a system akin to the 'putting out system' of early capitalism, where production is subservient to distributors' capital which is advanced to producers, the product then belonging to the financier.

Film distribution was not the main occupation of those who entered the business. Most of them were moneylenders who turned distributors in order to recover their money:

[7]Note that financing of production by distributors is by no means a peculiar feature of the Indian scene. This was commonly the practice in Hollywood and elsewhere. What is important is the industry's status in relation to that sector.

The chief characteristic of distribution in India is that to a great extent the firms handling the work are merely departments of financing houses . . . . Since the returns from a picture will be recovered only after it is in the market for some time the studio must have sufficient funds to carry on its activities. The financiers who stepped-in with this help took as security the returns from the picture and in the majority of cases retained the distribution with themselves . . . (Fazalbhoy *Review:* 28–9).

The 'minimum guarantee system', which is supposed to assure the producer a minimum return on each film, is also not as favourable to producers as it appears. The amount that is fixed as the minimum guarantee in this transaction is usually the amount loaned by the distributor to the producer during the making of the film. As a result the producer often gets no revenue from a film after production because the minimum return has already been given in the form of loans. It was also in the distributors' interest 'to see that returns from pictures are not so excessive as to enable the producer to pay them off' (ibid: 48).

The exhibition sector's role in this scenario largely complements that of the distributor. In the first place, distributors, to secure their long-term interests, establish control over theatres. A syndicate of distributors has been in operation in Bombay, monopolizing the theatres. The rise of the multi-starrer, and the saturation release strategy led to rental increases which reinforced the monopoly of a few distribution houses (NFP *Report:* 24). Theatres were scarce in any case because of unfriendly construction rules. Even when new ones were constructed all over India during the seventies after the rules were relaxed, demand continued to exceed supply in densely-populated cities.

There also emerged an intermediary class of 'theatre contractors' who booked theatres and sold time to distributors at higher prices. The logic of the industry also gave rise to the staging of 'fake jubilees' in some centres to create a good impression on audiences in late-release centres. In 1957, *Filmfare* decided to focus on the 'exhibition racket'. The sharp rise in rentals—between 1955 and 1957 according to the magazine, the average rental went up by Rs 700 in the case of small and second-run theatres and by Rs 2000 in the case of first-run houses—was the most tangible index of what was seen as a racket involving various forms of deceit.[8] In 1972, echoing the Indira Gandhi

[8]*Filmfare*, 24 May 1957, p. 3

government's slogan of 'Garibi Hatao', a *Filmfare* editorial entitled 'Zamindari Hatao' returned to the question of the black money hoards of the exhibitors and the exorbitant rentals. It pointed out that even foreign film theatres demanded black money payments when they screened Hindi films. It wondered how long the 'socialist government' would tolerate such 'antisocial' activities. The title pointed to the links between theatre owners and a more traditional, British-created form of landlordism. The government, which had recently proclaimed its commitment to ending feudal practices was called upon to smash the power of theatre owners and bring them into the modern capitalist economy as rationally-functioning entrepreneurs.

This brief account of the economic structure of the Bombay film industry demonstrates the dominance of merchant capital and the fragmentation and heteronomy of the production sector. Against this background we can now turn to a consideration of the form of manufacture widely adopted by the industry and its significance for the understanding of Indian film ideology.

The Heterogeneous Form of Manufacture

Marx makes a distinction between the heterogeneous and the organic or serial forms of manufacture. The first, heterogeneous mode is characterized by the separate production of the component parts of a product and their final assembly into one unit, while in the second a given raw material passes through various stages of production assigned to various workers or units within an integrated serial process (Marx, *Capital I:* 461–3). In Hollywood, as Staiger points out, the organization of production 'most closely approximates serial manufacture', and features mass production (although far removed from the 'assembly-line rigidity' of large industry) and a detailed division of labour, that is to say a division of labour developed in the factory production process and either intensifying or deviating from the more generally prevailing social division of labour. In Hollywood, the 'detailed division of labour mode became dominant when commercial film-making started emphasizing the production of narrative fiction films after 1906' (Staiger 1985: 93). The comparison with Hollywood is crucial because it establishes the centrality of the question of narrative to the 'economic' questions being considered here.

A broad equation can be established between each of the two film industries under consideration and a 'fundamental form of manufacture'. If Hollywood is dominated by serial or organic manufacture, Bombay is dominated by the heterogeneous form. Marx's example for the heterogeneous form is watch-making. The components of the watch are produced by different and separately functioning skilled workers, and assembled into the final product. If we consider that the Hindi film is conceived in this way, as an assemblage of pre-fabricated parts, we get a more accurate sense of the place of various elements, like the story, the dance, the song, the comedy scene, the fight, etc. in the film text as a whole. On the other hand, what makes this method of functioning unsuitable for Hollywood is the fact that a material substratum—the story—is the point of departure of the production process and its transformation into a narrative film is the final goal of that process. The needle, Marx's example for serial manufacture, is distinguished by the fact that the base material of the product is present from the beginning to the end of the process. In the watch the whole's relation to its material components is that of an ideal signifying process (the measurement and indication of time) to its material *means of realization.*

It is striking that the typical film produced by the Bombay film industry should bear so close a resemblance, in terms of its relation to 'raw material', to the example of watch-making. Here we encounter the limits of the analysis we have been pursuing so far, which is focused on the internal economic organization of the industry. The fragmented, episodic structure of the Hindi film text reminds us that beyond the combination of the mode of production and form of manufacture, there arises a problem of narrative that can only be resolved at the level of the social totality.

To summarize the argument, it is my contention that while the Hollywood production process is structured around the primary operation of transforming a given raw material, the story/scenario into a film; in the production process most familiar in Bombay, the separate development of the components of the film text render this process relatively unimportant. Indeed it could be said that the story here occupies a place on par with that of the rest of the components, rather than the pre-eminent position it enjoys in the Hollywood mode. The written script, which enabled 'disjunctive shooting schedules' and other measures aimed at economy and efficiency and necessitating the division of the task of writing into several stages is one factor of extreme importance to the Hollywood production process, whereas everyone who writes on Bombay cinema notes, that this is conspicuous by its absence there. The script 'became more than just the mechanism to pre-check quality: it became the blueprint from which all other work was organized' (Staiger 1985: 94).

Contrast this with the numerous and constant complaints in Bombay about the lack of a fully-developed script and the equally frequent and shortlived euphoria about signs of change. In the early 1950s, in the wake of one of the recurring production crises, the 'stereotyped films' were condemned universally along with the absence of 'co-ordination' and 'powerful or realistic theme(s)'.[9] A 'silent revolution' was discovered, demonstrating audience dissatisfaction with the existing formula films and the search for new formulas based on realistic stories[10] was launched. Story writers were said to be coming into their own with producers launching a search for 'original story material'.[11] The actor and left-wing cultural activist Balraj Sahni argued in an article that the screenplay and not the story was the vital element in film-making. 'I cannot imagine', he wrote, referring to one of the conventions of Bombay film-making, 'how the dialogue writing can be separated from the screenplay writing.' Sahni linked his idea of the pre-eminence of a holistically conceived screenplay with a 'revolution in men's minds' that had placed 'man' at the centre of the world. He urged film-makers to study the realist drama of the west, which 'will teach our screen writer the 'method' of realism' and help to emancipate him from 'his feudal outlook'.[12]

Each of the component elements of the Hindi film is capable of much internal variation but their consistency from film to film is ensured by the fact that these variations are not demanded by the narrative. Thus, there are an infinite variety of songs, many extremely talented musicians with a tremendous capacity for blending different traditions of music and creating a seemingly endless supply of catchy tunes. But the lyrics are written in a language which has its own set repertoire of images and tropes for themes like romantic love, separation, rejection, maternal love, marriage, etc. The songs adopt

[9]*Filmfare*, 7 March 1952, p. 6.
[10]*Filmfare*, 2 May 1952, p. 38.
[11]*Filmfare*, 16 May 1952, p. 37–8.
[12]*Filmfare*, 30 May 1952, p. 39.

a literary style which has a predilection for certain recurrent motifs: the *mehfil, shama/parwana, chaman, bahar, nazaaren*, and so on. This repertoire of images is drawn from the frozen diction of romantic Urdu poetry.[13] It is the task of poets, who figure here as traditional artisans with control over their own means of production, to supply these songs.

Dialogue, similarly, employs its own register of terms and idioms. Here we may observe one of the reasons why discussions of the need for a script also combine an exhortation to find realistic stories. For although it is rarely done, it is not impossible to prepare a fully detailed script for the kind of film described so far. But the problem lies elsewhere: the kind of narrative contexts that the given dialogue, lyrics, dances and stock characters make possible *do not require* a prepared script, simply because the variations in them are caused by innovations internal to the tradition of dialogue-writing, Urdu lyric-writing and dance history rather than the external pressure of the particularities of a narrative. The encounter between the good and bad elements in the fight scene is also a stylized enactment that follows its own logic of elaboration. Within the virtual space of the fight, what is enacted is a choreographed ballet, credited to 'fight composers' who have their own star value.

We are now in a position to state more precisely the manner in which a 'heterogeneous form of manufacture' operates in the Hindi film industry. It does so to the extent that the cinematic instance is not the dominant one in the production of the film text; to the extent that the component elements of the text arise in traditions that have a separate existence or in traditions that, arising in the context of film itself (like the star system), acquire an independence that retroactively determines the form of the text. The different component elements have not been subsumed under the dominance of a cinema committed to narrative coherence. The heteronomous conditions under which the production sector operates are paralleled by a textual heteronomy whose primary symptom is the absence of an integral narrative structure.

---

[13]Film lyricists produce versions of *ghazal, qawwali, thumri* and other musical forms with a distinctly 'filmy' flavour. Other traditions drawn from are those associated with Hindu weddings and other rituals and various folk forms. See Dale (1996) for a brief account of the almost 1000-year history of the *ghazal*.

Genre and Industrial Organization

In this context let us consider an interesting paradox. Most writers on the Indian cinema agree that during the studio era, while there was a weak but noticeable tendency to generic differentiation, post-independence history shows a tendency for generic distinctions to gradually weaken as a dominant form, most commonly known as the 'social', comes to reign supreme.

Rosie Thomas has described the emergence of the social succintly:

> By the 1930s a number of distinctly Indian genres were well established. These included socials, mythologicals, devotionals, historicals, and stunt, costume, and fantasy films. As song and dance are a central and integral part of films of *all* genres, the term musical is seldom used. Although genre distinctions began to break down in the 1960s, they are still relevant, not only to an understanding of the range of films made today and in the past, but because the form of the now dominant socials has in fact integrated aspects of all earlier genres (1987: 304).

Thomas's definition of the social indicates that the term is convenient rather than appropriate:

> The social has always been the broadest and, since the 1940s, the largest category and loosely refers to any film in a contemporary setting not otherwise classified. It traditionally embraces a wide spectrum, from heavy melodrama to light-hearted comedy, from films with social purpose to love stories, from tales of family and domestic conflict to urban crime thrillers (ibid).

This form not only subordinated the other generic tendencies to itself *externally* (i.e. by restricting the number of films with a distinctly different generic identity and/or by relegating them to the more provincial or sub-cultural exhibition outlets), but also by an *internal* subordination, whereby films in the dominant form included within themselves, fragments of genres like the thriller, the detective film, the gangster film, the costume drama and the devotional. The transition from studio production to the dominance of independent producers is one of the factors cited for the rise to pre-eminence of the 'social'.

Thus, on the one hand, the dominance of a few studios yielded to the new, extraneously backed power of a multitude of independent one-film producers, resulting in a fragmentation of the industry. On the other hand, in a parallel and contrary development, a tendency to generic differentiation, which was supported by the competing studios' desire to give a distinct identity to their products, was reversed and a super-genre swallowed up all the rest. Comparing the studio era with the situation at the start of the sixties, B.R. Chopra, one of the established producers in the industry, commented:

> In the past, producers were financed by progressive men who were interested in keeping up a banner like that of New Theatres, Prabhat, Ranjit, Sagar Movietone and Bombay Talkies. But today the financier advances money only to one single picture which has become a Unit by itself regardless of the banner under which it is made[14].

We can ignore the suggestion that the financiers of the past were all progressive. What is interesting in this passage is the idea that the new mode of film production had led to the conception of each film as a single Unit. The use of the capital letter suggests that what is being referred to here is a conception of each film in its comprehensive singularity, its status as a product specific to the particular combination of financier-producer-director-stars and undetermined by the need to distinguish it from products of a multitude of other similar combinations that together made up the Bombay film industry. Thus arises the ideology of the all-inclusive film, whose vision of the world tends to be multi-faceted, episodic and loosely structured. The post-independence Bombay film's aesthetic has often been traced by critics to Sanskrit dramaturgy but here we glimpse the historically more significant material determinations of the dominant film form.

The structuring of a film text around a single linear strand of narrative with one dominant affect—pathos, comedy, action, mystery, music, romance, horror—indicates the logic of a production process based on product differentiation and the development of 'special needs'. Where such a process has not advanced beyond the elementary stages, where an industry is composed of a large number of individual capitals 'not bound together by any objective social interconnection' (Banaji 1990: 237), the conditions for the planned differentiation of products do not exist. These two modes of capitalist production (by a firm and by individuals functioning in temporary alliances) thus result in two different modes of commodification.

In the Hollywood mode, the commodity unit is the individual film. Each film is marked by a high degree of internal unity and the values and skills that enter into its production are organized into a stable hierarchy, whose primary effect is that of a tightly-organized

[14]*Filmfare*, 29 December 1961, p. 19.

coherent narrative. By contrast, the independently-produced Bombay film is marked by the relative autonomy retained by the various elements that flow into the production process.[15] The system of film songs has an autonomous existence, as we have seen, and so do the dialogue and the star image.

This means that the process of commodification operates along lines that are determined by an unevenly-developed market capitalism, fragmenting the film text into its component parts. Thus the individual film tends to function more as a space for the exhibition of a combination of autonomous talents or values.[16] This space is organized by means of a minimal narrative framework.

Returning to the relation between the production practices and ideology, it is necessary to ask whether the haphazard and individualized mode of production that has survived in Bombay for such a long time is necessitated by the kind of ideology that the industry is committed to disseminating. So far, it has seemed as if the economic conditions of the film industry constitute a series of drawbacks, failures and constraints, an image produced by the industry's own perceptions. The analysis rests on a presupposition that the economic realities were acting as a constraint on the type of film that could be produced by the industry. But it is possible to pose a different question: if it is said that Hollywood, when assigned (or assigning itself) a certain ideological task,[17] developed a mode of production that would facilitate its achievement, can a similar statement be made about the relationship between the ideology of the Indian film and its mode of production? The question, in other words, concerns the instrumentality of the production process to an ideological goal: can we assume that this is true of all situations?

[15]But see Alexander Doty's (*Wide Angle* 10.2), 'Music Sells Movies' which points to a minor trend in Hollywood that seems to parallel ours.

[16]This explains the otherwise peculiar function of film titles in the Hindi cinema. Titles are often abstract, symbolic words and phrases: *Kismat* (Fate), *Pyar ka Mausam* (Season of Love), etc. They bear a relation to the text that is metaphoric and disjunctive, rarely metonymic. They are witness to the non-specificity of narratives. As such within a few years of the release of a film, the title becomes available for re-use. On the other hand, the point about a title like *Junglee* (The Wild One) is that it refers to a character trait of the hero which is quickly shown to be superficial. It is a sort of brand-name through which a star persona is identifiable.

[17]The details of which need not concern us here. There is a vast amount of writing on Hollywood ideology. Apart from J. Staiger (1985), who makes the specific point mentioned here, see G. Mast and Cohen (1992), B. Nichols (1993), and P. Rosen (1986) for a wide selection of representative writings.

The evidence points to two conflicting answers: on the one hand, there is the perceived failure of the attempt to gain mastery over the production process, to make it serve a determinate ideological project; on the other hand, the very impediments placed in the way of such consolidation by the powerful financiers may be said to have contributed (with whatever degree of 'intention') to the perpetuation of a backward capitalism in production and pre-capitalist ideologies in which relationships based on loyalty, servitude, the honour of the *khandaan* (clan) and institutionalized Hindu religious practices form the core cultural content. Thus, a state of affairs that appears to be the result of a series of 'failures'[18] may well be the one that the particular state form obtaining in India makes possible. Given this, it is difficult to agree with the oft-repeated assertion that the popular Indian film is 'precisely tailored to the tastes of the local audience'.[19]

Having examined the economic structure of the film industry, we have seen that beyond the distinctly economic constraints on this cultural institution, there remains the problem of narrative whose explanation has to be found outside the narrow framework of the industry's mode of production. We have seen that the prevailing mode of organization of the industry perpetuates itself because the dominant aesthetic form does not require the kind of integrated production process, which becomes imperative where the narratives are particularistic, focused on chunks of the real. Why does the standard Hindi film take the form it does? Why has it proved so difficult, and yet to some so necessary, to integrate the film text around a central, particularistic narrative?

The advocates of realism, narrative integrity, linearity and other virtues function in the history we have recounted as the would-be agents of a bourgeois revolution. Their repeated campaigns, all ending in failure, are symptomatic of the return, at every step, of a logic of form that is beyond their control, beyond the reach of the solutions they propose, a logic that could not be grasped in its totality because it is itself located at the level of the social totality, and determines the discursive possibilities available to cultural producers. Now, perhaps, as the basic conditions are changing, we may be able to catch a glimpse of this logic.

---

[18]On the problems arising from the use of 'failure' as a concept in historiography, see G. Spivak (1988).

[19]Nick Roddick, 'Sticky Wicket for Indian Films', *Screen International*, No 634 (January 9–16, 1988), p. 15.

What we observe in Hollywood, during the era of 'classical Hollywood cinema', is a historic turn in the logic of production whereby stories were situated at the beginning of the production process, in the position which, in other industries, is occupied by 'raw material'. This positioning of the narrative as the pre-eminent factor in the process, was what made it possible for Hollywood to establish, for about thirty years, a system of efficient mass production that has been the envy of the rest of the world. Such a shift, however, was facilitated by the fact that the aesthetics of realism itself was capable of being re-imagined in these terms. Realism's political significance becomes clear in this light: Andre Bazin, perhaps the most influential theorist of the cinema, associates realism with the maintenance of the values of liberal democracy. In his way of representing the true nature of realism, we glimpse the traces of a conception of realist performance as the occasion for production of meaning by audiences. Bazin manages to at once acknowledge the productive, creative role of the author, and negate it, by investing the right to interpret and produce meaning in the spectator as sovereign citizen. Such a conception of the aesthetic process is inconceivable without the historical process of capitalist expansion which gradually renamed every bit of the world as 'raw material'. The genius of Hollywood was to have discovered a way to combine the real process of transformation of raw material with the replication of that relation within the sphere of ideology.

How could the Indian industry reproduce that kind of unique historical event? Contrary to the fictive performance contract that prevailed in the west, what prevailed here can be represented as shown in the chart below. In this structure, there is no scope for the raw material relation: the representation of 'chunks of the real' which are made available for interpretation. The devolution of meaning requires no large-scale production system. There is a political problem here which outweighs all the efforts focussed on finding economic or purely cultural solutions to the industry's problems. Only if and when that transcendental point of emanation of meaning ceases to regulate the discourse of cultural texts will the occasion arise for searching for other ways of organizing the text. And when that happens, it may no longer be necessary or desirable to repeat the history of Hollywood: other possibilities may have emerged by then.

Fictive contractual relations in the (film) performance apparatus: Two types

Performance as:

1. Relay of Meaning (Heterogeneous manufacture)	2. Production of meaning (Serial manufacture)
Message from the Symbolic (God, King, star)	(No message from the Symbolic)
Transmission of message through performance (producers, actors)	Reality as raw material for meaning production (author/producer)
Reception of the message (audience)	Reception as meaning production by audience as bearers of Symbolic function

3

The Absolutist Gaze:
Political Structure and Cultural Form

The question of nationalism (or more precisely, the formation and the chances of consolidation of nation-states) in post-colonial countries has been the object of reflection in much recent work. In the 'Notes on Italian History' Gramsci developed the concept of 'passive revolution' as a 'criterion of interpretation' (Gramsci 1971: 114). In these notes, Gramsci was grappling with a central problem in the critique of political economy related to the development of capitalism beyond the borders of the primary capitalist states and involving a 'transmission' of 'ideological currents' from the 'more advanced countries' to the 'periphery' (ibid: 116–17). These reflections on 'passive revolution' and the related concept of 'war of position' have proved to be a very important point of departure for current thinking on the subject.

In one of the most ambitious applications of these concepts to the question of the postcolonial nation-state, Partha Chatterjee has argued, in *Nationalist Thought and the Colonial World* 'that passive revolution' is the *general* form of the transition from colonial to post-colonial nation-states in the 20th century' (Chatterjee, 1986: 50). In elaborating this thesis, Chatterjee notes how, according to Gramsci, there are 'organic tendencies of the modern state' which seem to favour the forces which carry out a protracted . . . 'war of position' rather than those which think only of an instantaneous 'war of movement' (ibid: 47). The open confrontation associated with the 'war of movement' does not suit the interests of emergent bourgeoisies in the underdeveloped peripheral regions. Under such conditions there are two possible options: either the pre-capitalist sites of resistance have to be modernized as a pre-condition of the establishment of a modern nation-state conducive to capitalist growth;

or a nation-state has to be established as the first step, to be followed by a process of reform from above which will gradually modernize the nation and expand the domain of capitalism.

In adopting the second approach, the national state banks on the colonial state machinery, which it inherits through the 'transfer of power' that marks the transition from a heteronomous state formation to a (relatively) autonomous one. An alliance of dominant classes[1] mobilizes the masses in support of its programme of development. However, this mobilization, and the transformation that it envisages, are limited in two 'fundamental ways':

> On the one hand, it does not attempt to break up or transform in any radical way the institutional structures of 'rational' authority set up in the period of colonial rule, whether in the domain of administration and law or in the realm of economic institutions or in the structure of education, scientific research and cultural organization. On the other hand, it also does not undertake a full-scale assault on all pre-capitalist dominant classes; rather it seeks to limit their former power, neutralize them where necessary, attack them only selectively, and in general to bring them round to a position of subsidiary allies within a reformed state structure (Chatterjee 1986: 49).

An interventionist state apparatus becomes the principal instrument of capitalist transformation in the absence of bourgeois hegemony over civil society (which is to say, in the absence of civil society). Capitalist control of the state apparatus is curtailed by the coalition within which the bourgeoisie has to function, and in which it can only pursue 'reformist and "molecular" changes' (ibid: 49).

Neil Larsen has also turned to the 'Notes on Italian History' in talking about the Latin American nation-states. Both Chatterjee and Larsen identify colonization as the crucial factor in the 'state first' model of capitalist development. The state in post-colonial societies 'finds itself enmeshed in an acute crisis originating in its own abstract negativity as an autonomous power'. Its principal tasks are the 'conquest of civil society' and the concomitant constitution of the 'unitary bourgeois subject' (Larsen 1990: 73).

The thesis that 'passive revolution' is the characteristic mode of transition to (and further development of) post-colonial nation-states

---

[1]See Pranab Bardhan (1984) and Achin Vanaik (1990) for a discussion of the dominant classes that constitute the ruling coalition in India. The bourgeoisie, the rich farmers and the professional classes have been identified by Bardhan (1984: 40-53) as the three principal constituents of the ruling coalition. See also Francine Frankel (1978) and Sukhamoy Chakravarty (1987).

enables us to retain a dialectical approach to the question of national autonomy/dependency. One of the problems faced by contemporary cultural theory is how to balance the perception of the cultural autonomy of post-colonial states with the reality of their dependent status in global capitalism. Even as we witness the steady erosion of the economic and political autonomy of these nations with the expansion of multinational capital and the military-political power of the NATO bloc, cultural theory takes on the responsibility of a compensatory assertion of absolute cultural autonomy for these beleaguered entities.[2] The paradox here is that the sources of this autonomy are seen to reside in the irreducible cultural differences between previously independently developing civilizations and communities, that is, in whatever already existed before the advent of a homogenizing capitalism. On the other hand, within the limits of a capitalist order the possibility of a difference and autonomy in a modern sense is predicated on the construction of a new national culture, itself dependent on political and economic autonomy.

Contrary to such axiomatic assertions of cultural autonomy therefore, this study will assume that there is a complex dialectic of autonomizing and heteronomizing tendencies within the field of mass culture where cinema is situated, and that the cultural forms arising from what Gramsci calls the 'transmission' of 'ideological currents' are a symptom of this dialectic. In particular, in a discussion of cultural forms, we must pay attention to the question of the production (and reproduction) of new subjectivities compatible with generalized capitalist development. The 'Citizen Subject', as Balibar has argued, is the elementary unit of the abstract State, an ideal unit whose actual realization is never complete, even in the most advanced of the capitalist countries. Nevertheless, this 'utopic figure' is, according to Balibar, 'the actor of a permanent revolution', a figure whose very positing, by the bourgeois revolution, inaugurates an unceasing struggle for the equality which was the unrealized premise of that revolution's philosophy (Balibar 1992: 54).

Although the Citizen-Subject remains an incompletely realized utopic figure in all instances, it is also the case that this non-realization itself takes specific forms in different nation-state formations. I will try to elaborate this by reference to Indian culture, where it can be

---

[2]Such, for instance, is the spirit behind the opening argument of Thomas (1985). Ashish Nandy's theory of popular Indian culture is also based on a similar assertion of an incommensurability of traditional and modern cultural sectors.

observed that the concept of 'citizen' remains an ideal attached to a unique individual, rather than an attribute that is automatically assumed to belong to all who inhabit the nation-state. Of course, in the political sphere, every citizen votes and thereby realizes his/her 'citizenness'. However, this sphere of symbolic equality is qualified not only by the real differences in wealth that undermine the equality (and indeed necessitate the discourse of equality as a disguise), but also by the uneven combination of ideologies which reproduces other political subject positions.

Post-independence Hindi narrative cinema has been dominated, as stated earlier, especially in the 1950s and 1960s, by a form that can be described as the feudal family romance. The dominant status of this form in popular cinema is a symptom of the nature of power in a ruling alliance in which the bourgeoisie is only one of several constituents. It is a compromise formation specific to the mutually beneficial co-existence, in independent India, of a colonial élite with a pre-capitalist social base and a bourgeoisie aspiring to the status of the dominant (if not the sole) partner in the coalition. The dominance of this form is evidence of the suspension of the process of re-constitution of the social around the figure of the citizen.

The feudal family romance, however, survives alongside tendencies towards the consolidation of realist and melodramatic aesthetic modes. While the feudal family romance is itself a 'melodramatic' form (corresponding to the stage melodrama of early capitalism), its romance form, hierarchical mode of address and its configuration of social space are in conflict with the aesthetic project represented by the new melodrama and realism. However, this conflict does not coincide with the idealist notion of a conflict between tradition and modernity. Rather, it represents a conflict between two ideologies of modernity, one corresponding to the conditions of capitalist development in the periphery, and the other aspiring to reproduce the 'ideal' features of the primary capitalist states. The following section will situate the feudal family romance in relation to the competing modes of film melodrama and realism in an attempt to chart the ideological forces at work in the project of Indian film culture. My attempt is to understand these cultural forms in relation to the processes of modernity, namely the formation of the modern state, the transformation of the social space into a value-generating order, and the project of expanding the field of operation of the figure of the citizen.

Realism and Melodrama

Both realism and melodrama have been acclaimed as aesthetic forms bearing an intimate relation to the democratic revolution. For a long time, it seemed as if realism alone was worthy of this distinction but in recent years, since the publication of Peter Brooks' *The Melodramatic Imagination* (1976) and a series of essays on film, beginning with Thomas Elsaesser's 'Tales of Sound and Fury', (see Landy 1991) the tide has turned in favour of melodrama. However, this shift has not been accompanied by any explanation of how and why these two forms can both claim to be *the* representative aesthetic form of a democratic society. The 'feminization' of mass culture has been shown to be a feature of cultural theory in the Modern West (Huyssen 1986). Thus, the gendered polarization of culture into a masculine sphere of autonomous modernist work of art, and a feminine sphere of heteronomous and formally diffuse mass culture, has led to an affirmation of melodrama as a feminine form and its pleasures as the denigrated but real and valued pleasures of female audiences.

However, melodrama, which in its early manifestations was too diffuse and fragmentary to be called a form in its own right, achieved its highest level of formal consistency precisely at the moment when it came to be specifically addressed to women, in the Hollywood women's melodrama (Gledhill 1987: 6) and in similar films made by the Bombay industry. On the other hand, a study of Indian film melodrama shows that in its most fragmented, patchwork texture, its most 'feminized' appearance going by Huyssens' argument, it was addressed to a wide, undifferentiated audience. Thus women's melodrama appears to be a specific branching off from a popular form; its achievement of a certain pre-eminence for a period in the history of Hollywood cinema may serve as an index to the prevailing social relations in American society, but the question of the conditions of possibility of melodrama remains unresolved.

The relation between melodrama and realism can be best understood by reference to the fiction of the social contract and the field in which the contract is held to be effective. Many of the early European and American stage melodramas were aristocratic romances.[3] In the search to identify a 'melodramatic imagination' it is possible to miss the fact that this 'form' does not derive its distinguishing properties from its thematic content, but from features that attest to its origins in a transitional social formation. It is the undifferentiated mass audience on the one hand, and the thematic eclecticism and episodic narration on the other that give melodrama its specificity (cf. Elsaesser on the many points of origin of the melodrama). It is futile to look for any 'essential' qualities of melodrama, any identifiable melodramatic imagination. As Mary Ann Doane (1987) has observed, the term melodrama has occasioned so many divergent explanations and applications that its usefulness as a critical term may well be doubted (Doane 1987: 71). While feminist film criticism has employed the term to designate the '50s family melodrama' of Hollywood, it has had a longer history in drama criticism as theatre has been the 'natural' habitat of the genre. In film criticism, while initially, as Pam Cook ('Melodrama and the Women's Picture' 1991) observes, melodrama was studied within the auteurist critical tradition, feminist intervention led to more generalized theoretical projects attempting 'a historical appraisal of the genre in cinema as a whole' (Cook 1991: 249; Gledhill 1987: 5). Beyond this, the very clear-cut genre differentiation that is characteristic of Hollywood cinema was itself seen to be overridden by the melodramatic worldview that all these genres shared (Landy 1991: 15). Thus, it could be said that all popular cinema is tendentially capable of being described as melodramatic.[4]

[3] A typical example is 'A Tale of Mystery' written by Thomas Holcroft in 1802 and based on a French original. Some of the most common plot devices of popular Hindi cinema are to be found in this play, in which an alliance between good aristocrats is threatened by the machinations of an evil aristocrat. J.B. Buckstone's 'Luke the Labourer' (1826) also has a familiar plot involving the downfall and restoration of a virtuous landowning family. Both the plays are included in Michael Kilgarriff's *The Golden Age of Melodrama* (1974), 34–52; 94–127.

[4] 'Today, the subgenre of the domestic melodrama is emphasized exclusively in attempts to define the filmic genre. Historical epics, gangster films, and horror films are seen as different genres, distinct from melodrama. This is at least partially a result of the tendency . . . of certain theorists to consider late nineteenth-century British and American melodramas as the precedent for filmic melodrama. Once the earlier history of melodrama is considered, we see the immense importance of the historical, supernatural, colonial, criminal, and mystery melodramas. They provide the antecedents for the historical epic, the gangster film, and the horror film. It certainly is necessary to consider the wide range of expression and subgenres that constitute the nineteenth-century melodrama' (Turim: 156). The Hindi cinema, compressing as it does the entire history of melodrama into a few decades of film production, is a uniquely appropriate site for the exploration of this cultural form.

The current accumulation of research seems to suggest in the case of Hollywood that no 'pure' melodrama exists in a separate state. 'Melodrama was at best a fragmented generic category and as a pervasive aesthetic mode broke genre boundaries' (Gledhill 1987: 6). Melodramatic and realist codes seem to occur in combination. Nevertheless, there remains the question of the different values associated with these two aesthetic modes. The realist aesthetic occupies a privileged place in the western imagination. In particular, the post-World War II emergence of Italian neo-realism on the international scene led to the equation of realism with democratic, anti-fascist ideologies while popular forms were described as escapist and corrupting (Landy, British Genres 1991: 19). To attribute such political functions exclusively to any aesthetic form is essentialist and anti-materialist; no aesthetic mode can be inherently democratic or reactionary. But the very existence of this hierarchy as well as the evolving compromise between the two aesthetic modes is indicative of the determination of the formal possibilities in capitalist culture by the hierarchies entailed by modern social structures.

Every representation of reality is not a realist representation. Realism is thus not so much a matter of the object of representation but a mode of textual organization of knowledge, a hierarchical layering of discourses. Colin MacCabe (1985), whose essay on realism elaborates this thesis, notes that the hierarchy of discourses in the 'classic realist text' is 'defined in terms of an empirical notion of truth'. In this type of text 'the narrative prose [here it is the literary realist text that is in question] functions as a metalanguage that can state all the truths in the object language . . . and can also explain the relation of this object language to the real' (MacCabe 1985: 34–5). The object language belongs to a world of indirection and opacity that is compensated by the transparent metalanguage. This metalanguage MacCabe describes as 'unwritten', not because it is not present in the novel but precisely because of its ambition to become a transparent medium for making visible the meanings immanent in the object language-world. In thus 'denying its own status as writing' (ibid: 36), the metalanguage of realist representation, I suggest, exactly corresponds to the in-betweenness of the figure of the *citizen*, who, as Balibar has observed can, by definition, be neither singular not collective.[5] The citizen-subject is a combination of the abstract unit of the bourgeois polity with the material, 'pathological' subject.

A difficulty arises when this definition of the classic realist text is sought to be applied to cinema. Here there is no manifest equivalent of the written discourse that aspires to 'unwrite' itself, the meta-language that, aspiring to a condition of absolute transparency, is nevertheless obliged to go through the materiality of writing. However, the camera's work of narration, 'which 'shows us what happens', functions as a metalanguage, providing 'the truth against which we can measure the discourses' (MacCabe 1985: 37). 'The narrative of events—the knowledge which the film provides of how things really are—is the metalanguage in which we can talk of the various characters in the film' (ibid: 38). What is significant here is the implication that in cinema the metalanguage moves closer to the condition of invisibility, while remaining identifiable in the traces of the work of narration.

But it is not only in cinema that such a potential disappearance of the metalanguage is observable. In his investigations of 'peripheral modernity', Neil Larsen has demonstrated how, in its further adventures within the literary domain, the metalanguage proves that it can indeed conserve all its ideological effects even as it completely disappears from the space of the text itself. Larsen's analysis of a story by Juan Rulfo, 'La Cuesta de las Comadres', while tracking the changing disguises of the metalanguage of realism, also introduces the element that is crucial to its broadened understanding: the question of the state.

[5]'The citizen properly speaking is *neither* the individual *nor* the collective, just as he is *neither* an exclusively public being nor a private being' (Balibar 1992: 51).

Here mention must be made of Elizabeth Deeds Ermarth's *Realism and Consensus in the English Novel* which argues that 'fictional realism is an aesthetic form of consensus' maintained by 'the agreement between the various viewpoints made available by a text' (Ermarth 1983: ix–x), such agreement witnessing the existence of a cohesive community. Ermarth does not regard this consensus as a 'consensus-effect', nor does she relate its emergence to the figure of the Citizen and the fiction of the contract, although in linking realism to the emergence of the Subject/Object duality (ibid: 77), she could be said to indirectly acknowledge the connection. Because her notion of 'consensus' is tied to the idea of 'community', Ermarth's use of the term remains ideological and does not connect the production of the consensus-effect with the destruction and dispersal of 'communities' at the beginning of the history of capitalism, a connection which enables us to see that the consensus-effect is an ideological evocation of community in the service of the dispersed mode of cohesion specific to contractual bourgeois society.

The story is narrated by an old farmer in a regional dialect[6] (corresponding to the 'object languages' whose reception the metal-anguage of realism tries to mediate). It recounts 'what at first appear to be two unrelated series of events: the sudden and unexplained depopulation of the small community of *ranchos* named in the title, and the equally suspicious activities of Remigio and Olidon Torrico, the two local *caciques* who have remained behind' (Larsen 1990: 57). This story, with its surprise ending, in which the narrator comes round to confessing to a murder, catches the reader unawares. 'For a reader attuned to the narrative signposts and motivations of a conventional prose realism, the initial effect produced by 'La Cuesta de las Comadres' is one of perplexity and shock' (ibid: 58). The reader is left without the reassuring mediation that a metalanguage provides. The source of the shock, thus, is the 'uncodedness' of violence 'within the cultural whole' (ibid: 59). A second reading that is aware of the ruse, Larsen observes, may suggest 'that this sense of an interior plenitude of spoken cultural substance is not self-sustaining but rather the effect of the *absence* of any obvious rationalizing authority on the level of the narrative discourse as a whole' (ibid: 59), in other words precisely that hierarchizing discourse of the metalanguage that is at once there and not there. But if it is not there in the text, where has it gone, and how does it produce its effects *in absentia*? Larsen's argument is that while it has disappeared from the horizontal axis of the narrative, its effects are produced on a vertical axis, from a place outside and above the text.

> The erasure of 'direct authorial word' from the horizontal axis of the narrative . . . appears . . . to be the result of its transfer or displacement, to a paradigmatic position from which it is able to govern the flow of narrative as if through filtration. The semic material upon which this vertical writing operates is not composed of words or meanings in the standard morphological sense but of whole narrative utterances, macroscopic blocks of a store of oral narrative, which the invisible authorial writing selects and arranges in a predetermined syntax (ibid: 61–2).

Thus the appearance of popular language independently of a dominating metalanguage does not constitute a freeing of the former from the latter. 'The transparency of writing to its regional object, understood transculturally as a failure or at least a deferral of the

---

[6]An English translation (without the 'dialect', of course), entitled 'The Hill of the Comadres' is available in Juan Rulfo (1967): 17–28.

bourgeois episteme, perhaps tells us something we are loath to hear—that this same "cognitive structure" has now learned to represent itself exlusively in the cultural/aesthetic signs of its Other' (ibid: 62).

Larsen relates the 'aesthetics of vertical writing' to 'the politics of the state as nonstate' (ibid: 63). When the rationalizing discourse of realism does not appear, it is because 'the state, the very center of extra-literary authority, has itself become a horizon of representation' (ibid: 67). In the transition from the classic realist text of European literature to this realism of peripheral modernity marked by a strategic suspension of rational mediation, the missing link is the figure of the citizen which, in its in-betweenness, performed the double function of the state-collective, and voice of narration, the present discursive agent of a self-absenting authority. The citizen as the mediating figure between state and individual is an elusive mechanism of social organization in conditions of underdevelopment. The 'regional and "barbaric" circuitries' that resist the formation of 'civil society' necessitate a different hegemonic strategy: 'the consensual stability of civil society must be sought through the direct control of these non-state circuitries themselves rather than through the traditional atomizing approach of the liberal metropolitan states (constitution of the modern 'citizen')' (ibid: 63).

From here we can proceed along two diverging routes to the further critique of realism. The first would remain within the framework of the discursive hierarchies of the realist text, encompassing both the classic realist text of the western tradition and the vertically controlled realist representations of peripheral modernity. The various 'nationalist realisms' like Italian neo-realism, and the realist experiments in Indian 'new cinema' as well as the manifestoes of realism like Bazin's which emphasize its political liberalism, fall within this problematic.[7] Most extensively elaborated in the writings by and about the Italian neo-realist film-makers, this aesthetic movement finds itself functioning as one of the mechanisms of the modern state's hegemonic project, giving *substance* to the state's claim to represent the 'nation' that it encompasses. The nation, which Robert Fossaert described as 'the discourse of the state'[8] is produced by various means: aesthetic realism is one of them. The

---

[7]Harry Levin' s cryptic observation, that realism has some connection with 'real estate' (Levin 1963: 68) begins to make sense in this context.

[8]Cited in Larsen (1990): 70.

land and the people, represented in their objective there-ness, constitute this substance.

The second route open to the critique of realism is the one isolated by MacCabe in his second essay on the subject. In a discussion of Hollywood cinema, MacCabe reminds us that by the Bazinian definition, these films are not realistic. However, the case for Hollywood realism is made, as already mentioned, by considering that the goal of realism, 'a transparency of form'—is achieved by Hollywood through cinematic practices of signification, whereas 'Bazin's criteria for distinguishing between films can only be based on non-filmic concerns' (MacCabe 1985: 60), i.e considerations of a qualitative kind centred on 'any narrative procedure which tends to make more reality appear on the screen' (Bazin).

Although by making visible the productive role of the camera and the suppression of contradiction in the realism of the Italian school, MacCabe makes a case for the fundamental unity of neo-realism and Hollywood realism, there is a secondary axis of difference between these two modes which the essay comes close to denying but eventually leaves open. If, then, we assume that there is a significant difference between these two modes of realism, how can this be defined? I have suggested above that the distinguishing mark of the first mode, which for convenience can be called nationalist realism (or realism arising at the level of the political instance), is its engagement in the project of producing the nation for the state. The Indian new cinema of the early seventies, especially the first three films of Shyam Benegal, employs this mode (see Chapter 8).

The second mode, identified with Hollywood, and more pertinent to our immediate concern, which serves as an ideal that the popular Hindi film sometimes strives to emulate, arises in the context of a desacralized social order where the free individual is the elementary unit. Here the determining factors include the organization of society into a self-reproducing value-generating order, a mode of regulation of the free circulation of individuals by means of a symbolic equality and citizenship. The realist imperative in this context consists in according primacy to the features of a rationally-ordered society—relations of causality, progression along a linear continuum marked by motivation, credibility, and action submitted, in the ultimate instance, to the narrative possibilities arising from the operation of the rule of law; the realist text in this sense is a sign of bourgeois hegemony.

This form of realism, contrasted with the melodrama of the

standard Hindi film, bestows an immanent unity (as opposed to a unity that derives from a transcendental plane) on its content. Coming into its own with the consolidation of the modern state, it is distinguished by a transformation of the field of perception such that the spectator's gaze is attracted by the unfolding of a sequence of events focussed around a central character, and whose meaning is constructed through the diegesis, under the aegis of legality.

In such 'rational fictions', the motivation of episodes in their sequencing ensures that a legally justifiable spectacle ensues as a result. Principles of credibility, necessity and relevance hold sway. Such a form does not tolerate 'extraneous' interpolations. The effectivity of the social contract is symptomatically manifested in the agreement to subordinate spectacle to the rules of credible, causal progression of narrative. The narrative contract is a clause of the social contract. Through its operation, the rationality of the bourgeois world is demonstrated and ratified. Narrative restraint—credibility— is a chastisement of non-rational ambitions. To flout the norms of narrative credibility is to flout the law.

I shall employ the term *mise-en-valeur* to designate this work of textual organization that produces the real as rational.[9] When Bombay film-makers talk about realism, they have in mind precisely this project of a *mise-en-valeur* which would streamline the standard film text with its episodic and fragmentary form deriving from stage melodrama, eliminate features that interfere with a unified linear narration, achieve a system of generic differentiation which would

[9]I have chosen this term because it resonates with the other term—*mise-en-scene*—that has become the standard term in English for the organization of profilmic space. The association helps to understand the meaning of the second term, which pertains to the text as a whole and the way in which the elements within that whole are organized. However, the term is not my own: it was used by the French colonial administrator Gallieni to describe a stage in the process of colonization that followed after the first stage of 'pacification' which involves the military. In the second stage, the administrators take charge, in order to dissolve the traditional communities, to establish a new pattern of relations between the colonizer, the colonized and the natural resources of the pacified region which would be conducive to a modern system of value-generation (see Gallieni 1949: 242–7). While my use of the term is somewhat different, there remains an area of overlap with Gallieni in so far as the ongoing project of modernization in peripheral countries like India continues to be centred on precisely such a reorganization of human and natural 'resources' into a capitalist production system. Indeed, the term can be applied to the general process of capitalist expansion around the globe, which proceeds with a similar mix of coercion and administrative initiative and is directed towards the elimination of blockages in the circuit of value-generation, like traditional communities' resistance to the development of new needs. A link is thus suggested here between political economic processes and the transformations registered in the cultural sphere.

break up the heterogeneous components of the 'social' super-genre and enable their separate development and exploitation,[10] subordinate the quasi-autonomous factors of the production process to the overall supremacy of the main narrative trajectory and so on.

Mise-en-valeur operates at the level of the economic and legal instances of modern social formations. It has two sides, deriving from these two instances. On the one hand, the legal instance imposes the requirements of credible, rational progression of narrative and subordination of the 'moral' world to the functioning of the legal system. On the other hand, the economic instance calls for streamlining and product differentiation, a rational distribution and ordering, across the text, of affective values, a textual economy that favours internal unity. In combination, these two logics make possible a realism that differs from the politically inspired national realism. However, these two modes of realism are not always to be found in a pure form. Instead, it would be accurate to say that individual texts lean more strongly towards one or the other. At one extreme, the spectator's gaze coincides with the frame itself and operates a vertical control over the space of the narrative, and in the process approximates the relation of state to nation. At the other extreme, the random configurations of the narrative are focussed by anchoring the spectator's gaze in a relation of identification with a central character, and thus the citizen as the individual embodiment of the legal order is called into being.

The Feudal Family Romance

Indian film melodrama, and its most important precursor, the Parsi theatre,[11] together compress the almost 200-year history of European/American melodrama into less than 100 years of discontinuous evolution. Indian film melodrama has affinities not only with the film melodrama of the west, but also, and more significantly, with

[10]See an article by Dadasaheb in *Filmfare*, 8 January 1954, p. 11 which recommends that shorter films with no songs be shown along with shorts on the music and dances of India; Chetan Anand (*Filmfare*, 25 May 1956) said each film should be in two versions, of which one would be 'short, dramatic, intense and thematic' and suitable for export to the West; during a period of raw stock shortage film-makers were urged to make use of the situation to produce 'shorter, more integrated films': *Filmfare*, 24 August 1962, p. 3.

[11]Balwant Gargi 1962: 154–61. Also relevant is Gargi's discussion of the regional theatres, particularly that of Bengal. See also Anuradha Kapur (1993).

the stage melodrama of early nineteenth-century Europe and America. David Grimsted's study of American melodrama in the first half of the nineteenth century is helpful in tracing the formal and thematic similarities between this tradition and Indian cinema.

Thus Grimsted observes that early American melodrama's 'class structure remained generally feudal and predominantly populated with kings and peasants, lords and ladies'. Within this broad framework, variations were possible, 'slaves, peasants, and mechanics were all allowed at times its most elevated roles' (Grimsted 1968: 208). Characteristic situations included babies being switched in their cradles, children thrown into rivers and rescued by gypsies, servants or monks who were sworn 'to 20 years of secrecy', secret marriages, princes in disguise, etc. (ibid: 175). While 'it was a belligerently egalitarian feudalism', the twists and turns of the plot would succeed in cancelling this egalitarian displacement, most commonly through last minute disclosure of the lowly character's noble birth (ibid: 208). The dislocations of social rank which enable narrative movement in these melodramas are also found in fairy tales and aristocratic romances; the incipient egalitarianism of these plays could also be read as a mechanism of aristocratic self-legitimation, a way of figuring the prince's or noble's organic relationship with his subjects.

A similar feudal structure provides the basic framework for a majority of Indian film melodramas. From the immensely popular *Kismet* (1943) made by Bombay Talkies to the early post-independence *Andaz* (1949) and *Awara* (1951) and further, to the dominant feudal family romances of the 1950s and 1960s, this basic structure reasserts itself. In most films this structure appears in an attenuated form but occasionally one encounters it in all its splendour.

Khandan (Bhim Singh 1965) is a good example. The narrative centres round the threat posed to the unity of a feudal landowning family by the intrusion of alien values embodied in the figures of the villain and his sister played by Pran and Mumtaz, the Singapore-returned relatives of the landlord's selfish wife. Their arrival signals the introduction of greed, western social norms and dress, the conversion of traditional wealth into cash, speculative business ventures (Pran takes cash from his aunt and invests it in a circus) and a voyeuristic sexuality. In contrast to the folk rhythm of the songs sung by the villagers, the Mumtaz character and her lover, wear tight shiny clothes and sing a fast dance number full of English words in a setting that looks more like a city park than a rural landscape. Their coming is preceded by the arrival of a poor orphaned woman (Nutan) who, while working as a servant, nurtures the handicapped hero and shows herself worthy of admission into the family. The conflict of values results in a partitioning of the joint family's property between the two brothers, who had till then lived together in harmony.

The villain's attributes are significant: his name, Navrangilal, signifies a changeable, unstable nature, while his parentage (born of an Indian father and a mother who is seen as non-Indian because Goa, her place of birth, was still a Portuguese colony) indicates a new national type that is antithetical to the organic and longstanding heritage that the landowning élite claimed for itself. On arriving in India, he declares it his 'fatherland' and is reminded of the preferred description, 'motherland'—the latter signifying a way of relating to the land that is characteristic of the countryside.

Preceding the villain's arrival, the landowning class's preferred relation to modernity is articulated in the course of a family chat. While the older members of the family talk ironically about the 'darkness' that electricity has brought to the community, the hero (who was paralysed when he climbed up an electric pole to retrieve a kite) refers to the benefits of electricity, signalling a possibility of assimilation of the technological aspects of modernity into the old order. The social order ushered in by the new national type, represented by Navrangilal, however, is firmly rejected. The celebration of Janmashtami and readings from the *Ramayana* indicate this class's conception of the legitimacy of its socio-economic power. Another more contemporary source of legitimation is Gandhianism, with its emphasis on the stability of village communities, and the role of the wealthy as trustees. The power of the modern to destroy this order derives from certain weaknesses internal to the order, such as the absence of male heirs (since the hero is the son of the younger brother, the line of inheritance is not direct, thus creating a gap which the wife's family tries to widen in order to appropriate the wealth) or, as in the case of the hero, a debility caused by the advent of modernity. The restoration of the old order at the end coincides with his being cured of this handicap. The feudal order has its own scopic regime which comes into conflict with that of the new order. The voyeuristic look is prohibited. With the arrival of Pran, however, we are presented with the only voyeuristic composition in the film, where Pran in the foreground, with his back to the camera, looks at Nutan, her body framed internally by a door, as she sweeps the yard.

This basic narrative structure, where the unity and jouissance of the feudal family, its control over its accumulated wealth, is threatened by usurpers and modern values, is repeated in numerous films of this period. The stability of this structure in the period preceding the early 1970s is proved by films like *An Evening in Paris* (1967) and *Love in Tokyo* (1966), where, even though the action unfolds against an international setting, the essential features of the feudal family structure remain firmly in place. From the organic space of the north Indian village to the high-tech tourist spots of the world, the feudal structure displays a mobility that demonstrates how powerful its ideological hold was and to an extent still is. This structure could incorporate consumerism and other 'modern' features without damage as long as it did not slide into a position of affirmation of new sexual and social relations based on individualism. The 'foreign' values that came in for vicious criticism occasionally were a code word for democracy and a capitalism based on the generalization of free labour.

The powerful hold that this structure has had on the narrative possibilities of the Indian cinema is evident in that an emerging middle-class ideology opposed to the feudal family structure still requires a staging of this conflict between the feudal and the democratic as in Rajkumar Santoshi's *Damini* (1993; see Chapter 9). In such films, which stage a transition from the aristocratic melodrama to a democratic version, we are reminded that melodrama is not inherently democratic, as some commentators have argued, but is a structure within which a struggle between classes, between old and emergent forces, is enacted. Thus we must posit a break between early melodrama, with its aristocratic themes, and the middle-class melodrama, in which we encounter a form that has made a compromise with the dominant realist aesthetic.

Of the crime films of the fifties, *Kala Pani* (Raj Khosla 1958)[12] also employed a broad democracy versus feudalism approach, in its organization of the detection plot. The detective story is one of the popular forms that teaches the cultural values of the new capitalist hegemony. In his cultural writings Gramsci referred to the absence of a detective story tradition indigenous to Italy, and the consequent popularity of serialized detective stories from other countries, which is viewed as a symptom of the failure to constitute a new national

[12]See Vasudevan (1993) on the significance of the Indian crime film of the 1950s.

culture (*Cultural Writings* 1985: 254–5; 359–62; 369–74)[13]. In India, Guru Dutt and Dev Anand, together with directors like Raj Khosla tried their hand at the detective film. Although these films—like *Kala Pani* and *C.I.D.* (Raj Khosla 1956)—had a very elementary plot, the narratives had a distinct anti-aristocratic thrust.

In *Kala Pani,* the hero's investigation of a 15-year old murder for which his father was wrongly convicted, unfolds in a social space characterized by the coexistence of the feudal and the modern in an uneasy consensus enforced by the feudal elements who continue to control the institutions of the modern state. On the side of the good are the hero, his parents, his lover (the daughter of a lodge-keeper), and his friends (who include a penniless poet, a retired and penitent police officer and a waiter). The feudal order is represented by a Dewan, who is the real murderer, and his lawyer, also a colonial aristocrat as his title ('Rai Bahadur') suggests, who represents the colonization of the democratic legal apparatus by feudal interests. There is also the in-between world of the courtesans, where the murder took place, peopled by ambiguous figures like Kishori, who blackmails the Dewan with an incriminating letter and later surrenders to the new values represented by the hero, by assisting him in his search for justice.

The occasion for the narrative is the discovery by the hero that his father, whom he believed dead, was alive and serving a life-term for murder. This secret had been maintained by his mother and uncle, both of whom were anxious to spare him the shame of dishonourable parentage. *Kala Pani* thus revolves around the distinction between honour (which has to be maintained by secrecy, by suppression of the unpalatable) and conscience (which requires the uncovering of truth, the coincidence of word and reality). In this struggle the legal system is democracy's ally, although it must be freed from the control of the feudal class. In a revealing scene, the Dewan suggests to his lawyer that they eliminate the intruding hero, who is digging up the past, whereupon the lawyer reminds him that the aristocratic order does not exist anymore. The murder took place in 1943, linking the aristocratic order with the era of British rule. The police officer who convicted the hero's father declares that he

---

[13]The relation between hegemony and aesthetic forms is also touched upon by Roy Armes (1971), who observes that the 'prevalence of short story over novel, in Italy as in Germany, is a reflection of wider issues: until quite recent times any sort of coherent social view has been impossible because of the political disunity of the country' (p. 23).

had borne the guilt of having wrongly accused an innocent man and had resigned from his job at India's independence, so that its fledgling legal order would not be tainted.

The 'truth' that the hero of *Kala Pani* seeks is a legal truth, based on the legal discourse's emphasis on precision of language. As such it enables an escape from the moral categories of shame and sinfulness which, in their diffuse and flexible application, do not allow for exoneration. Thus, the father's immorality is beyond question: even if he did not kill the courtesan, he frequented the brothel. Sinfulness is established on the basis of such association. But the question that the hero undertakes to solve is a *legal* question, concerning his father's guilt in the murder of a courtesan. It is this shift, from the morality of sinning by association to the legality of guilt by commission, that reactivates a legal apparatus and a new style of narrative involving investigation (the hero poring over newspaper reports that are 15 years old), and mystery. It also mobilizes the *nation*, represented by the newspaper and the reading public, against the diffuse *biradari* and *samaj* (community) which allocate honour. Such instances notwithstanding, the family romance centred around aristocratic or otherwise exemplary figures retained its hold through the sixties.

Early melodrama tends to privilege the moral sphere over the legal (Grimsted 1968: 225–6). One striking feature of *Andaz* (1949) is the position occupied by the legal structure *vis-à-vis* the moral imperatives of the feudal family.[14] The heroine, who transgresses the feudal moral code by engaging in a series of covert romantic exchanges with a stranger during the absence of the man who is pre-ordained to be her husband, ends up killing the stranger in order to prove her innocence and is tried and sentenced to prison. In the end she declares her punishment as justly deserved, not for the murder, but for her transgression of the moral code. Here the law is figured as being in consonance with the feudal family's worldview, rendering a justice that restores a moral order that is, strictly speaking, beyond its jurisdiction.

Speech in the early melodrama is conventional, contrived, excessive. 'Even when a specific object was mentioned, the reference was usually both metaphorical and highly conventionalized.' It was a language suited to the idealized, extraordinary world that was represented, a world of moral absolutes which did not afford a

---

[14]See discussions of *Andaz* by Ravi Vasudevan (1993) and Paul Willemen (1993).

'taste of real life' because 'Elevation was the primary aim' (Grimsted 1968: 231). Language in melodrama is not derived from realist speculations about the necessities of the situations and characters represented. The characters are objects of emulation or disapproval rather than identification.[15] As such they speak a language suited to the primary function of representing the conflicts of a moral order. They are, as Paul Willemen has suggested, agents or functions, rather than characters in the realist sense, and as such they are conceived in a non-psychological manner, liberating them from the obligation to speak like 'real people' (Willemen 1993: 185; Elsaesser 1991: 69).

Discussions of Hollywood melodrama have not paid much attention to this question of language or dialogue, which is all-important in considerations of western stage melodrama. There is a reason for this: in Hollywood melodrama, the camera's role as an instrument of signification and the visual codes of representation acquire primacy over the dialogue, which is reduced to a complementary function. In the movement towards the consolidation of a separate genre of women's melodrama, there also occurs a subordination of the stage melodrama's textual anarchy to the control of a realist aesthetic code.[16] The excesses of dialogue are in the process pared down considerably. The feudal family melodrama of Indian cinema, however, retains the autonomous signifying function of dialogue intact. Dialogue-writing is a specialization in the Indian film industry, with its own minor star system. In Chapter 2, I argued that this pattern of autonomization of skills and talents led to the prevalence of the heterogeneous form of manufacture in the Bombay film industry. The narrative structure of the feudal family romance is an effect of this separation. This feudal order claims a divine sanction for its power and authority, a claim that is reinforced by the references

---

[15]From the beginning, melodrama, as a theatrical tradition, was defended as a means of popular education, in which 'people were not shown the world as it is, but rather as it should be' (de Pongerville, a French writer, cited in Hyslop 1992: 65.) Hyslop discusses the debate over melodrama in which Pixerecourt, known as the 'father of melodrama', defends it as an instructional medium with a high moral purpose. She argues, against Peter Brooks and Thomas Elsaesser, that the 'democratic' nature of melodrama cannot be taken for granted (pp. 67–8).

[16]Thus E. Ann Kaplan notes that 'in the modern period (unlike melodrama in other cultures), in Europe and North America the genre used realism. This was because, in order to consolidate its power, the bourgeoisie desired art that mirrored its institutional modes, forms, rituals, making them seem natural, nonideological, "given".' (Kaplan 1992: 12). For a very useful comparative history of national melodramatic traditions, see Maureen Turim (1993).

to the epics and their semi-divine heroes (although historically, the power and wealth of the landowning class derives from the social order instituted by British colonial rule). Representations of this order and the threats posed to it are enunciated from its own point of view, while making this point of view coincide with the will of a divine authority. Thus speech in such a configuration can only be *already interpreted* speech, whose meanings are readily visible on the surface (cf. Barthes (1973) on myth). By contrast, in the realist text the spectator/reader holds the interpretive authority (at least formally) and is therefore presented with a speech that is *immanent* to a represented scene.

At stake here is also the feudal order's firm resistance to the 'invention of the private' which is a mark of the transition to a modern state. For speech in melodrama is cleansed of its private, interpersonal character and elevated to the status of a symbolic discourse. According to Peter Brooks, melodrama penetrates the 'surface reality' of everyday life to get 'under the surface of things' where a 'mythological realm' of 'large moral entities' comes into play. From this topography, Brooks, derives the notion of a 'moral occult' that is the stuff of melodrama. Perhaps it would be more accurate to say, of the early western stage melodrama and Indian film melodrama in any case, that it aspires to the transcendental, ceaselessly sublimating the realities of existence into mythical moral categories because these are the currency of human interaction in the pre-modern symbolic order maintained by the church and the monarchic state. The language of melodrama reduces practical activity to a mythical residue.

Due to its rigid commitment to a moral project, this primary narrative segment of the early melodrama cannot, as Grimsted put it, give us a 'taste of real life'. However, these plays incorporated scenes representing ordinary life situations, with recognizable people speaking a more familiar language. 'Less elevated in principle and sentiment than the heroine', these characters were either servants (in European plays) or simply poor people, 'lively, good-natured and often in love with one another'.

> In contrast to the characters in the central structure of the melodrama, they partook more of purely human qualities and less of superhuman virtue or subhuman baseness. The good were likely to be worldly-wise, and the bad to have a roguish charm. If seldom many-sided human beings, neither were they moral abstractions (Grimsted 1968: 183–4).

This aspect of early melodrama too is reproduced in the Hindi film. The above description could be applied word for word to the 'comedy track' that was a standard feature of Hindi cinema all through the sixties. Comic characters played by Johnny Walker, Tuntun, Agha, Manorama, Dhumal, Bhagwan, Mehmood, Rajendranath, Jagdeep, etc. figured in these comedy scenes often as servants in the feudal household, or as the hero's or heroine's accomplices. The hero's male friend and the heroine's female companion often went through a romance that ran parallel to the main narrative and involved some very worldly negotiations and deceptions in which, for instance, the female comic's father, who aspired to marry his daughter to a social superior, would be deceived into agreeing to the comics' alliance. The hero's comic accomplice is often conceived of on the lines of Hanuman, the monkey-assistant of the epic hero Rama.[17] This fact perhaps led some critics to regard the comedy track as a distinctly Indian feature deriving from Indian theatrical traditions. However, the association with Hanuman is an additional coding of a feature integral to the structure of the melodramatic form, just as the feudal family's colonial wealth and power is given a divine legitimation by associating it with the moral order of the epics.

The Structure of Spectation

What the two modes of realism discussed above share is a premise that the world represented on the screen is, in Christian Metz's (1986) words, a world that is seen without giving itself to be seen. This premise, the true mark of realism, is what distinguishes it from melodrama. The difference emerges sharply in a little story told by Rossellini, about how he deals with non-professional actors:

> I watch a man in life and fix him in my memory. When he finds himself before a camera, he is usually completely lost and tries to 'act', which is exactly what must be avoided at all costs. There are gestures which belong to this man, the ones he makes with the same muscles which become paralyzed before the lens. It is as if he forgets

[17]Hanuman, the very embodiment of devotion and dedication to the master's cause, is the presiding deity of bachelor clubs, hire-cycle shops and lower-class body-building cults. As the quintessential subaltern subject, he is the figure of identification for the Bajrang Dal, the vigilante arm of Hindu nationalism.

himself, as if he never knew himself. He believes he has become a very exceptional person because someone is going to film him. My task is to return him to his original nature, to reconstruct him, to *reteach* him his usual movements (Rossellini 1979: 98).

While Rossellini wants to capture this person *as he really is*, the latter, upon seeing the camera, instantly begins to pose for it, to speak to it. He then has to be taught to 'be himself'. This story could be read as a parable about the difference between realism and melodrama. Rossellini's approach is that of the realist, who wishes to capture a reality that does not give itself to be seen, while the ordinary man cannot relate to the camera's presence without attempting to create an ideality—a combination of proper demeanour and proper speech—that, in his eyes, would be worthy of public circulation. It is not that the man 'forgets himself'; on the contrary, it is only when confronted by a camera that he remembers his existence and seeks to produce, from within himself, the distinction between what he really is and what must be represented. Realism disapproves of this because it wishes to retain the task of *representation* for itself. Melodrama, like the peasant before a camera, can be defined as a representation that gives itself to be seen.

But this realist convention is also the primary requirement of the voyeuristic look of the spectator in the cinema. As Laura Mulvey has argued, the separation of the object from the look directed towards it is central to the constitution of the 'active' voyeuristic aspect of scopophilia. 'Although the film is really being shown, is there to be seen, conditions of screening and narrative conventions give the spectator an illusion of looking in on a private world' (Mulvey 1975: 9), of 'unauthorized scopophilia' (Metz 1986: 264). Taken in its double function as both a voyeuristic relation and a realist convention, this structure of spectation is distinguished by a displacement of the contractual relation from the site of the performance to a place outside it. There is no longer a contractual coming together of performer and spectator for a mutually agreed purpose. Instead, there is established a contractual link between the members of the audience, including the film-makers, thanks to which the object-world can be represented in its there-ness. It is this latter contract that is at the base of the metalanguage of realism and it is because of the operation of this contract that it is possible for the metalanguage to effectively disappear in its material aspect without eliminating any of its effects.

But there is a second, narcissistic aspect of scopophilia which is a function of ego libido (Mulvey 1975: 10), and involves the mechanism of imaginary identification with an ego ideal. This mechanism has the narrative function of organizing the field of perception around a central figure with whom the spectator identifies. It could be argued that this mechanism functions to supplement the invisible metalanguage of the contract with an internal contractual relation. This is necessary because the contractual relation that supports the metalanguage does not include all in its purview, and is mostly closed to subaltern subjects, especially women (but also the lower castes and the proletariat in general), who are regulated by the contract without being its signatories.[18] Excluded from the abstract space of the social contract, the subject requires another kind of anchoring in the real, another axis of relation with the world, which subtends the performance relation. The star, who, despite appearances, is best understood as a reality reference for the subject, is one such 'charismatic' supplement (Dyer 1991). As Mulvey observes, 'the cinema has distinguished itself in the production of ego ideals as expressed in particular in the star system, the stars centring both screen presence and screen story as they act out a complex process of likeness and difference' (Mulvey 1975: 10).

The contractual space ends where the domestic space begins. This is the space of femininity and love, the space where modern film melodrama unfolds. The two limits to the contract's effectivity are thus the family and the world of the subaltern. These are the sites in which many modern narratives are situated, although the watchful eye of the citizen's law is always present, whether in the form of male characters representing the rational world or an invisible frame of intelligibility coinciding with the sphere of the state.

This structure of spectation in which the spectator occupies an isolated, individualized position of voyeurism coupled with an anchoring identification with a figure in the narrative is specific to western popular cinema and a small tendency within Indian cinema. Turning to the Hindi feudal family romance we find that its organization of the look differs from the above model in being governed by a pre-modern institutionalized structure of spectation embodied in the tradition of *darsana*. There is no study of the politics of darsana (literally 'seeing') that would enable us to identify

---

[18]See Kant (1983), pp. 61–92 on who can be a citizen, i.e. a signatory to the contract.

its principal characteristics.[19] But in its most widely employed sense, darsana refers to a relation of perception within the public traditions of Hindu worship, especially in the temples, but also in public appearances of monarchs and other elevated figures. Typically this structure is constituted by the combination of three elements: the divine image, the worshipper and the mediating priest. In common parlance, the act of going to the temple is perceived as involving the 'taking' of darsana (*darsan lena*) by the devotee and the 'giving' of darsana (*darsan dena*) by the divinity in question. (This is in Hindi. In the south Indian languages the equivalent expression translates as 'making' or 'doing' darsana) The practice signifies a mediated bringing to (god's) presence of the subject, who, by being seen by the divine image, comes to be included in the order instituted and supported by that divinity. The mediation of this relation by the priest is not incidental but is integral to the structure. The priest performs the task of bringing the devotee to the divinity's attention. In this structure, the priest has monopoly over the verbal invocation by means of which the perceptual link between devotee and divinity is brought about and rendered meaningful.

The devotee's muteness is a requirement of the entire process. The devotee's look, moreover, is not one that seeks to locate the divinity, to inspect it and be assured of its existence. It is not a look of verification but one that demonstrates its faith by seeing the divinity where only its image exists and by asking to be seen in turn. It is not surprising that in the more individualized modes of worship that have developed on the fringes of this central institution, the devotees close their eyes and connect with the deity through *words*. This development constitutes a threat to the monopoly over language that the priest enjoys in the orthodox structure but given the persistence of this monopoly over language(s) in other spheres of modern society, there continues to operate a set of relations akin to those characteristic of the temple darsana structure.

Before the transformation of the cinematic field in the crisis of the early seventies, the darsana structure imposed a set of protocols of perception that differed from the two inter-related aspects of scopophilia. In the first place, contrary to the voyeuristic relation, in

[19]I have come across only two studies of darsana, by Diana Eck (1981) and Lawrence Babb (1981), neither of which, however, deals with the political dimension of this institution of spectatorship. Ravi Vasudevan has also noted the significance of the notion of darsana to the study of popular Indian cinema.

the *darsanic* relation the object gives itself to be seen and in so doing, confers a privilege upon the spectator. The object of the darsanic gaze is a superior, a divine figure or a king who presents himself as a spectacle of dazzling splendour to his subjects, the *'praja'* or people. Unlike the hero of the democratic narrative, who is, by common understanding, 'any individual subject', the hero of the feudal family romance is not chosen randomly by the camera but belongs to the class of 'the chosen' in the extra-filmic hierarchic community.

The object of the darsanic gaze is only amenable to a symbolic identification: 'in imaginary identification we imitate the other at the level of resemblance—we identify ourselves with the image of the other inasmuch as we are "like him", while in symbolic identification we identify ourself with the other precisely at a point at which he is inimitable, at the point which eludes resemblance' (Zizek 1989: 109). Imaginary identification, however, is enabled by the comedy track, where more familiar, less exalted figures enact a more worldly drama of everyday life. The structure of this staggered identification process powerfully links up, as already noted, with the relation between Hanuman and Rama in the *Rāmāyana*, especially as elaborated in popular discourse. This aspect particularly is strongly apparent in the regional cinemas of the south where male comic actors often declare an abiding loyalty to the reigning male star, both on screen as well as off.[20]

It is in relation to the figure of the woman, according to Mulvey, that 'the gaze of the spectator and that of the male characters in the film are neatly combined' (Mulvey 1975: 12), giving rise to the 'split between active/male and passive/female' (ibid: 11). It is crucial to determine how Hindi films, while inviting the darsanic gaze, are able to deal with this form of voyeurism. One explanation is that typically the Hindi film combines two modes of representation ('realist' narration and a series of punctuating tableaux) as Ravi Vasudevan has insightfully argued. As such it can include scenes of voyeuristic fixing of the female figure as object, while elsewhere asserting the unavailability of the female figure for the spectator's enjoyment. But there are other clues that point to another possible explanation. One such clue lies in the fact that the erotic exhibition

---

[20]Dwarakish, a popular comic actor in Kannada films, was once shown with an open shirt revealing a vest on which the face of Rajkumar, the top male Kannada film star, was printed. This recalls the popular calendar image of Hanuman ripping open his chest to reveal the image of Rama in the place where his heart should be.

of the female figure is mostly confined to the presumably non-diegetic space of the song. (Where it is not so confined, the voyeuristic look is attributed to the villain, as in the *Khandaan* scene discussed above and is coded as irredeemably evil.) The song-and-dance is a form of spectacle that belongs to the order of contracted performances like stage dances, cabarets and the striptease. As such it calls for a direct perception of the spectacle rather than a perception mediated by the identificatory relation. The frontal orientation of the screen image, especially in the song-and-dance sequences, makes the erotic spectacle less capable of functioning as a device of male-to-male identification. This is not to say that the Hindi film narrative does not privilege the male; however, this privilege does not derive from such cinematic strategies.

Another deployment of the darsanic gaze can be seen in Hindi cinema of the post-70s, especially in the Amitabh Bachchan films. The most interesting example of this is the 1989 film *Main Azad Hun* (Director: Tinu Anand), which is a remake of Frank Capra's *Meet John Doe* (1941) with an original darsanic twist that is different from the many variations on the ending that Capra is said to have tried.[21] In the Hindi version Azad dies. In the original, John Doe is prevented from committing suicide by the intervention of the reporter and the people, who assure him that the movement bearing his name will continue and will succeed in its mission of asserting the rights of 'the common man'. But it is not the difference between dying and living that makes the ending of the Hindi version so unique. It is the fact that, after his death, Azad's videotaped message to the people (who are figured not as 'other John Does' who are inspired by him as in the Capra film but as followers, or more precisely, fans) is played on a giant screen in a sports stadium in a drama of resurrection and apotheosis staged by the reporter and her associates. This mode of inviting the darsanic gaze is characteristic of the populist films of Amitach Bachchan. But in *Main Azad Hun,* made after Bachchan's political decline had begun, the power and charisma of the popular hero is appropriated by his managers who wield his image as a weapon in the political struggle for the people's support. The popular hero's relation with the people is thus mediated by a priestly class consisting of journalists and other middle-level agents.

Thus, in the Hindi film the gaze is mobilized according to the

---

[21]See Charles Wolfe (1989) for the story of how the film's ending became a national issue, and for a sampling of variations on the ending.

rules of a hierarchical despotic public spectacle in which the political subjects witness and legitimize the splendour of the ruling class. In the horizontal organization of the image-series that characterizes the realist narratives, the spectator's gaze is powerful in its active voyeuristic holding of the image but at the same time its control is forever threatened by the possibility that the distance that separates the look from the object may widen into an unbridgeable gulf. The pleasure of voyeuristic capture derives from the overcoming of this very threat. However, the despotic spectacle creates its own field of perception into which the subject must enter in order to see and be seen—the spectator's gaze here is not threatened by the perils of voyeurism.

In a society of castes and traditional ruling élites, the 'private' cannot be represented in public (or, to put it differently, images cannot be represented from a 'private' point of view) because such a representation violates the ruling class's scopic privileges (this is taken up in detail in Chapter 4). In this context it is pertinent to recall that for the British colonial government, cinema censorship became important not only to suppress overtly nationalist and anti-colonial films made in India, but also to prevent the colonized from seeing images (especially in American films) of white people engaged in activities that exposed the well-kept secret that the white race was also human. Ruling classes protect themselves by claiming to protect their women and it was the 'damage done to the image of British women through the films, mainly American, screened in India' that led to the introduction of pre-censorship of films in 1918. Indeed, the recommendation by W. Evans that 'films suited to an Indian audience' (Baskaran, nd) should be encouraged was not unrelated to a perceived need to wean Indian audiences away from the films about white society which made them contemptuous of British authority.[22]

[22]See also the *Report of the Enquiry Committee on Film Censorship* 1969; Margaret Dickinson and Sarah Street's *Cinema and State: The Film Industry and the British Government 1927–84* (1985), shows that the British had their own ideas of nationalism which included a sense that the colonies were part of the 'nation', although this claim was made only in the context of a perception that 'trade follows film', that audiences were 'hypnotised into purchasing items' they had seen in American films. But there was the additional fear of exposure of the 'private' realm of white society to Indian eyes. In a parliamentary debate on the subject, Lord Newton declared: 'Imagine what the effect must be upon millions of our coloured fellow citizens in remote parts of the world who perpetually have American films thrust upon them which frequently present the white man under the most unfavourable conditions' (Dickinson and Street 1983: 16). Then as now, American films represented a 'cultural invasion', though for different reasons.

The history of Indian cinema shows that it has not been easy to overcome this injunction against the subordination of spectacle to an individualized point of view.[23] Far from being a 'natural' derivative of India's cultural heritage, therefore, the Indian popular film is the product of a specific political conjuncture whose historical force has not yet been exhausted. A struggle for the reorganization of film spectacle around an individualized point of view has been waged by a section of the industry. The universalization of the figure of the citizen is the political goal whose ideological supplement is the point of view narrative. However, in the early decades of independence, the 'public' spectacles staged by the 'social', with their emphasis on corporate identity, retained their position of dominance. At times, when new generic tendencies emerged, threatening to segment the audience, the 'social' reasserted its dominance through strategies of annexation that re-installed the absolutist subject at the helm of the narrative. *Sholay* achieved this in the seventies, against a sudden eruption of 'cowboy' and bandit films featuring small-time villains and cabaret dancers in leading roles, addressed to a predominantly proletarian B-movie audience (see Chapter 6). But there was an earlier instance of a similar 'return of the social' in the sixties, which demonstrates the centrality of the absolutist gaze to this super-genre. Here it was the middle-class audience that posed the threat of 'secession' from the consensual 'social'.

Why Rajendra Kumar Had to Die

In the detection plot of *Kala Pani*, we have seen how the individual hero's quest opens the space for a point of view narrative. Another generic tendency could be seen, beginning perhaps in the late fifties, and representing a move towards a Hollywood-style women's melodrama whose subsequent fate is illustrative of the nature of the struggle mentioned above. Films like *Chirag Kahan Roshni Kahan* (Devendra Goel 1959), *Dhool ka Phool* (Yash Chopra/BR Films 1959), *Dil Ek Mandir* (Sridhar/Chitralaya 1963) centred on the question of women's position in a modernizing society. These and other films represented an unmistakable generic tendency, with the actor Rajendra Kumar, who acquired a reputation as a 'women's star' often playing the male lead. These films were notable for their promotion

---

[23]On the centrality of narrative point of view as well as point of view narration to cinema's aesthetic identity, see Jacques Aumont, *Quarterly Review*: 11.

Raj Kapoor breaching the bond between Dilip Kumar and Nargis in *Andaz* (Mehboob 1954). Courtesy National Film Archive of India, Pune.

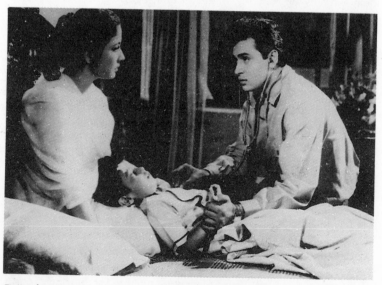

Rajendra Kumar and Meena Kumari in *Chirag Kahan Roshni Kahan* (Devendra Goel, 1959), a hero willing to belong wholly to the woman. Courtesy National Film Archive of India, Pune.

of middle-class consumerism in the course of narratives of love, betrayal, sacrifice and reunion. Of these *Dhool ka Phool* is perhaps the most remarkable. It tells the story of a woman who, abandoned by her lover, gives birth to a child, whom she in turn, abandons in a moment of fear and helplessness. Brought up by a kind old Muslim who is ostracized by his community and spurned by the Hindus for his act of kindness, the child becomes the focus of a narrative movement that ends with the Muslim man handing the child over to the mother, while the father is punished for his crime by being denied access to the child. *Chirag Kahan Roshni Kahan* concerns a forbidden romance between a widow with a child and a man who becomes fond of her child. In *Dil Ek Mandir* a forgotten romance is rekindled when a woman accompanies her husband to the hospital, where he is treated by her former lover. In all these narratives we see an attempt to represent the woman's point of view or to centre the narrative on a woman caught between desire and an oppressive tradition.

In *Dil Ek Mandir* the narrative movement is facilitated by a serial attention to the three main characters' points of view. Each of the characters is shown in interaction with the other two. Thus Rajendra Kumar and Meena Kumari have to work through the unfinished story of their romance; Meena Kumari has to establish her devotion to her husband; and Raaj Kumar (the husband) extracts a promise from Rajendra Kumar that in the event of his death the latter would marry Meena Kumari. The issue of widow remarriage is introduced in the form of a pact between two men about the future of a woman.[24] Although the film finally restores the status quo and eliminates Rajendra Kumar, its narrative structure is especially designed to allow for the elaboration of the thematics of love as a relation of mutuality in conflict with the compulsions of marriage. The husband's legitimacy is restored only after a full acknowledgement on his part of the legitimacy of his wife's relation with the doctor.

In 1964, a year after *Dil Ek Mandir*, Raj Kapoor released his megafilm *Sangam*. Critics regard this as a turning point in Kapoor's career because it was seen to mark the beginning of a shift away from the 'progressive' orientation of the fifties, when in collaboration

---

[24]When this pact is first broached there is a barely visible cutaway to a church seen through a window and lit by a flash of lightning, suggesting that widow remarriage has Christian sanction and thereby mitigating the scandal of a husband's proposal of his own wife's marriage to another man. At the same time, it also points to the fact that in India, for historical reasons, the reforms associated with modernity are perforce also linked up with a Christian world-view.

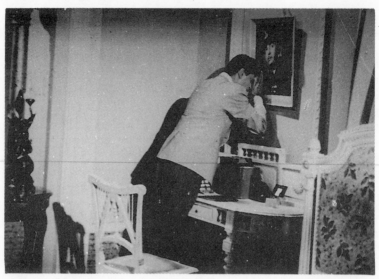

Guilty of love, Gopal (Rajendra Kumar) is full of remorse on hearing that Sundar (Raj Kapoor), presumed dead at the front, is alive and about to return home. *Sangam* (Raj Kapoor 1964). Courtesy National Film Archive of India, Pune.

Radha (Vyjayanthimala) is horrified when she realizes that Gopal (Rajendra Kumar) has written a love letter to Sundar in her name. *Sangam* (Raj Kapoor 1964). Courtesy National Film Archive of India, Pune.

with the socialist K.A. Abbas, he made films like *Awara* and *Shree 420*, towards big-budget extravaganzas (cf. Chakravarty, 1993: 216).

However, *Sangam* was an important event in Indian popular film history for a different reason. It represented a decisive (though not irreversible) generic reannexation of the fledgling women's melodrama by the national super-genre called the social, a genre predicated on the deployment of the absolutist gaze. This conquest was staged through a combination of strategies. The first of these was the expansion of the representational space of the narrative to include the defence of the nation-state as a factor in the unfolding of the story, thus reducing the family as site of melodramatic thematics to a position of unmistakable subordination. Secondly, the text incorporated a long segment, with little narrative value, shot on foreign locations and offering the pleasures of consumerism on an intensified scale. Thirdly, buttressed by these extraneous sources of power, the plot expanded to include both pre-and post-marital romantic conflicts. In *Dil Ek Mandir*, the narrative begins after the marriage and thus makes the pre-marital romance an event in the past, which the characters must come to terms with in the present narrative. In *Sangam*, the woman's romantic inclinations are allowed to develop *before* the marriage, thus opening up the possibility of choice and the need to find justifiable ways of denying her that choice. In thus giving itself a nearly irresolvable problem of woman's desire, *Sangam* risks more than the other women's melodramas mentioned above, but manages to find a resolution through the deployment of the compulsions of patriotism. The film can therefore be read as an allegory of resistance to generic differentiation where the latter tendency represents the fragmentation of the social body into 'interest groups'.

The central device of this narrative strategy is the *unseeing* hero, the 'blind' lover, played by Raj Kapoor. This is the figure of absolutist subjectivity, more visibly mobilized here than anywhere else, but nevertheless a characteristic ingredient of the popular film. The story begins with the three main characters as children, the two boys vying for the attention of the girl who gives early indications of being attracted to Gopal (Rajendra Kumar). While both the males are attracted to Radha (Vyjayantimala),[25] they are also attracted to each other by a strong homosocial bond of *dosti*, which in Hindi cinema functions as the code of fraternity that binds men into a

---

[25]The characters' names reinforce the allegorical reading: It is not just any couple but the mythical, ideal couple Radha and Gopal, that must be split in order to re-assert the privileges of Sundar, to submit the conjugal scene, once again, to the inspection of an absolute authority.

separate society. The code of dosti takes precedence over that of heterosexual love and in case of conflict, the latter must yield to the former. Thus, in a conflict over love between male friends, the woman remains out of the picture, while the two males decide between themselves who will have her (another instance of this thematic is to be found in *Naya Daur*). The bond of dosti is then, a prototype of the compact among men that institutes the social contract.

The conflict in *Sangam* arises not because both the men fall in love with the same woman, but because one of them establishes a reciprocal love relation with the woman *before* settling the issue of who will have her with the other man, thus breaching the code of dosti. The most difficult representational dilemma that the film creates for itself arises as a consequence of the above breach of the code: since the woman, Radha, has clearly expressed her love for Gopal, the film must justify both his breach of commitment to her, as well as the union between her and Sundar (Raj Kapoor), which takes place after she has been silenced by the combination of dosti and national honour. The segment in which this transfer of rights over the woman occurs begins with Sundar joining the Air Force as a pilot during a war. His plane crashes and he is declared dead, leaving the field open for a romance to develop between Gopal and Radha. Just as the romance is about to take a significant turn, Sundar returns, having survived the crash and made his way back into Indian territory. When the three meet together again, a shocking revelation is made. Recounting his experience of the crash and subsequent escape from enemy territory, he tells Radha that the only thing that preserved his courage in the most trying circumstances was a letter she had written to him after he left for the warfront. Radha, however, did not write the letter. It was written by Gopal in her name. Gopal stifles her protests by lying and pleading silently with her not to betray the secret. This scene reveals to the audience an obscene secret that resulted from a conflict between the two codes of dosti and love. From Radha's point of view a redeeming resolution would be an open declaration by her and Gopal of their love for each other. But the narrative drive is towards another resolution that, forcing Radha to marry Sundar, then turns to the elimination of Gopal (who now becomes an unpleasant memory from her past) and in the process, her complete submission to a love that she did not reciprocate but which, backed by the might of the state, never encounters the need to justify itself. Gopal's claim on Radha is delegitimized by the act that betrays his vacillation between the two codes of dosti and love.

Sangam was released two years after the surprise attack by China, which shattered many illusions and exposed the vulnerability of the new nation. The tensions with another neighbour, Pakistan, were to erupt in war in the following year. Thus the film was topical, but unlike patriotic films such as *Haqeeqat*, it did not take on the burden of nationalist propaganda in a straightforward manner. Instead, it employed war in order to resurrect an absolutist subjectivity as the anchoring point of national unity. It used war as the legitimizing ground for an assault on the domestic enclosure, prising it open to insert the absolutist imperative, to repudiate the sanctity of mutuality and reciprocity as signs of true domesticity.

On the other hand, any austerity implied by this negation of domestic love by the imperatives of absolutism is compensated by the lavish consumerism, the access to the pleasures of western capitalism that the heroine enjoys, as a reward for her sacrifices. The long segment shot abroad, mainly devoted to tourism, to consuming the sumptuous sights and pleasures of advanced capitalism, and, not least, to the pleasure of representing India to the outside world, stands in sharp contrast to the forebodings of a duty-bound, self-sacrificing career for the woman that the plot might have prepared us to expect.

In effect the father has overridden the son's desires, and kept the woman for himself, a truth that the film does not fail to acknowledge, if only indirectly, in the humorous song *'Main kya karoon ram mujhe budha mil gaya'*. By being blind, Sundar remains powerful. He does not look for an answering desire in Radha to confirm his own; nor does he see the ample evidence of Radha's preference for Gopal. Both Radha and Gopal, on the other hand, are rendered powerless by being reduced to their own particular points of view. Both become guilty by simply having desired each other because their desire, in its mutuality, has the effect of shutting out the world around it, of making them, but especially him, forgetful of the duty of the patriot[26].

---

[26]The unseeing male lover is a frequently encountered figure in the Hindi film. Only rarely, as in *Deedar*, is he actually blind. In *Deedar* (1951) the blind hero meets a destiny that is the very antithesis of the all-powerful Sundar's in *Sangam*. His love proves incapable of winning the woman back from her mutual love relation with a doctor. However, his powerlessness there signifies a sacrifice that ennobles him and makes him the patron of the couple. Thus, in *Deedar* the blind lover, through his act of self-effacement (he finally becomes blind again and retreats from the scene of love), creates a space for the constitution of nuclear couples. By contrast, in *Sangam*, the blind lover's tyranny breaks the couple in order to reaffirm by force the unity of the nation. A more detailed study of the 'blind lover' would be required in order to draw out all its implications for a national ideology. The hero of *Chhalia* and the Muslim character in *Dhool ka Phool* are also relevant to this problematic, as is, of course, the legendary Devdas.

It is a fellow-soldier at the front who tells Sundar the story of his betrayal by a friend, entrusted with the protection of the soldier's wife, had an affair with her, a story that Sundar regards as repeating itself in his own life when he learns of the relationship between Radha and Gopal. Perspective or point of view here gets coded as self-interest, self-absorption, a mark of deception and guilt. This coding is not entirely mistaken in so far as Metz has defined cinematic voyeurism as a 'shamefaced voyeurism'. But the power of the injunction against individualized perspective is an extension of the power of a state whose authority rests not on the consent of citizens but on a pact entered into by the '(pre)chosen'.[27]

The Hindi women's melodramas were male-centred, as is indicated by the presence of Rajendra Kumar in many of them. But at the same time they raised the question of women's desire, and albeit with adequate patriarchal scaffolding, broached questions connected with the emancipation of women from the oppression of feudal orthodoxy. To that extent Rajendra Kumar himself came to stand as an emblem of female desire. It is thus not a coincidence that in *Sangam* the death of Rajendra Kumar also extinguishes Radha's desire and cleanses her marriage with Sundar of the dishonour that her desire represents. The quasi-autonomous woman's film thus gets re-annexed to the social genre which symbolizes the form of national integration favoured by the coalition of modern and pre-modern ruling élites.

The mobilization of the state apparatus in the service of a perspective-free national subject's enjoyment also reminds us that Raj Kapoor had a special status in Nehruvian India especially because of the role played by his films in providing a cultural dimension to Indo-Soviet friendship. Raj Kapoor was able to get the help of the Air Force as well as shoot some scenes during the Republic Day parade, both involving a scale of operations that few Indian film-makers could dream of seeing through at the time. *Sangam* was also the first and probably the most lavish of a series of sixties films to be shot on foreign locations, which implied a whole range of government approvals.

[27]Mehboob's *Andaz* where similarly the heroine's illicit (because) desiring, relation with another male ends in the latter's death, is more open in its affirmation of the feudal family's drive to maintain its status. There too Nargis and Dilip Kumar were linked by a mutual, intimate and guilt-ridden exchange of glances and Raj Kapoor was blind. The blind hero who represented the feudal family in *Andaz* has become the patriot in *Sangam*.

The killing of generic differentiation begins, of course, at the level of film budgets. The low-cost women's melodrama has to compete with a big-budget social which incorporates the former and thus provides a combination of pleasures for a wider audience. It drags the fledgling genre into a space where its freedom to explore women's issues is constrained by the national concerns that relativize their importance. But the difference in expenditure also translates into a difference between the types of social space represented in the text. The crucial scene where Gopal's obscene secret is revealed shows how in the 'public space' of the social super-genre a woman's questions must remain unasked. When Sundar declares that it was Radha's letter that kept his courage up at the battlefront, Radha begins to deny having written the letter. But she is cut short by Gopal who jumps in to 'remind' her that she had given him the letter to be mailed to Sundar. This is accompanied by a beseeching look that asks her to go along with the lie. At this point there is an extended exchange of looks between Radha and Gopal during which Radha's face registers first perplexity, then suspicion and finally a full realization of the murky horror of the betrayal that she cannot even protest against. Although this scene is explicit enough to give us a clear indication of Radha's recognition of her betrayal and secret prostitution, *Sangam* succeeds in finding a resolution without answering the woman's unasked but obvious question. The fact that Sundar does not *see* this long exchange of looks indicates that it belongs to a world of privacy that cannot intrude upon the narrative as public spectacle. The spectator's own muteness is signalled by the fact that his/her witnessing of this private moment remains unacknowledged by the narrative.

The dominance of this spectatorial relation is thus a symptom of the continuation of the despotic/monarchic organization of public space. In the next chapter we will see how this mode of organization of public space is reinforced by means of a prohibition of representations of kissing.

4

Guardians of the View:
The Prohibition of the Private

In the post-independence era, a much discussed feature of the censorship code for Indian films has been the prohibition of scenes of kissing. As the enquiry committee on film censorship led by G.D. Khosla reported in 1969, this prohibition was based on an 'unwritten rule' (*Report* 1969: 93). The written rules prohibited 'excessively passionate love scenes', 'indelicate sexual situations' and 'scenes suggestive of immorality', all of which were derived from the British code of censorship applied in Britain as well as (with modifications) in British India (ibid: 20). No reference to kissing as such, as a target of prohibition, is to be found in the censorship guidelines.

In the first place, the ban on kissing may be related to a nationalist politics of culture. The most frequently offered justification of this informal prohibition has been that it corresponds to the need to maintain the Indianness of Indian culture. Kissing is described as a sign of westernness and therefore alien to Indian culture. In keeping with the logic of this justification, this principle has never been applied in the censorship of foreign films. Further, there has been the occasional Indian film shot abroad, in which the Indian characters have to observe the ban, while the usually white couples, who appear in the background are allowed to break the rule (for eg. Raj Kapoor's *Sangam*). The 'double standard' whereby foreign films were censored according to a different code was justified on the basis that the audiences for these films were different from the ones for Indian films, with some even arguing that this was appropriate since 'foreign pictures cater to a higher stratum of society' (ibid: 82). There also appears to have been (at least in the late sixties, when the committee was doing its work) significant popular support for this ban, with a survey revealing that 51 per cent 'expressed the view that kissing scenes should be deleted from Indian films even if kissing and embracing was a natural part of the story' as against 33.3 per cent who voted for a more 'liberal' code (ibid: 83). According to the gender division of votes, more men (52:45) voted for a stricter code than women.

Discussion in the film magazines in the wake of the committee's report proved to be quite revealing of the opinion within the industry. The committee's recommendation to lift the ban did not meet with the sort of universal welcome that might have been expected from an industry that was supposed to be united in its objection to the excesses of censorship. Indeed, many notable film personalities wrote articles opposing the introduction of scenes of kissing.[1] It was not until the mid-eighties that films began to appear in which some awkward and perfunctory kissing scenes were included, as if to merely register the lifting of the ban.

One must avoid the temptation of concluding, as some 'enlightened critics' have done, that the lifting of the ban in itself

'I am an Indian girl and according to Indian custom, that . . . that's only after marriage.' Sharmila Tagore denies Shammi Kapoor a kiss in *An Evening in Paris* (Shakti Samanta 1969). Courtesy National Film Archive of India, Pune.

[1]See articles in *Screen* during the months of August and September 1969.

represents some form of liberation, although the existence of the prohibition would seem to validate the 'repressive hypothesis' (Foucault 1987). The standard opinion is that the ban on kissing is a manifestation of a form of prudery, a residual Victorianism in Indian culture which constitutes a national embarrassment. But, as everyone acknowledges, there is a great deal of sexual 'vulgarity' in Indian films. The so called 'cabaret dance', and other song and dance sequences are evidence of a sexual permissiveness that contradicts the idea that Indian censorship is a transparent reflection of a Victorian attitude to sexuality.

How do individual films negotiate this prohibition? For it is an observable fact that whatever the self-appointed interpreters of 'Indian culture' may say about the cultural status of kissing, the very fact that a prohibition must be imposed in order to keep it out of sight means that the culture in question is not as homogeneous as it is made out to be. At the level of content, then, we see in Indian films (at least) three different ways of dealing with the ban. The first way is to stage the prohibition itself, as in the scene from Hrishikesh Mukherjee's *Ashirwad* (1969), where as the lovers move towards each other for a kiss, a fade out overtakes them and prevents, not the act itself, but its appearance on the screen. In this way the film reminds us of the ban and at the same time ridicules it. This is the cinematic equivalent of the 'enlightened' attitude, disdainful of the meaningless prohibition but resigned to the power of the bureaucracy to impose it. It hints at the non-coincidence of representation and its content, in the process representing censorship itself as an extraneous limit, a constraint that *curtails* representations but does not determine them.

Another approach is to thematize the prohibition as a cultural truth and a duty, thereby inscribing it within the represented content, instead of treating it as a political act of curtailment. This happens for instance, in *An Evening in Paris* (1967), where the contrast provided by the foreign location, with its alien mores, serves to highlight the uniqueness of the national culture and the responsibility of the characters to uphold it. Thus, the heroine in this film invokes Indian custom to refuse the hero's demand for a kiss. In such films the reality implied by the prohibition is literally produced as truth at the thematic level. The idea of cultural/moral duty is a striking feature of this approach and points to the elevation of particular moral codes in force among some Hindu castes to the status of a national truth. It is significant that the threat posed by a transgression of custom is not only to the family or the institution of marriage, but to the nation itself, as if the expansion of the sphere of sexuality threatened to break open the national borders and destroy its identity. As such it raises the question of the nature of the relation between sexuality and national identity and reminds us of Fanon's assertion, in the course of a discussion of the contestation over the veil in Algeria, that the 'phenomena of resistance observed in the colonized must be related to an attitude of counter assimilation, of maintenance of a cultural, hence national, originality' (Fanon 1965: 42). This need for counter assimilation as a guarantee of national originality focusses on women's cultural behaviour. It is women who are regarded as the guardians of the national culture, it is women's appearance that becomes the mark of distinction. Thus, while colonialism leads to changes in men's clothing (with the European shirt and trousers becoming standard at least in cities), what women should wear becomes a subject of national debate.

But there is a third way of negotiating the prohibition which complicates the picture. Typically this approach is employed in song sequences: the dancing couple retreat behind a bush or a tree and after a pause the heroine emerges into the frame wiping her lips. This public confirmation of a private act has cultural associations with a certain feudal practice of communal eroticism that consists of the display of the marks of sexual initiation on the female body. In the 1992 film *Beta*, the heroine's *sahelis* (female companions), singing in chorus, ask her to explain a series of marks on her body—the smudged *bindi*, the crumpled clothes, etc. This form of eroticism, which displays the female body for communal inspection, consists of a retreat of the sexual act itself to a zone of privacy while exhibiting the evidence of its consummation. And, not surprisingly, the alleged sexual conservatism of Indian censorship has not prevented such a display of the female body in spite of widespread public protests. What is it that makes the kiss so objectionable while other forms of sexual display pass the censors without much difficulty?

Here it is necessary to recall one more complicating factor—the informal nature of the prohibition. Such unwritten rules have a way of themselves seeming to be the obscene result of some illicit cohabitation. For one cannot help but ask who thought up such an idea, how it came to be adopted by a group of people licensed to exercise moral authority, who gave the sanction to this at the level of the government, and how it was possible after all this to keep it informal. Viewed from this angle the issue suddenly explodes into questions about the nature of informal authority in a democratic society, the nexus between the state (which is understood to be functioning according to written and legislated codes) and other sources of authority which function on the strength of less systematized but no less effective modes of power. In brief, the prohibition of kissing, a meaningless prohibition of a harmless act, may well reveal some dirty secrets of the state.

We have so far desisted from attempting to verify the truth claim on which the prohibition is based, i.e. the claim that kissing is alien to Indian culture. Such a claim would be impossible to verify and raises questions about the attempt to imagine a homogeneous 'Indian culture' in a country with such a variety of ethnic, religious and linguistic groups. But should we venture to take a step in this direction, we are at once reminded that no one is really making such a claim. We discover a vagueness that goes hand in hand with the appearance of a dirty secret that the whole business of enforcing the ban takes on as we approach it. The secret that it most reminds us of is that of the Emperor's new clothes, one that could be held up as the truth as long as it went unscrutinized. As soon as the child declares that the emperor is naked, what is revealed is not the 'truth' but the fact that community consensus is what maintains the social order intact. By breaking the silence, as Slavoj Zizek has pointed out, we disrupt the 'intersubjective network' without which our very existence as a community is endangered (Zizek, *Looking Awry* 1991: 11).

But even this imprecise justification has a further significance. Thus, a witness who was interviewed by the censorship inquiry committee, justified the prohibition in these words:

> You cannot have the same yardstick both for the western films and for the Indian films. There have to be two standards. Our culture is different from the western way of life. Our dresses, our emotions, our background are different. For instance in India, when two people meet, they do not begin to embrace and kiss each other in public, though they may do so in private. In the west, people do embrace and kiss in public (*Report* 1969: 81).

The meaning of the private/public divide that emerges from this explanation is worth examining in detail. This witness's confusion of the categories is not simply an error of thinking but an imprecision integral to the nature of the prohibition and its social function. The error consists in equating cinematic representation with the representation of the public sphere. In this account there is no recognition of the possibility, which we otherwise take so much for granted, that while the representation circulates *in* public spaces, it need not necessarily be *of* the public. Far from being an idiosyncratic view, this idea is actually an accurate description of the consensual ideology that undergirds the popular cinema as a national institution.[2] The contradictory attitudes to kissing (which is banned) and the erotic display of the female body as spectacle (which is widespread) in the popular cinema is explained by this very ideology of the public sphere. The female body as spectacle is a public representation, a putting before the public, of an erotic imagery that does not violate the code that prohibits the representation of the private. This is because (1) such spectacle occurs in song-and-dance sequences which are conventionally coded as contracted voyeurism, rather than an unauthorized view of a private world; and (2) where they are not so coded, they serve, as Mulvey has pointed out, as points of narrative arrest. Kissing on the other hand, and by extension the details of a sexual relation between two people, belong to the realm of the private. It is significant that among the recent popular films that feature scenes of kissing this occurs usually in the song-and-dance sequences, as if the intention were to embed this in a stylized space where the kiss would become another novel movement in a dance.

It is not without significance that of all the features that attract the censor's scissors the prohibition of the kiss alone is justified by an argument for cultural non-correspondence. On the other hand, as Kumar Shahani has pointed out, the word *shudra* is not allowed to be used in a film although it refers to a real social hierarchy (Shahani, *Framework* 30/31: 88). This is also an unwritten rule in the censorship code. It would therefore be fruitless to speculate whether there is some validity to the truth claim made in this regard: the truth is of little consequence here because if the criterion of cultural authenticity is applied, far more than the kiss would have to be deleted from every Indian film. What is more to the point is to ask why this realist demand is made in relation to this particular representation.

---

[2]The same explanation has been repeated endlessly by almost everybody who defends the ban. Rosie Thomas, commenting on the ban, also cites this argument, and characterizes it as 'puritanical'. According to her the ban 'came only with the puritanical reformist zeal after Independence that saw *kissing in public* as an immoral Western import' (Thomas 1987: 320; my emphasis).

The Invention of the Couple

In reality then, what the prohibition targets is the representation of the private through a meaningless ban on kissing. In order to understand what this means it is necessary to survey the history of capitalism and colonialism leading to the organization of the private that came to be a distinct feature of capitalist societies: the nuclear family, centred around the couple. Some remarks by Alain Grosrichard are extremely pertinent here: Grosrichard speaks of the 'invention of the couple' by Rousseau who, like many French writers of his time, was preoccupied with the spectre of despotism (1979: 222–3). How does this 'invention' of the couple solve the problem of despotism?

Grosrichard's book consists of a complex analysis of the European 'fiction' of Asiatic Despotism. Instead of trying to demonstrate the falseness of this discourse by marshalling contrary historical evidence, he asks what function this fantasy served for the Europeans who so assiduously pursued this idea of the despotic regime. Such an approach enables him to locate Montesquieu, Rousseau, Voltaire, Diderot, Bernier and other writers' preoccupation with the nature of despotism in relation to their fears about the degenerate monarchies that they were witness to. It also succeeds in recreating the picture of this despotic regime as one governed by a chain of command which runs from God down to the last position of power in local communities. The absolute power of the despot allows no scope for challenging his authority, but the despotic regime is at the same time rife with transgressions. These transgressions take the form of a subterranean proliferation of 'perversions' which survive through the elaboration of secret codes of communication. Absolute power thus begets rampant decadence. The European thinkers who recognized this relation concluded that any transformation of the microsocial would depend on a permanent securing of the state against the recurrence of despotic regimes. The despotic regime is founded on an acknowledgment of the psychoanalytic assertion that 'there is no sexual relation': here the relation of the phallic authority to the members of the harem is mediated by the eunuch, who is the sexual 'in-between', and polygamy is one of its necessary consequences.

In response to this, Rousseau (and Diderot) construct the couple, as an accomplishment of the impossible (sexual relation). The couple is the 'political subject' that guarantees a State that is free from the risk of despotism (Grosrichard 1979: 223). Here we may recall Carol Pateman's argument in *The Sexual Contract*, which asserts the dependence of the social contract on a (logically) prior sexual contract. The sexual contract, it is to be noted, is not a contract between the man and the woman who form the couple, but between the men, who all agree to recognize one another's right to a space of (despotic) sovereignty: the family and the woman who, within it, becomes the man's property (Pateman 1988: 2). It is this dual contract that alone produces the conditions of possibility of a modern state, where the phallic power is not incarnated in the living body of a despotic king but instead is distributed among the male contracting members of society, the *fraternite* that formed the third element of the slogan of the French Revolution. Thus the very stability of the post-despotic state rests on the stability of the micro-despotism of the nuclear family. The fiction of contract marks a transition from the rule of fathers to the rule of brothers (ibid: 77–9).

The cinema, emerging in the historical space of the modern, is committed, as Raymond Bellour has said, to the endless reproduction of the couple, in narratives that bring about or restore the conjugal scene (Bellour 1980: 183). However, while the cinema in the west has only to *re*-present the transition from the familial to the conjugal —'the resolution of Oedipus'—as an endless cyclical process that has already been inaugurated (Bellour 1986: 78), in Indian cinema the modern state is present as only one of several patriarchal authorities competing for domination. As such we find that in the dominant filmic narrative the drive towards the affirmation of conjugality is reined in by the restoration of the clan to its position of splendour and power; the couple, in other words, is repeatedly reabsorbed into the parental patriarchal family and is committed to its maintenance. The modern family romance occurs in the popular Hindi film only in an embedded form, under the aegis of the compound authority of a feudal and a modern patriarchy. This is amply illustrated by a phenomenon that has been often noted, that in Hindi films (at least in the sixties), the 'police always arrive late'. In other words, the climax of the romance would usually consist of a battle between the hero and a primary villain, with lesser villains being fought by the hero's accomplices in the background. And the police usually arrive only in time to witness the decisive defeat of the villain and to endorse the justice rendered in their absence. This phenomenon tends to be read as a satire on the incompetence of the police. But something more is involved here: the late arrival of the police attests not only to the endorsement of a feudal system of justice by the representatives of the modern state, it also enacts the formal alliance between these two sites of power which retain their separate identities. Thus, to borrow Marx's terminology from a different context (Marx, *Capital*, 1977: 1019–28), here the subsumption of the feudal family romance in the modern is only formal, not real. Real subsumption would render the family a transitory functional entity committed to re-enacting the conjugal scene in the lives of its children, after which it must, as Hegel says, dissolve itself (Hegel 1967: 117–22).

The 'new family' in Hegel takes the place of the old one which was committed to 'preserving the family and its splendor by means of *fideicommissa* and *substitutiones* (in order to favour sons by excluding daughters from inheriting, or to favour the eldest son by excluding the other children),' a proclivity that Hegel characterizes as 'an infringement of the principle of the freedom of property . . . like the admission of any other inequality in the treatment of heirs' (Hegel 1967: 121). The family that does not dissolve itself into the families of its children and instead regards its own enjoyment as the ultimate aim contravenes the ethical life that Hegel is elaborating as the integral external embodiment of the modern state. The old family institution 'depends on an arbitrariness which in and by itself has no right to recognition, or more precisely on the thought of wishing to preserve intact not so much this family but rather this clan or 'house' (ibid: 121) or, in the Indian context, the *khandan, gharana* or *vansh*.

The kiss that seals the Christian marriage and inaugurates a zone of privacy, thereby dissolving all other intermediate claims to authority except that of the state, is the very same kiss that is prohibited on the Indian screen, between Indian citizens. The private is only invented in and through this relationship of the family to the state (the end result of the contract that inaugurates the new patriarchy), whereas in the old family, which is also, at the same time, an authoritarian regime, the private does not exist. As such the unspoken ('informal', like the prohibition) alliance between the modern state (which is only formally in place) and the numerous premodern points of power and authority (which could also be stated in another way: the state is the embodiment of the alliance of premodern centres of power and has no substance of its own) prohibits the invention of the private, the zone of intimate exchange and union, where in the Hegelian ideal, the members of the couple become as one. Thus, while the spectacle of the female body poses no threat to this informal alliance that constitutes the Indian ruling bloc, the scene of intimate exchange where bourgeois female subjectivity (the 'law of woman' being for Hegel the 'law of the inward life' and opposed to the 'law of the land', finding its proper sphere of influence in the family, which is the woman's 'substantive destiny') may emerge, challenges the claim of the intermediate patriarchal authorities to unrestricted control over the space of conjugality.

As a space marked by a discursive shift (the appearance of private languages, the possibility of unsanctioned practices), the private is a self-enclosing libidinal exchange that various authorities seek to oversee.[3] Any representation of this private space and its activities in the public realm thus constitutes a transgression of the scopic privilege that the patriarchal authority of the traditional family reserves for itself. Such a representation threatens to draw a circle around the couple, thus realizing its autonomy, its independence from the self-appointed sanctioning authority and at the same time makes the modern state the overseeing authority and the guarantor of the couple's autonomy. This moment also marks the inauguration of the history of realist voyeurism.

The prohibition of kissing, as we have seen, is attributed to 'Indian culture'. The prohibition, according to this understanding, blocks the centrifugal force unleashed by the kiss that would threaten the integrity of the culture. Absence is translated as a negative injunction. We are dealing here with what psychoanalysis terms the 'Big Other', which Zizek describes as 'the agency that decides instead of us, in our place', an invisible hand, which in our case takes the form of Culture (Zizek, *For They Know Not* 1991: 77). The prohibition of certain practices is attributed to this Other of the symbolic network, by reference to which what is prohibited is also said to be non-existent. This paradoxical prohibition of the non-existent is the basis of the consensual formation that ensures the stability of the community's identity.

Why must the non-existent be prohibited? It is a question of desire, of a certain tendency of desire that cannot be integrated into a homeostatic system (such as the nation-state is envisaged to be), a desire that threatens to break out of the limiting circuits of the national body to seek its fulfilment 'elsewhere', this elsewhere being, precisely,

[3]See Jacques Donzelot, *Policing the Family* (1980).

the culturally non-specific, deterritorialized space of modern consumer culture.

Going beyond this we must pose the question that brings the historical into the picture, that is why this specific prohibition is so important to the stability of the social formation. Why should the ban be anything more than a meaningless act that was stupidly continued for a long time? Indeed, if the ban on kissing as such is the issue, there is nothing more to be said about it. But if it is acknowledged that this meaningless prohibition extends beyond the kiss to a certain notion of the 'private', and that it is imposed in the service of an informal alliance of patriarchies, then the picture becomes more complicated.

In Basu Bhattacharya's *Anubhav* ('Experience' 1971), a film which self-consciously attempts to deal precisely with this question of a 'private space', the problem that threatens the family is defined by the heroine as the lack of *lagao* (attachment) between husband and wife. The couple then proceed to create this absent connection, which consists in producing a space of intimacy, of closed or restricted exchange. The problem of the couple is the problem of the formation of a middle class, where the possibility of restricted exchange is

A middle-class housewife, trying to set her house in order, encounters a remainder from the past: Dinesh Thakur and Tanuja in *Anubhav* (Basu Bhattacharya 1973). Courtesy National Film Archive of India, Pune.

predicated, paradoxically, on the possibility of the free circulation of autonomous subjects. It is the initial free pact between 'consenting adults' as the law puts it that is the condition of possibility of a private space.

Thus, in *Anubhav* the wife's pre-marital romance with the man who has now re-entered her life as her husband's employee, consisted in no more than 'a few hours of conversation' in which the subjectivity denied to her in her parental home found a space to emerge. Having resolved to restore the space of intimate exchange between herself and her husband, the heroine's first act is to dismiss all the servants. The servants have occupied and fully control the domestic space. In their midst the marriage is a daily spectacle and their intrusive presence is the mark of a lack of closure in the relationship. They stand in for a traditional overseeing authority, penetrating the conjugal space with the inspecting glance.[4] While in the eyes of this overseeing authority the marriage retains the external features of conjugality—cohabitation, economic co-operation, etc.—its internal subtance is absent, the love or lagao that guarantees a nuclear family's autonomy. It is the Hegelian ideal of the Christian marriage, distinguished by spiritual unity that is represented as an absence. In bringing it about, support is drawn from the only servant who refuses to leave, claiming for himself a special status in the family: he is the non-intrusive, supportive remainder of the dissolved parental family.

It is in the context of a state-form in which the relations between the citizen and the state (itself guaranteed by the Law of the Father) are mediated by unreconstructed patriarchal codes that the injunction against the representation of the private becomes intelligible. A state that has to oversee the expansion of capitalist production through the maintenance and sometimes intensification of pre-capitalist modes of exploitation is obliged to maintain a protected sphere of cultural traditionalism: women and the peasantry are often the objects of this paternalist attention. This is not to suggest that the patriarchal nexus that maintains this protected culture is actually successfully regulating the modes of reception of new cultural forces by the people. Such regulation would be difficult if not impossible. But what it does accomplish is the naturalization of the ideological notion of a conflict between tradition and modernity and the prohibitive force of tradition.

[4]That the servants can function as a surrogate of the feudal patriarchal authority should not surprise us: the eunuch in the harem was precisely such a figure, a servant who was like an extension of the master's body.

To summarize, the prohibition of kissing is a symptomatic cultural protocol whose origins lie in the need to prevent the dissolution of pre-capitalist patriarchal enclaves, to rein in the forces of democratic transformation. It is not the transparent expression of a pre-existing cultural predilection but a 'meaningless' (the moment we recognize that it is not meaningless, not just stupid or merely puritanical, it ceases to function effectively) prohibition that regulates the public circulation of images as an obligation of the contract between new and traditional élites. Its tangible result in cinema (which has been the central national cultural institution because mass illiteracy poses obstacles to literature playing a similar role) is a blocking of the representation of the private.

The Prohibition of Cinema

The prohibition of the private in a way amounts to the prohibition of cinema itself. For what is at stake here is the specific scopic regime that is activated by the cinema and its social significance in the context of a capitalist social formation. In a section of 'The Imaginary Signifier' entitled 'The Passion for Perceiving' (1986: 260–7) Christian Metz elaborates on the specificity of the scopic drive within the cinematic relation. The practice of cinema is dependent on the activity of the scopic and the invocatory or auditory drives, both of which relate to their objects at a distance. In voyeurism, there is a constitutive distance between the object (what is looked at) and the source of the drive (the seeing eye). 'The voyeur represents in space the fracture which forever separates him from the object; he represents his very dissatisfaction (which is precisely what he needs as a voyeur), and thus also his 'satisfaction' in-so-far as it is of a specifically voyeuristic type'. The looking drive (and with modifications the auditory drive), thanks to this function of distance in its very unfolding, cannot ever afford the illusion of 'a full relation to the object' (ibid: 261).

These features of the scopic drive are however common to all visual and auditory modes of representation. The specificity of the cinema arises, according to Metz, from 'an extra reduplication' of this relation of absence or lack of the object. In the first place, the absent object is infinitely more varied in the cinema and secondly, its absence is not simply marked by the distance that separates the spectator from the stage, as in the theatre, but by the absence of the object from the stage (or its cinematic equivalent, the screen) itself.

The cinema 'only gives it [the object] in effigy' (Metz: 262). When the actor was present (during the shooting) the spectator was absent, and when the spectator arrives, the actor has already left (ibid: 264): this 'missed encounter' that constitutes the essence of cinematic voyeurism (reminiscent, we might add, of the missed encounter between the two agents of the 'original' economic activity of barter, when money intervenes to split the exchange relation into its component parts, buying and selling as independent activities) makes cinema a distinctly capitalist cultural phenomenon. Metz contrasts cinema with other 'more intimate voyeuristic activities' like 'certain cabaret acts, striptease, etc', where 'voyeurism remains linked to exhibitionism, where the two faces, active and passive, of the component drive are by no means so dissociated; where the object seen is present and hence presumably complicit . . . .' (ibid: 262–3). This presence, 'and the active consent which is its real or mythical correlate (but always real as myth) re-establish in the scopic space, momentarily at least, the illusion of a fullness of the object relation, of a state of desire which is not just imaginary' (ibid: 263).

This vestige of a mythic fusion with the object, which survives in the theatre, is 'attacked' by the cinema signifier in so far as the consent of the object on the screen cannot be taken for given. Cinematic voyeurism thus turns out to be 'unauthorized scopophilia' (ibid: 264) and its difference from the theatre can be further contextualized in the 'socio-ideological circumstances that marked the birth of the two arts'. Thus:

> cinema was born in the midst of the capitalist epoch in a largely antagonistic and fragmented society, based on individualism and the restricted family (= father-mother-children), in an especially superegotistic bourgeois society, especially concerned with 'elevation' (or facade), especially opaque to itself. The theater is a very ancient art, one which saw the light in more authentically ceremonial societies, in more integrated human groups (even if sometimes, as in Ancient Greece, the cost of this integration was the rejection into a nonhuman exterior of a whole social category, that of the slaves), in cultures which were in some sense closer to their desire (=paganism): the theater retains something of this deliberate civic tendency toward ludico liturgical 'communion', even in the degraded state of a fashionable rendezvous around those plays known as *pieces de boulevard*.

It is for reasons of this kind too that theatrical voyeurism, less cut off from its exhibitionist correlate, tends more toward a reconciled and community-oriented practice of the scopic perversion (of the component drive). Cinematic voyeurism is less accepted, more 'shamefaced' (Metz 1986: 265).

Cinema thus reflects the dispersal of the 'community' that is characteristic of capitalist societies. But the 'unauthorised scopophilia' of the cinema 'is at the same time authorized by the mere fact of its institutionalization' (ibid: 265). This ' "reprise" of the imaginary by the symbolic', whereby a 'legalization and generalization of the prohibited practice' becomes the established reality of capitalist societies links cinema to certain clandestine but sanctioned spaces like the licensed brothel. In spite of the legitimacy that institutionalization provides, however, this place of leisure remains a "hole" in the social cloth' (ibid: 266).

In Indian popular cinema we observe a tendency to resist the extra-communal tendency that Metz regards as constitutive of cinematic culture. The mandatory 'cabaret' scene in many Hindi films, marked by a tendency to frontal representation (where the dancer often looks straight into the camera, in violation of the 'recipe of classical cinema' which forbids such a direct address, and which originates in the logic of cinematic voyeurism), this spectacle is clearly 'theatrical' in Metz's sense. That which is offered as spectacle for the cinematic voyeur is distinguished by the fact that it 'lets itself be seen without presenting itself to be seen' (ibid: 264).

This disjuncture, which Metz tends to locate at the points of cinematic production and projection can also be related to the aesthetics of realism. What Metz broadly reads as a difference between the theatre and the cinema can also be seen as a historically datable difference between pre-realist and realist theatre, with the latter inaugurating the aesthetic that Metz identifies exclusively with cinema.[5] Realist theatre and classical cinema manifest a common attempt to erect an invisible but unsurpassable barrier between the spectator/reader and the object, a barrier whose traces are precisely those injunctions against direct address, as well as the tendency to represent the private, that which does not present itself to be seen. By contrast Indian popular cinema, with its rejection of realist principles of representation accords more with those forms of voyeurism in which the complicity of the object is a crucial real or mythical assumption. It is the representation of the private that

[5]As stated earlier (see Introduction), it is the combination of elements (eg. realism + camera + . . .) that gives cinema the capitalist specificity, the emblematic quality, which is disavowed in the Indian case.

engenders the 'shame-faced' voyeurism of the cinema and presupposes the reality of the subject's solitude in the act of voyeuristic perception, and the dissolution of the substantive communal relation into the atomistic individualism of capitalist social relations.

Thus, at the heart of the film industry an informal injunction goes to work to prohibit the representation of kissing and thereby generates a chain of implied prohibitions: the prohibition of representations of the private, the prohibition of cinema (in the western 'emblematic' sense), and, we are now in a position to add, the prohibition of the open acknowledgement of the capitalist nature of the new nation-state. Where socialism was only invoked as ideology, and Congress socialism was no more than a protective shield for the development of indigenous capitalism, the emerging capitalist culture had to be disavowed and this disavowal was the only (negative) proof of the existence of socialism.

The Indian popular film bridges the gap between the screen and the spectator (a gap which in Hollywood cinema is bridged only by the spectator's participation in the unfolding of the narrative, a process which highlights his/her complicity) through the effect (produced by various means, of which the prohibition of kissing is only one) of an underwriting of the voyeuristic relation by the Symbolic. This is made clear by the reading of the politics of the darsanic gaze in the previous chapter, where we saw that the subject is invited to participate in a spectacle as witness to the splendour of that which presents itself to the subject's gaze. The cinema, according to Metz's definition, takes place in a reserved space, where the functioning of the symbolic is suspended (or left outside, standing guard) in order to allow the activity of 'unauthorized scopophilia'. By contrast, the cinema in India unfolds as if under the aegis of the Symbolic.

When the members of the couple turn to each other for a kiss, what occurs (or what is feared) is a decisive shutting out of the Other, whose gaze then at once becomes, or is reminded of its, shamefaced voyeurism. This gesture of withdrawal by the object throws the subject back onto itself, and acts as a reminder of the subject's solitude, the condition of individuals in a capitalist society. The couple's withdrawal into an inviolable privacy threatens to set the image loose from its mooring in the contracted voyeuristic relation, sending it spinning away on an unpredictable course (as the couple literally does in Adoor Gopalakrishnan's *Swayamvaram*, 1972), leaving the spectator similarly rudderless, the imaginary unity then coming permanently under the ever present threat of an irreparable rupture. In prohibiting this withdrawal, the cinema produces and maintains the illusion of a community, the alertness of all subjects to the existence of all others or the alertness of the Subject to the existence of all subjects.[6]

The subject's desire, constitutively unpredictable in its choice of object, is a disruptive element that the national ideology—Barthes once described ideology as 'the Cinema of a society' (Barthes 1973: 3) —of communal cohesion has to manage. Indeed, desire (as desire for the modern that cinema is and represents) is often replaced by the curious notion of need as an explanatory factor for the Indian people's enthusiastic reception of the popular cinema. The opposition constituted by the terms need and desire in the context of a theory of (Indian) cinema has implications at the level of a theory of the modern Indian state and its location in the global capitalist system. In order to examine these implications, I turn to a text by Ashish Nandy which elaborates a need-based theory of 'commercial cinema'. This discussion will also disclose the real stakes of the ideological project of Indian popular cinema: in prohibiting representations of the private, this cinema blocks the recognition of the breakdown of precapitalist community bonds and the learning of new modes of solidarity based on the shared interests of the working classes.

The Disavowal of Capitalism

In a spirited defence of commercial cinema, Nandy asserts that it speaks for the masses and has a claim to legitimacy as valid as that of the 'art cinema' in its own sphere.

[6]It goes without saying that the illusion of communal cohesion can only be maintained with the active complicity of the audience. It is not a question of an imposed illusion. One encounters, in cinema halls, signs of this complicity whenever a scene of intimacy between two characters appears to go on for .longer than is appropriate to the maintenance of the community effect. Shouts will be heard from someone or the other, expressing discomfort with the proceedings. In Bangalore, this used to take a particular, curious form. At such moments someone would invariably shout, 'Thaattiningo!' The word means a palmyra fruit which is usually sold on city streets at night (usually after 9 or 10) to preserve its juiciness. The everyday experience of the nocturnal intimacies of couples being disrupted by the call of the fruitseller is evoked by the shouts and the awkwardness of the moment, which threatens to remind the spectator of his voyeurism, is thus overcome.

The basic principles of the commercial cinema derive from exactly the core concerns of the Indians caught between the old and the new, and the native and the exogenous. That is, the strength of the commercial cinema lies in its ability to tap the fears, anxieties and felt pressures of deculturation and even depersonalisation which plague the Indians who do not find the normative framework of the established urban middle-class culture adequate for their needs (Nandy 1987: 72).

The primacy accorded to need in Nandy's discussion gives him a reason to defer the question of the aesthetic. Thus, his comparative treatment of 'art', 'middle brow' and 'commercial cinema' does not question the legitimacy of the art film (Nandy 1988b: 61). The comments made in favour of the commercial cinema are qualified by others stating 'however much we may bemoan the entry of mass culture . . .' indicating an uneasiness on the aesthetic question which is all-important for the art cinema. A second consequence is that the notion of cultural need, which implies that different groups have different needs, leads to the argument in favour of a sectoral division of culture: 'art films cannot and should not hegemonise the entire cultural space available to the Indian cinema' because 'there is need for at least a tripartite division of spoils among the high, middle and low-brow cinema in India' (Nandy 1988b: 60–1).

Nandy produces a folk culture for us out of a supposed intimate fit between a displaced proletariat (uprooted from their relatively stable rural existence and thrown into the uncertainties of urban life) and its favourite cultural institution, the commercial cinema. The usefulness of this cinema lies in its ability to heal the wounds of deracination. This is at the individual level. On another level, this cinema also helps preserve the endangered traditions of the modernizing nation-state by making tradition the 'normative fulcrum' of self-expression, thereby providing the displaced masses with a take on modernity from their own standpoint. Nandy urges 'us' to recognize that this cinema, while meeting the needs of the masses, also satisfies 'our' longing for the preservation of tradition. It is by giving the masses what they want that we can be sure of getting what we want.

This reading of popular cinema marks a break with the more common aestheticist tendency to treat it as not-yet-cinema, a formless and anarchic bricolage of titillation, violent spectacle and moral conservatism. But having left the aestheticist critique behind, Nandy does not quite manage to free his arguments from a temptation to simply reverse the equation. His text has a strong tendency to equate the defence of the commercial cinema with a defence of the people, the masses and their (supposed) role as the preservers of tradition in a modernizing society. He explains his position thus:

> Now that modernity has become the dominant principle in Indian public life, when much of the oppression and exploitation in the society is inflicted in the name of modern categories such as development, science, progress and national security, the logic of the situation demands a different kind of political attitude towards cultural traditions. However much we may bemoan the entry of mass culture through the commercial cinema, the fact remains that it is the commercial cinema which by default is more protective towards traditions and towards native categories (Nandy 1988b: 61).

Nandy's claim is that popular cinema speaks for the people and their traditions and against the encroachment of the principle of modernity. And yet he also asserts that it is in the context of the domination of the principle of modernity that this cinema must be defended. Thus commercial cinema, if it is indeed as he describes it, would seem to the fighting a lost battle. Read in conjunction with the idea that different sectors of culture serve different needs, this seems to carry a disturbing implication that popular cinema should be protected because of its ability to serve, not as the site of a transformative critique of modernity, but as a rejuvenating, healing ideological refuge from it. Where these 'native categories' have been irreversibly emptied of any real social effectivity, cinema mitigates the trauma of the masses' encounter with the new by preserving the illusion of a persistence of tradition. This affirmative theory of the popular would thus appear to have as its guiding principle, an administrative concern with normalcy, law and order. Here we encounter the theoretical justification for the disavowal of the capitalist nature of the Indian nation-state. This disavowal is partial, confined to the psychic sphere of the proletariat and accordingly, finds it possible to divide cultural spheres into incommensurable sectors. We of the middle class, who know that modernity can no longer be defended against, and who participate in its expansion with our commitment to the western aesthetic standards that make a Satyajit Ray film so appealing—we are not being asked to commit ourselves to a rejection of modernity or to a denial of its arrival. We are being invited, on the other hand, to confine the modern revolution (or, more accurately, the consciousness of it) to our sphere of existence, not to insist on its extension to the people, for whom the illusion of the normative function of tradition provided by the cinema is a therapeutic necessity.

The discourse of and on popular cinema has always involved a dialectic of modernity and tradition in which the point of enunciation cannot be unambiguously located in one or the other for all time. And even where we are able to clearly identify the perspective, in individual films, the 'traditional' is by no means identical with the interests and desires of the dispossessed and displaced masses. It is problematic to employ tradition and modernity in this sense as terms of analysis. It is true that popular films deploy this binary frequently and that thematic conflicts are structured around it. But to treat it as if it were a transparent representation of some real conflict between these two concepts is to fall into an ideological trap. For the construction of 'tradition' is part of the work of modernity. This is not to deny the material effectivity of the binary in the social. On the contrary, our questioning of the binary necessitates the investigation of the relation of these representations (of conflicts between tradition and modernity) to the real relations that characterize the social formation.

Sectoral need theory neglects the relational aspect of any social divisions that it may identify. In *Anubhav,* as we have seen, the couple's resolve to produce a private world is supported by a self-effacing patriarchal servant figure. In a scene at the beginning of the film, this old man gives the hero, a newspaper editor, a massage while the latter works late into the night.[7] In the conversation that ensues, the servant gently criticizes the master for working too hard and long and not enjoying the fruits of his labour. Thus the servant makes visible to the man an important truth about his existence. The film tries to realize the positive suggestion contained in the servant's remark. But this suggestion is never allowed to reflect back on the working life of the servant himself, who as we can plainly see, has no fixed working hours and no 'private life' either. The obvious naturalness of the terms of this relationship, in which the servant is made to pronounce a truth that applies to the master but not to himself, also depends on a version of the sectoral theory of needs. The proletariat's right to a fixed working day, a 'modern'

---

[7]An almost identical scene occurs in Gulzar's *Aandhi*, with the same actors, A.K. Hangal and Sanjeev Kumar playing the roles of servant and master: clearly no accident, given that both *Aandhi* and *Anubhav* figure in the list of middle-class films (discussed in Chapter 7) which, in the late seventies, attracted audiences drawn by the promise of social distinction.

right, if asserted in such a context could upset the neat division of the social into sectors.

In his description of the commercial cinema, Nandy refers to its ability to 'tap the fears, anxieties and felt pressures of deculturation and even depersonalisation'. Given the emphasis on culture as a need, it is not surprising that desire does not figure in this list. Desire, once introduced, threatens to lead the subject astray (into the spaces of modernity, reserved for the middle class and the connoisseurs of art cinema), whereas the point of the exercise is to bind the subject to a place in a need-based, self-reproducing cultural economy. The desired image of the masses is an image of the masses as lacking desire.

Need is that which can be met by a specifiable and unchanging object. Hunger, for example, can be satisfied by food and only by food. By making culture a sphere of need, Nandy integrates the psychic into the modern economy and identifies the cinema as that which meets the needs of the population. Culture becomes a sphere of nature, not one in which meanings circulate, producing frames of intelligibility by means of which the relations of power and production are justified. That there may be a demand for a different social order, that cinema provides various explanations for the contradictions of capitalist society, that tradition as the 'solution' for these contradictions may be an ideological construction disseminated by popular Hindi cinema, these are ignored. By this reckoning it must be said that while the other sectors of the economy have failed to meet the basic material needs of the masses, the culture industry alone has succeeded in effectively meeting the demand that is placed on it. If we push this argument further, it may turn out that the culture industry's success in meeting this need gives the other sectors of the economy and the exploitative system itself some respite. For if the basic needs were to become more important to the masses at any time, would the cultural need continue to remain the same? And conversely, if the basic needs were ever to be adequately met, would the masses then not be in a position to demand a different kind of entertainment, even one that is not predicated on a disavowal of modernity? Is it then Nandy's argument that when the people are hungry, commercial cinema is the best thing for them?

It is not simply a question of opposing need to desire but of acknowledging the dispersal of communities and then figuring whether the people's interest in cinema signifies the desire for a transformation that will acknowledge their entry into modernity, or whether they regard the cinema as speaking on their behalf when it disseminates tales of feudal morality. The primary attraction of the cinema is its modern character, whereas once drawn into the theatre, we may be presented with traditional ideologies that try to deny the changed circumstances that are the very condition of possibility of a cinematic culture. What the ideology of cultural need denies is the possibility that human beings may desire the transformation of their conditions of existence, that a utopian element may inhere in cultural activity.

While often anchored in familiar narratives that reinforce traditional moral codes, the popular film text also offers itself as an object of the desire for modernity. The fragmentary text of an average popular film is a serial eruption of variously distributed affective intensities whose individual effects are not subsumed in the overarching narrative framework. As an effective medium of propagation of consumer culture, popular cinema has managed to combine a reassuring moral conservatism with fragments of utopian ideology and enactments of the pleasures of the commodity culture. The very familiarity of the narrative makes it a useful non-interfering grid within which to elaborate the new.

But consumer culture is itself not a neutral 'content' which fits indiscriminately into any available narrative framework. While functioning within the grid of the traditional moral tale, it at the same time conflicts with that tale and makes for contradictions at the level of narrative. These contradictory features can be read as reflecting the contradictions of a capitalist society functioning on the basis of pre-capitalist social relations. Popular films represent the utopian ideal that consists of not only the pleasures of commodity culture but also the microsocial forms such as the nuclear family, which is at once an ideal consuming unit that the industrial economy's logic calls for, as well as an alternative to the existing patriarchal enclaves within which subjects are situated. It is then a question of emerging from feudal social relations into capitalist ones, an epic narrative of the transpatriarchal migration of subjects, a struggle within the social for a radical transformation which cinema represents and resolves in its own way.

The State of Love

It is the discourse of romantic love that the popular film deploys in its representation of this ideal. As argued above, the tale of romantic love has continued to be embedded in an overarching framework derived from the feudal family romance. Thus the romantic couple's courtship takes place in a space of controlled anonymity.[8] They meet by accident in a public space, as if it were a question of two 'citizen-subjects' encountering each other and falling in love in the course of a long courtship: but what begins as an accidental encounter between two individuals turns out to have been predestined. While initially their love invites the disapproval of one or both the families, last minute turns in the narrative disclose certain pacts entered into by the families, which had sanctioned the love relation even before it took place. Thus, the centrifugal force of the love relation is reined in and the family in its feudal self-governing form re-secures its boundaries. This is a narrative pattern that was endlessly repeated in popular cinema throughout the sixties and in spite of many transformations, has not entirely disappeared. The family capital was one of the key issues in the unfolding of the narrative. The son's love adventure ran parallel to the plotting by close relatives to grab the family fortune through manipulative matchmaking, embezzlement, etc. (*Waris* is a representative film of this type.)

The emergence of the discourse of romantic love has been traced to North Africa and medieval Europe (Spain and southern France), although, if we consider the 1000–year history of the *ghazal*, or the Indian *bhakti* movements, an earlier or parallel Asian origin is suggested (Dale 1996). The second great era of the elaboration of this discourse in Europe was the Romantic age, from which the modern conception of love derives (Singer 1984: 1, 23, 283 ff). (Needless to say, it is the concept of love that can be said to have a specific place of origin, not the affect itself). As a concept, romantic love is 'an ideal for changing the world or . . . a psychological state' (ibid: 3). Love's transformative potential lay in the idea that it was an 'intense, passionate relationship that establishes a holy oneness between man and woman' (ibid: 23). This ideal of oneness, which was an attribute of religious love before the emergence of courtly love, represents a secularization of religious devotion and as such

[8]This pre-marital encounter is often a mere ritual of aristocratic socio-sexual arrangements as is clear in a film like *Chhalia* (Manmohan Desai 1960).

came into conflict with religious dogma (ibid: 32). Romantic love, like the courtly version, 'finds its divinity in the act of loving' (ibid: 293).

In India it was the medieval bhakti movements and personalities who elaborated a discourse of spiritual love with romantic overtones. Thus the songs of Mirabai, the sixteenth-century devotee and self-proclaimed bride of the god Krishna, express devotional love in a language drawn from the institutions of sexuality: courtship and marriage (Alston 1980). But romantic love as a social practice transforming relations between individuals did not emerge from these moments. Persian and later Urdu poetry, flourishing in India's aristocratic Muslim society, elaborated a discourse of love that Hindi cinema took over wholesale when it turned to the inexhaustible thematics of love. This discourse had no social currency, its intricate conceits and metaphors were more suited to poetry than to everyday language. As such its use was largely confined to songs.

Mainstream Hindu society, which has continued to be governed by the caste system, was in no position to generate a discourse of love. There were attempts at social revolution which consisted precisely in challenging the caste division and proclaiming a direct link between the devotee and the divine. Such was the revolutionary slogan of the bhakti movement in twelfth-century Karnataka, one instance of the early protests against the monopoly over religion by established orthodoxies. But these movements did not succeed in their mission to transform Hindu society. After 1947, Hindi cinema borrowed the discourse of love elaborated in Persian/Urdu poetry and superimposed it on the traditional sexual relations of Hindu society. However, its elaborate conceits and refined language continued to serve as reminders of its aristocratic origin, which meant that love itself came to be associated with a certain soulfulness and otherworldliness.

In this context it is of interest that the last few years have seen a sudden proliferation of the use of the English language expression 'I love you'. From Hindi films to the regional language cinemas of the south, songs and dialogue everywhere are littered with this expression. It is sung to a variety of tunes, subjected to the most unpredictable conceits (as in the song which begins *'yeh ilu ilu kya hai?',* a question about the meaning of the expression, which then expands into a musical primer of love). In part this is one more instance of popular cinema's pedagogical function as an initiator of the masses into consumer culture: in the past, new fashions, dance forms and other practices of (western) capitalist culture were similarly introduced. Thus, not too long ago, the song 'I am a disco dancer' taught the national audience the 'meaning' of disco, spelling out the word as if it were an acronym.

But beyond this consumerist function, the utopian aspiration to social transformation that the concept of love embodies also finds itself invoking a certain state-form as its true ground (cf. Bellour 1980). A striking illustration of this intersection of consumerism, romantic love in its congealed form as an English expression, and the modern nation-state is provided by Mani Rathnam's highly popular Tamil film *Roja* (1992; see Chapter 9). The following lines of dialogue, in which the English expression is employed, are exchanged by a newly married couple, who take a holiday in Kashmir when the husband is sent there on an assignment. After an exhausting erotic game of running around the hotel room, the two plunge into bed. The husband is a Madras-based cryptographer, employed by the intelligence wing of the state, while the wife is from an interior village of Tamil Nadu. (The italicized words are spoken in English):

> 'Hey village girl, if I say something to you in English, will you be able to understand it?
> 'Say it, let's see.
> '*I love you.*'

Here in these three lines we have the initiation of a closed exchange which can create the private space of the couple. But in these same lines we also get a glimpse of the (impossible) condition of possibility of that closure.

In this exchange what comes across is a strongly felt compulsion to consummate the marriage by means of the English language utterance. It is as if a lack had remained, after the marriage ceremonies, that could only be filled by the intervention of this ritual declaration. The expression, delivered to the adressee, transports the couple into their own private space. In this process the hitherto unapproachable precinct of romantic love is domesticated, by inhabiting it. But this space of symbolic consummation, by whose grace a private space is made possible, is also the most public space of all: like the first person pronoun that circulates freely among all those who enter the symbolic network, and is unavailable for exclusive possession, the expression, 'I love you' transports the speaking subject and the addressee into a different symbolic network, one in which the declaration is the true legitimation of the couple.

Being in English, this expression and the symbolic network into which it transports the couple, are also marked as a social privilege, a mark of social distinction. What is this Other whose recognition is invoked and guaranteed by this expression? This Other, the witness to a coupling that is beyond the formal coupling sanctioned by traditional authority, is as yet unformed, unidentifiable, its only trace being the obsessively recurring English expression that attests to the fact that something is being called into existence. Would it be farfetched to speculate that this Other is precisely the modern state in which the romance of the nuclear family and the state would dissolve or sublate all other mediating categories?

In any case, popular cinema displays no unequivocal preference for a traditional standpoint in its narratives of conflict between the traditional and the modern. On the contrary, one of its constant preoccupations is with the propagation of commodity culture within the context of traditionally regulated social relations. In the process it sometimes represents the utopian aspiration to transform the social in keeping with the promises made by capitalism and the modern nation-state.

PART II

5

The Moment of Disaggregation

Aaina hamen dekhke hairansa kyun hai?

—*Shahryar*

P art I developed a general theoretical framework for the study
of popular Hindi cinema through an investigation of the
conditions of possibility of the dominant textual form, the
'social'. We have seen that in the post-independence era a modular
and 'public' textual form rose to dominance, whose ideological
mission was to produce a coherent subject position in a situation
where the democratic revolution had been broached and then
indefinitely suspended. Three mutually-reinforcing factors served
as the conditions of possibility of this textual form: (1) backward
capitalist conditions in the film industry; (2) a transitional state-form
determined by the interests of the dominant coalition, characterized
by the deferral of bourgeois dominance; and (3) the persistence of
pre-capitalist ideologies and the continued authority of traditional
élites.

Against this background I turn in Part II to a conjunctural analysis
of developments in the field of film culture during a brief period of
political and ideological crisis of the Indian state. The attempt here
will be to develop a 'historical construction' of the transformations
in the field and their ideological significance. A historical construction
is not a 'reconstruction' in all its detail, of the events of the period in
question. It is an attempt to understand the historical significance of
a constellation of events by focussing selectively on certain aspects.

The hypothesis constructed and substantiated here can be stated
as follows: a period of intense political upheaval beginning in the
mid-sixties brought into crisis the political form of the national
consensus (represented by the dominant integrationist role of the

Congress party). Since the forces unleashed by this crisis were re-contained by an authoritarian populist government, only a limited transformation of the political field occurred. Re-organized in a looser, somewhat disaggregated form, including a more visible though fragmented opposition, the political system was able to absorb or marginalize radical challenges through populist mobilization.

Within the ideological sphere, the film industry faced a challenge to its established aesthetic conventions and mode of production. It was able to survive the crisis by a strategy of internal segmentation which enabled it to absorb the challenge of a politically-mobilized and demanding audience, and at the same time to reduce the threat of a state-sponsored rival production apparatus. The segmentation produced three distinct aesthetic formations—the new cinema, the middle-class cinema and the populist cinema of mobilization.

This chapter will explain and specify the political and institutional factors behind the pressure for change within the film industry, and the manner in which segmentation evolved as a solution to the crisis. The process of segmentation will be discussed in relation to the theoretical problem of genre formation as a feature of capitalist culture.

In political history, the period in question roughly coincides with the first phase of the Indira Gandhi era, from 1966—when after Lal Bahadur Shastri's death, the Congress Party elected her to take over as Prime Minister—to the state of Emergency which was in place for 18 months from 1975 to 1977.[1] This period was marked by the decline and fragmentation of Congress and the beginning of a series of political challenges from the left and the right to the Congress-managed 'consensual' stalemate between the defenders of traditional privileges and free-market principles on the one hand, and the forces agitating for the realization of the new nation's professed democratic and socialist ideals on the other. According to some political theorists, the consensual stalemate, which amounted to a negotiated suspension

---

[1]In view of the goals of my project, I make no attempt at providing clear cut-off points for the 'period'. There can be no exact overlap of political and cultural logics of periodization. Taken separately, the period of crisis for the film industry could be said to begin in 1969 with the launching of the new FFC policy. But it is more difficult to say when the momentum of a new thrust comes to an end. Politically, 1969 and 1977 can serve as more stable cut-off points because it was in 1969, with the split in Congress, that Indira Gandhi's transformation of Indian politics began and it was in early 1977 that the first phase of her rule came to an end with the lifting of the emergency and the electoral defeat.

or retardation of the democratic revolution, required two conditions: 'a low level of popular mobilisation, when the lower orders of the electorate voted on the advice of superordinant interests of some kind'; and 'a loose and largely federal political machine in which negotiation of local support, at local prices, were [sic] left to local bosses of the Congress' (Kaviraj, *EPW* 1986: 1699).

Indian politics, according to Kaviraj, was coalitional in two senses. There was first of all the class coalition, whose significance is structural, and entails 'long-term costraints'. This structural feature is threatened but did not undergo any significant transformation during the Indira Gandhi era. Politics is also coalitional in a second sense, at the level of 'parties or political formations'. 'Around a central, disproportionately large party of consensus were arranged much smaller parties of pressure, which imposed a coalitional logic on both government and opposition political groups.' The right and left factions within the Congress party had more ideological affinities with opposition parties like the Communists and the Swatantra than with each other. Thus the Congress itself was a coalition that enforced a coalitional logic on the functioning of the party system as a whole (ibid: 1986, 1698). Both these coalitional structures have a bearing on the ideological question. While the general theoretical framework elaborated in Part I must be understood by reference to the class coalition, the historical construction attempted in Part II refers itself to the local crisis in the mode of political functioning of the coalition.

The crisis in question begins with the unmistakable signs of popular dissatisfaction in the late sixties, an indication 'that lower orders of people were becoming less inclined to vote on the basis of primordial controls' (ibid: 1699). The particular strategies adopted by the regime (authoritarian populism based on a direct appeal to the masses over the heads of the intermediate leadership), were determined by the challenges to the consensus from both left and right and a recognition of the need to transform the political form of the consensus. Through the late sixties and early seventies, the political situation in India remained volatile, with a wide variety of movements occupying the centre of the political scene. While one segment of the communist left was making political gains through participation in the electoral process, another Maoist segment aligned itself with the rebellious peasantry and rural working class and appeared to be gaining ground in the countryside. Urban working-class militancy was at its peak in this period, and a combination of forces led by the ex-socialist Jayaprakash Narayan mounted a strong offensive against Congress dominance.[2]

The crisis can be usefully described as a deep disaggregation of the socio-political structure resulting in the delegitimation of the consensual ideology of the state. Given the central role of the Congress in maintaining the political equilibrium up to this point, it is not surprising that the party became a prominent site of the unfolding of the crisis. The fragmentation of the Congress, beginning with the various dissident formations that sprang up in the 1967 elections, at the state and regional level culminated in what was popularly known as the 'Indicate-Syndicate' split in 1969. The former group, led by Indira Gandhi and defined by its left-oriented programme, broke away and quickly marginalized the Syndicate with a reorganization of the political machine that rendered the existing modes of political negotiation obsolete overnight. In the Nehru era, the ability of the Congress to either marginalize or absorb rival political tendencies had enabled it to produce and maintain the cohesion-effect. Its modular unity reflected the unreconstructed articulation of a variety of old and new enclaves into a national political network. The disaggregation of this structure manifested itself in the form of a serious political crisis with several possible resolutions.

This crisis represented the culmination of a democratic ferment which promised a transformation of the social order. During British rule the nationalist movement had mobilized the masses with the promise of democracy. After independence, the people were repaid in the heavily devalued currency of citizenship, whose only tangible benefit was universal adult suffrage. The new regime found that the long process of colonial exploitation had left the economy too weak, that the infrastructure for self-reliant industrial growth had to be built almost from scratch. In view of this constraint on capitalist growth, the Nehru era, with its programme of state-led economic growth and 'gradual revolution' found itself relying upon the continued operation of the ideology of the despotic colonial state and the feudal order it had instituted.

The forces opposed to this order gathered strength in the post-Nehru era. Thus, this eventful period represents a revolutionary upsurge whose potential was hijacked by the Indira Gandhi government and channelled into an authoritarian interregnum.

[2]For a detailed description of the political ferment of this period see Francine Frankel, chapter 9–13, pp. 341–582. See also Biplab Das Gupta (1974), Sumanta Banerjee (1980), Achin Vanaik (1990)

'Social Tax' Versus State Competition

The crisis in the ideological instance of popular cinema took the form of a segmentation of audiences, the obsolescence of the feudal family romance, the pressure to develop new textual forms. It was the period in which the 'social', whose cultural status was remarkably similar to that of the Congress on the political plane, underwent a multi-faceted transformation. While one significant causal factor behind this drive for transformation was the politicization and mobilization of the masses, another was the state-sponsored movement that sought to give substance to the idea of a national cinema. These two factors were related, because the decisive step towards a new approach to film financing by the Film Finance Corporation (FFC) in 1969 was made possible by the Indira Gandhi government's interventionist policies. These were strongly stated by her and the information and broadcasting ministers in her cabinet, Nandini Satpathy and I.K. Gujral. The latter, in the course of an exhortatory speech, told the industry that its demand for a reduction in entertainment tax would be considered seriously if it was willing to pay a 'social tax' instead.[3] Thus, government co-operation in developing the capital base of the industry was to be purchased by a commitment by the industry to the production of films with progressive themes, to provide cultural support for the developmental goals of the 'socialist' government. The industry's leaders were habituated to making pledges of loyalty to the policies of the ruling party, but on this call for commitment unanimity was out of the question. The maintenance of a posture of deference towards the

[3]*Filmfare*, 4 July 1969, p. 29. Gujral championed the Film Council proposal with great passion. The progressive role of cinema would only be guaranteed by a well-organized industry communicating with government through 'a single highpowered authority capable of acting as a guide and mentor, as well as a responsible executive agency for undertaking worthwhile programmes of establishing professional norms and a rational code of intersectional relationship' (ibid: 27). In his presidential address to the seventeenth *Filmfare* awards assembly in 1970, Gujral expanded on his vision by arguing that politicians and artists were united by the bond of 'the people'. He contrasted the regressive tendencies in cinema with the 'genuine national style of expression' that had been developed in theatre, literature and painting. That the intervention was conceived as a measure to break the hold of the popular industry by setting up a rival sector is borne out by his assertion that while Bombay was merely following foreign models in its 'retarded growth', the question for India was which cinema would dominate. Offering to 'share power' with the industry, Gujral asked for a reciprocal abandoning of 'laissez-faire' and greater social responsibility (*Filmfare*, 22 May 1970, pp. 29–33).

leadership was all that the industry could manage.[4] The most that such government pressures on the mainstream industry achieved was to inspire some producers to include, within a formally unaltered framework, 'progressive' elements which they hoped would win government approval.[5] Sometimes this led to the granting of entertainment tax cuts or exemptions.

However, the Film Institute and the Film Finance Corporation together formed part of very different kind of intervention which was to have a lasting impact. While the institute offered training in the technical as well as performance aspects of film-making, the corporation, after a few years of lethargic and unimaginative functioning, launched a financing policy aimed at the development of 'good cinema', which for most people associated with the project, meant a cinema that was realist, narrative-centred, developmental, and culturally distinctly Indian. Although the change in policy had been initiated in 1964 by Indira Gandhi when she was the Information and Broadcasting minister, its decisive implementation roughly coincided with the arrival of a number of trained directors, actors and other technicians from the Film Institute.

The FFC had hitherto functioned somewhat like other state financial institutions, supplementing the budgets of mainstream film-makers (and of individuals with international standing like Satyajit Ray). Now, changing course to became a producer, the corporation entered into direct competition with the mainstream industry. Although the protests were muted in deference to the prevailing mood of populist mobilization, this development caused great panic in the industry. The industry had for a long time been demanding that the FFC should expand its operations by increasing the capital available for lending, to provide state support for the transformation

[4]Even this form of feudal allegiance without specific commitments on policy came under severe strain in these years of political turmoil. Thus, at a meeting addressed by the prime minister, I.S. Johar who was at the time the head of a producers' organization, responded to the prime minister's criticism of the industry (Mrs. Gandhi is reported to have said: 'We do have an impression that this industry is only interested in making money'!) by reminding her of the 'obscenity of poverty' (*Screen,* 2 January 1970, p. 1). This led to an uproar in the industry, with several major figures writing letters of protest, publicly dissociating themselves from Johar's position and even writing letters of apology with a promise of good behaviour to the prime minister (*Screen,* 9 January 1970, pp. 1,6; 16 January 1970, p. 1).

[5]Some tried easier ways to align themselves with the 'socialist' power. Thus, Shyam Behl, in his *Gold Medal* (1970), had sequences shot at the annual Congress session, and presented a reel containing these scenes to the prime minister (*Screen,* 20 February 1970, p. 1).

of production relations within the existing industry. But it had not anticipated the form of expansion that the FFC finally chose. While depriving the industry of even the meagre finance hitherto available, it now established a parallel industry with an alternative aesthetic programme. No longer content to produce newsreels as an instructional supplement to the entertainment film, the government was now expanding the sphere of state-sponsored production to the aesthetic realm. However, the crux of the matter was not the ideological dangers of state-sponsored cinema (which were minimal since the FFC policy was administered by an independent body),[6] so much as the economic danger of the emergence of a formidable competitor.

The implications of the new FFC policy gradually became clear with growing signs of audience interest in the promise of novelty, and wide support from the press for the experimental ventures. The industry was also preoccupied with the more immediate dangers foreboded by rumours of an impending nationalization, Gujral's active pursuit of the Film Council idea, the calculations within the industry about the mode of accommodation with the government's new socialist agenda, etc. As president of the Film Federation of India, Sunderlal Nahata called for internal unity and discipline as the only way of side-stepping the encroachment by the government which was seen as the main purpose for the institution of the Film Council. Unity was to be supplemented with a stance of co-operation in the national project:

> Big social changes are taking place in the country. Society has been awakened to the realities and socialistic trends are on in the country for the welfare of the nation . . . the government can ill-afford to ignore our problems when we prove to it that we share in the responsibilities to contribute to the welfare of the nation in our own humble way as any other industry does.[7]

But with the visibility achieved by Mrinal Sen's *Bhuvan Shome* (1969), which won awards and had a limited but surprising commercial run, it became clear that a substantial challenge was gathering strength. In the past, figures like Satyajit Ray had developed their own individualistic trajectories which precluded any

---

[6]Several prominent members of the FFC board, led by Hrishikesh Mukherjee and B.K. Karanjia, resigned in 1976 when the Emergency leadership started interfering in the affairs of the corporation (*Filmfare*, 11 June 1976, p. 35).

[7]*Screen*, 14 November 1969, p. 8.

Shome's body learns strange new dialects: Utpal Dutt in *Bhuvan Shome* (Mrinal Sen 1969). Courtesy National Film Archive of India, Pune.

institutionalized aesthetic programme. The industry had found it possible to acknowledge Ray as the 'Master' and a national cultural hero, without jeopardizing its own system of production and values. As Bikram Singh observed at the time, 'It is mainly the institutional forces and the strength they began to gain in the late sixties which the established film industry has found less easy to ignore than it did Satyajit Ray.[8] While providing opportunities for a variety of styles and political and aesthetic positions, the new aesthetic programme was unified by an oppositional stance towards the commercial cinema. The political dimension of the challenge posed by this initiative was not lost on the mainstream industry. In a review of Mrinal Sen's *Interview*, *Screen*, while acknowledging its strengths, called it biased, and nervously observed that the film may appeal to a 'now growing type of Indians' but not to a 'normal' audience.[9] Among the many compromises that the mainstream industry explored as a means of defusing this challenge, one was particularly significant for the manner in which it sought to blunt the political thrust by foregrounding the 'artistic' dimension of the new movement.

In response to Nandini Satpathy's speech at the National Awards

[8]*Filmfare*, 10 January 1975, p. 26.
[9]*Screen*, 11 December 1970, p. 19.

presentation reiterating the cultural policy of the Indira Gandhi government, *Screen* published a long 'critical study' of the speech. Noting that the speech seemed to be an indication of the policy of the 'new radical leadership', the writer drew attention to Satpathy's approving comments on the 'new wave' films. The government was mistaken in thinking that these films fulfilled the aims of cultural policy, the writer warned. 'Mrs. Satpathy could be wrong about the Indian "new wave". Its inspiration appears to be outlandish and there is little of Indian reality in its products.'[10] By contrast, the Bombay film 'has been a vehicle of Indian thought, culture and ideals'. Moreover, the government was warned that by encouraging the 'new wave' it was playing with fire. The virtues of the Bombay film lay in their 'innocuous' story-telling technique, while the 'committed film-maker, committed to advance a particular ideology, can pose a serious danger to society'. On the economic side, the 'new wave' was a loss-making venture and it was 'unethical', a 'grievous misconception of priorities' to encourage such indulgence in a poor country. The article concluded by suggesting that instead of the new FFC programme, an academy of motion picture arts should be set up with Satyajit Ray—'the undisputed master of the medium'— at its helm.

The mainstream industry had good reason to invoke the authority of Ray to serve as an aesthetic focal point that would reduce the importance of the political dimension. Ray's opinions on the 'new wave' were first aired in an article 'An Indian New Wave?' published in *Filmfare* (8 October 1971) and again in a review article 'Four and a Quarter', published in *Indian Film Culture* in 1974.[11] In the first of these, Ray drew attention to the practical constraints on the ambitions of the new film-makers. Debunking the trendiness of their enthusiasm, Ray pointed out that narrative was central to cinema, that 'experiment' was costly and bound to fail where audiences were untrained in cinematic language. This criticism was based on the assumption that experiment necessarily entailed an imitation of 'Godard', a code-word for experimental cinema. Welcoming the new FFC policy, Ray nevertheless implied that products of such a policy were not going to succeed with the audience at large. Besides, films like *Bhuvan Shome*, which had been hailed as the harbinger of a new movement,

[10]*Screen*, 18 February 1972, p. 4.

[11]Both are now available in Ray's *Our Films Their Films*, pp. 81–99; 100–7 respectively.

were old-fashioned narrative films after all. In his response the critic Bikram Singh pointed out that while Ray found foreign experiments always suited to their time and place, he wanted Indian film-makers to know in advance the effect of their experiments on the audience, the commercial viability of the films, etc. The viability criterion amounted to a pre-emption of experiment.[12] Ray's rejoinder and Singh's counter-response[13] only reinforced the basic point of difference. Ray's argument was circular: he regarded narrative as central; he opposed experiment because it was anti-narrative; he found that the films made under the FFC aegis were narratives after all; he therefore questioned its claim to be a 'movement'. It was a no-win argument. If the new film-makers wanted to be called a movement they must experiment; if they experimented, they were out of touch with reality. Mrinal Sen, in a letter purporting to be an extract from a letter to a friend, summed it up thus: 'to me it (Ray's article) doesn't mean much except that he emphasizes on the necessity to build opinion for the "prevention of alleged cruelty to money-backers". And this, to my mind, hardly builds an aesthetic case . . . .'[14]

Ray's emphasis on narrative was shared by most people in the FFC. As the project unfolded, it was narrative that became the most visible mark of the new cinema's difference from the popular. However, the dispute between Ray and some in the FFC was over political and institutional questions. Ray's arguments were anchored in a notion of the film-maker as an individual artist who must function in a market that imposes its own rules. He was pragmatic in his recognition of market constraints but this did not impair his image as an artistic genius. The new film-makers would introduce a political element into the aesthetic field, by claiming for their experiments a significance that went beyond the 'improvement' accomplished by good narratives. At this juncture, Ray decided to side with the commercial industry by invoking pragmatic considerations, rather than serving as a supportive elder figure for the new enthusiasts.

The biggest obstacle to the FFC's project was the strong nexus between the theatre owners and the financier-distributors, on account of which the new films found themselves without exhibition outlets. The construction of theatres by the government was seen as the only possible solution, but despite such appeals only one or two

[12] *Filmfare*, 14 January 1972, pp. 21–3.
[13] *Filmfare*, 25 February 1972, pp. 51–2, 53.
[14] *Filmfare*, 24 March 1972, p. 51.

feeble attempts were made in this direction. This impasse was one of the factors that led to compromise formations such as the middle-class cinema, whose most widely known practitioners, Basu Chatterjee and Hrishikesh Mukherjee, were both associated with the FFC project, but made most of their films in this period with private finance.

Segmentation

The main sponsors of the middle-class cinema included the N.C. Sippy family, Tarachand Barjatya, B.R. Chopra, Suresh Jindal, etc., most of whom were established figures in the mainstream industry. This cinema was distinguished by its narratives of upper caste, middle-class life with ordinary-looking deglamourized stars. It consolidated itself by elaborating a negative identity based on its difference from the mainstream cinema, thus appropriating one of the main slogans of the FFC-sponsored 'movement'. An inter-textual reference system developed thanks to the regular appearance of a set of stars, the iconography and language of the middle-class household, a constant use of the popular cinema as a point of counter-identification, even direct references to other middle-class films (as in Gulzar's *Mere Apne* in which a poster and a radio advertisement for *Anand* figure prominently). While remaining firmly within the structure of the established industry, middle-class cinema represented the first serious and successful attempt at a planned segmentation of the industry based on the perception of a changed market and the threat of a rival's potential monopoly over that market. The middle-class cinema took over that aspect of the FFC's 'realist' aesthetic project which consisted in narratives of identification, centred on the urban upper-caste family, a demand for authentic urban middle-class characters who were recognizably ordinary, etc. The two films which are usually cited as the first successes of the new FFC policy, Mrinal Sen's *Bhuvan Shome* and Basu Chatterji's *Sara Akash* both presented this aesthetic of authenticity and simplicity. When it came to commercial exploitation, however, the main cultural 'resource' proved to be Bengali middle-class culture, which for historical reasons had developed early and boasted of a rich literary tradition.

Significantly, while FFC failed to create exhibition space for its films, the middle-class cinema movement within the mainstream industry was strong enough to prompt a suitable expansion of exhibition outlets. In many cities new theatres with reduced seating capacity were built specifically for the middle-class film. The Nartaki-Sapna complex in Bangalore, which was built in the early 70s, reproduced architecturally the relations between the mainstream film industry and its new branch, the middle-class cinema. Nartaki is an enormous theatre which showed only the biggest of the big Hindi films at that time. Sapna, which is still associated with the 'realist' cinema; is a single-level theatre wedged into one corner of the ground floor of the building. Sapna was soon followed (and elsewhere, preceded) by other such small theatres clinging to bigger ones. Thus permanent exhibition space was created for a new sector of the industry.

Certain FFC principles were thus appropriated and developed into a viable segment of the industry relatively easily due to the fact that those who had included the middle-class aesthetic principles in the FFC 'manifesto' were themselves responsible for initiating their commercial exploitation. Hrishikesh Mukherjee and Basu Chatterjee were key figures in developing the commercial middle-class cinema with the financial backing of people like N.C. Sippy. Other principles, however, seemed doomed to a slow extinction until Shyam Benegal emerged, literally from nowhere, to exploit their commercial potential. As editor of *Filmfare,* B.K. Karanjia provided crucial media support for all aspects of the new cinema movement. But Mukherjee and others like B.R. Chopra and even Karanjia, were unapproving of, and sometimes extremely hostile to the radicals who had used the opportunity provided by the new FFC policy to make films ranging from the openly political to the experimental. Such experimentation, which resulted in films like Mani Kaul's *Uski Roti* or Kumar Shahani's *Maya Darpan,* was ridiculed as an élite preoccupation for which the masses had neither the time nor the inclination. (Many writers on Indian cinema spontaneously echo this populist argument, with the result that the names of Kaul and Shahani have become a convenient shorthand for the denunciation of experimentation.) A common sense demand for easy intelligibility was deployed to mobilize public opinion against experimentation. For the proponents of middle-class realism, the role of new cinema was to function as 'leaven' to improve the quality of the mainstream product.[15] Not to compete with, but to supplement—was the slogan that Karanjia, for example, developed with vigour in *Filmfare.* Coupled with the even

[15]*Filmfare,* 1 January 1971, p. 31.

more forceful argument of economic viability, this amounted to an effective prohibition of aesthetic exploration aimed at developing a cinematic discourse distinct from both the 'realism' of instantaneous consumability and the aesthetic of the dominant popular cinema.

As a powerful player in the world of the commercial film industry, B.R. Chopra had much to say on the dangers of the new development. Chopra had acquired a reputation as an innovator by virtue of having made successful films without songs (*Kanoon, Ittefaq*). The latter was marketed as a turning point in Indian cinema: it was short; it had taken only a few weeks to complete; it had no songs. Chopra, who presided over a symposium on 'parallel cinema', leading to a walk-out by some new film-makers,[16] attacked the very notion of a parallel cinema movement and heaped abuse on the pretensions of 'a crop of pseudos', who 'in the name of art and realism, (had) introduced new kinds of vulgarities'. He attributed the art versus commerce split to the evil of democracy, which he defined as 'rule by mediocrity'. Film, 'which was once the entertainment of the intelligent middle class' had been destroyed by democratic forces which 'had taken over cinema and converted it into a mediocre art', leading to a compensatory art film movement. The solution was a 'healthy' cinema that was free from the compulsions of democracy. The middle-class cinema was thus not only a partial commercialization of the goals of the FFC project, it was also seen as a protection against the lures of political cinema.

But it is puzzling that a segment that was manifestly handicapped by a variety of impediments should cause so much panic in the industry. One reason for this was the perception that the privilege of serving as India's 'national cinema' would be more or less monopolized by the FFC sector. The auteurist FFC films were natural candidates for awards and for foreign festival entry. Such a turn of events also presaged government indifference, if not hostility, to the mainstream industry, which meant that the process of bargaining with government for concessions, incentives, and other forms of co-operation could well cease altogether. The industry's claim to national *cultural* significance would lack any credibility.

Although there was no possibility of a significant popular success of the experimental films, their continued production under the supportive aegis of the government implied real long-term consequences for the mainstream industry. The alarm would not

[16]*Screen*, 17 January 1975, p. 15.

have assumed such proportions if it were not for a fear that there existed a growing interest in precisely the kind of aesthetic shifts that the political cinema was attempting. While the 'normal' audience was still there, a 'new type' of audience was perceived as growing. There was a real possibility that a substantial segment of the audience for cinema would be drawn to an alternative cultural space, thus cutting into the size of the middle-class audience for popular cinema. Although the press and popular opinion continued to propagate the myth of a cinema exclusively addressed to a mass, proletarian audience, the middle-class audience (as Ashish Nandy has pointed out) is the decisive factor for the survival of the industry. The genius of the middle-class cinema lay in its ability to construct an aesthetic based on disidentification with the popular cinema while remaining within the financial and talent structure of the mainstream industry. But there remained a political excess which the identificatory realism of the middle-class cinema was unable to accommodate because its field of representation did not include the domain of the urban working class or the countryside, where the feudal order was being challenged by violent uprisings in which urban middle-class youth were prominent actors. It was through the construction of a *developmental aesthetic* that commercial cinema eventually managed to exploit this political excess.

While the lack of exhibition spaces kept most of the experimental films off the market, one of the incentives for a commercial exploitation of urban middle-class political discontent was the exhibition space that became available with the lapsing of the contract with the Motion Picture Producer's Association of America (MPPAA) for import of Hollywood films, as pointed out by Shyam Benegal himself (Rizvi and Amlad 1980: 8). Until this happened, though the 'demand' for a political cinema did exist, there was no sector in the industry that was competent enough to exploit it. 'Blaze', an advertising company, had entered distribution and, sensing the existence of a market for a cinema different from the popular as well as the 'middle class' variety, engaged one of its ad-film makers, Shyam Benegal, to direct *Ankur,* thus inaugurating the commercial exploitation of the political dimension of the FFC's aesthetic project.

The politically committed film-makers who benefited from the new FFC policy had no common aesthetic programme. Some adopted Brechtian aesthetic principles, while others pursued an aesthetic based on a critical appropriation of the techniques of melodrama. Some of the successful films were pure political thrillers in the Costa

Gavras tradition, while a fourth category of films made in the regional languages, focussed on rural India, with its feudal social order, the community rituals, etc. This last category provided the material from which Benegal forged the developmental aesthetic that came to be celebrated as *the* political cinema *par excellence*. This aesthetic was based on the appropriation of regional realism, and its elaboration as national cinema, while retaining the regional content as the object of a strategy of framing that produced a spectator position, allied with the developmental perspective of the state.

Thus, the FFC's intervention in film production can be read as a story of the establishment of a research and development facility, which conducted a variety of experiments from which the commercial cinema picked up and exploited the most viable forms, leaving the less viable ones to be pursued by individuals who came to be identified with aesthetic preoccupations irrelevant to the national culture. Commercial viability depended on the amenability of the forms to ideological re-inscription. The cross-over process filtered out critical experimentation resistant to the prevailing ideologies. What remained of the FFC's interventionist aesthetic programme was undercut by the 1975 *Report of the Committee on Public Undertakings*, which recommended commercial viability as the primary condition for film-financing.

The Construction of Amitabh Bachchan

While these developments were made possible by a combination of widespread politicization of cinema audience, especially the middle-class and the students, the declining efficacy of the feudal family romance prompted a move by the commercial cinema towards an aesthetic focussed on the mobilization-effect. The legendary star-figure of Amitabh Bachchan, the single most important mass cultural phenomenon of the seventies and after, with a fame stretching from the subcontinent to North Africa, was constructed through a series of contingent occurrences within a relatively short period of two to three years.

The Bachchan persona, identified with a primordial anger and populist leadership qualities, was, ironically, given its first exposure in Hrishikesh Mukherjee's *Anand* and *Namak Haram*. In Mukherjee's films, Bachchan's roles were varied. But beginning with Prakash

Mehra's *Zanjeer*, a series of films isolated and elaborated the image of the 'angry man', which soon pushed the other Bachchan persona out of popular memory. While Mukherjee continued to cast Bachchan in his films (*Abhimaan, Mili, Chupke Chupke, Alaap*), the 'industrial hero' had overtaken the middle-class character.

The disaggregation of the national audience should not be taken to mean an empirical division of the population into distinct consumer groups. Although a section of the population clearly patronized only foreign films and indigenous art films, the rest of the national audience was not so clearly segmented, and even after the decline of the feudal family romance, the audiences for the emerging generic tendencies were not mutually exclusive. However, new expectations arising out of the political upheavals of the period produced the conditions for exploration of new forms, narratives and characterological innovations. Disaggregation brought to the fore, class, gender and generational differences which the social had contained within its overarching feudal form. Thus, to give just one example, while the 'social' usually incorporated consumerist references to the latest fashions and other preoccupations of youthful audiences, these did not contribute to a distinct 'youth culture' because the paternalism of the reigning feudal ideology resisted any delinking of youth from its sphere of authority. But during and after the seventies, commercial culture gained access to a student/youth audience without paternalist mediation even if these films ultimately worked towards restoration of a reformed familial bond. (In *Hare Rama Hare Krishna* the reform of parental authority comes after the death of the Janice character played by Zeenat Aman.) This is a clear sign of an emerging capitalist tendency towards a disaggregated commercial culture.

In the context of the commercial film industry which was in the process of a many-sided and unpredictable transformation along with manifest tendencies to audience segmentation, the Bachchan phenomenon, though apparently 'in the spirit of the times', is best understood as a unifying phenomenon which re-established the popular film industry on a new foundation. While radically different from the feudal form that had dominated the scene for almost twenty years, the Bachchan film was nevertheless the means by which the industry transformed itself internally, providing it with a new identity that was capable of combining the novel aesthetic possibilities opened up in the period of crisis with fragments of the old form. The mobilization effect was the most significant new element, whose force was capable of holding together a new form of modular text in which the old ingredients would reappear but under a new aegis.

In the era of the feudal family romance, the star-image and the acting role were linked by the prevailing Hindu codes of iconicity. The roles of aristocratic or upper-caste heroes and heroines were played by actors carefully chosen for their looks, which had to match a certain conception of the 'heroic'. This attempt to approximate upper-caste and aristocratic ideals of physical beauty dates back to the time of Dadasaheb Phalke, who in one of his writings, outlined the ideal features of the actors who would play lead roles (Phalke, *Continuum* 1988–9: 65–9). Star glamour in such a context was indistinguishable from the 'innate' glamour or the splendour of the élite.

With the Bachchan phenomenon, however, we see the emergence of a new function for the star image. Now it is not just a question of exceptional physical features.[17] Nor does it follow the Hollywood tendency, as described by John Ellis (1992), where acting roles and star-persona exist side by side, with the films serving as instanciations of a star's image. In this western model, the star's image is built on the combination of ordinary and extraordinary traits that are developed in stories published in star magazines. Crucially, a clear line separates the star from the acting role, although there is a degree of seepage of star value into the acting role.[18]

The Bachchan persona is different because in it there is a degree of integration of star-value with narrative that is unprecedented in the Hindi cinema. What this demonstrates, however, is not the unfathomable power of the Amitabh mystique as much as the demands placed upon the star image by a new form of narrative in which the innate charm of the aristocracy was no longer the obvious central content of the text. The Bachchan phenomenon cannot be analysed in isolation from the construction of this new narrative form, in which the writer duo Salim-Javed played an important role. With the disintegration of the feudal family romance, the entry of 'ordinary' heroes into the popular film became possible, perhaps even necessary. Dockworker, mineworker, railway porter, police

---

[17]Amitabh Bachchan's acting ambitions were initially ridiculed by some producers who found his face unherolike; Hrishikesh Mukherjee's role in launching Bachchan is crucial precisely because unmindful of the unattractive physical features, he cast him in his narrative films and provided a showcase for Bachchan's unorthodox talents. Bachchan's first role, however, was in K.A. Abbas's *Saat Hindustani*.

[18]See also, Dyer (1987).

officer, small-time crook: these were some of the roles Amitabh played in his career, roles that were predominantly lower class and integral to the evolution of the aesthetic of mobilization (discussed in Chapter 6).

Such ordinariness brought with it a dilemma: the old hero's pre-eminence had derived from the hierarchies of a social order that were reproduced within the film text. The middle-class film, on the other hand, adopted a code of ordinariness that excluded both the divine splendour of the aristocracy and the political passions of the proletariat to create a circumscribed representational field where narrative requirements prevailed over the self-valorizing logic of the star system. But from the mainstream industry's perspective, ordinariness, in reinforcing the primacy of narrative movement, is a threat to the old order, in which as we have seen in Part I, heterogeneous manufacture, predicated on the assembly of pre-existing 'craft' products and congealed values was the prevailing mode of production. While the political ferment of the Indira Gandhi era was strong enough to render the old form obsolete and give rise to pressures for change, it did not bring about a complete transformation of the aesthetic bases of the industry. The problem that the industry faced was how to continue to function with the existing mode of production without the readymade narrative framework of the feudal family romance. The FFC project's long-term threat was a reorganization of film-production on the basis of the centrality and autonomy of the production sector. This was the factor that prompted a search by established industry figures for compromise solutions involving a workable mix of star and narrative values. Salim-Javed also identified themselves with this project for internal reform. But the resolution that imposed itself finally was one which would make this change of direction unnecessary. This resolution was made possible by the intensification of the value deriving from the star system through the infusion of political power into the figure of the star on the model of the populist cinema of Tamil Nadu. The star became a mobilizer, demonstrating superhuman qualities and assuming a power that transformed the others who occupied the same terrain into *spectators*. As the auratic power of the represented social order diminished, there was a compensating increase in the aura of the star as public persona.

The Politics of Genre

Before moving onto a more focussed analysis of films from these three segments, it would be useful to draw out the implications of the historical construction attempted here for the question of genre. Specifically, how is the segmentation of the industry discussed above related to or different from genre formation?

The question of genre has been a notoriously difficult one for critics of Indian cinema. Some critics evade the difficulties by simply identifying the mythological and the social as the principal Indian genres. Others recognize that generic differentiation in the Hollywood sense is not evident in Bombay cinema, although in the early studio era similar distinctions were prevalent.[19] In a recent essay, Rashmi Doraiswamy (1993) acknowledges the difficulties surrounding the question, but decides to use the 'personality type' as the basis for making generic distinctions. In Chapter 3, we have seen how incipient generic distinctions are undermined by the expansive identity of the 'social'. However, the 'social' has eluded a precise definition, serving simply as a label for a large quantity of films which resist more accurate differentiation.

One of the reasons for the relative weakness of generic differentiation in the Hindi cinema could be the prevalence of a particular mode of production in the industry, as argued in Chapter 2. Besides, the possibility of cultural production under such circumstances

[19]Sudhir Kakar (1980) has observed that there was a caste system of film genres, the mythological being the Brahmin of them all and the Nadia-style stunt films being the shudras. This would seem to have given way to the era of the secular social, incorporating the brahmanism of the mythological as well as the shudra antics of the stunt film. It is thus not surprising that in the crisis period under consideration, the decline of the social led to the resurgence of the 'shudra' genres like the stunt film, with 'shudra' stars (in the sense of being exploited minor stars) like Jyothilakshmi and Vijayalalitha reviving the Nadia phenomenon. (See G. Karnad (1994) and B. Gandhy and R. Thomas (1991) for discussions of the Nadia films.) In Hindi cinema, in the era of the dominance of the social, there was a sub-culture of gladiator films and 'thrillers' featuring stars like Dara Singh and Feroze Khan, Sheikh Mukhtar and Ansari. These were shown in cheap theatres frequented by a predominantly Muslim sub-proletariat. One of the reasons for the tremendous success of the first few Salim-Javed films was the strategic use of motifs from urban Muslim culture and Muslim folk religion which was an invitation to a hitherto marginalized audience. On the other hand, the 'Brahmin' mythological did not enjoy a corresponding resurgence. This may suggest that the social had effected an irreversible secularization of the mythological (Kakar, 1989: 25), although the revival of the latter on television in recent years complicates the picture.

bespeaks a whole array of other factors, including a distinct political structure and an ideological impasse. The pulls and pressures of such a social organization impose certain conditions of possibility, certain constraints on cultural production and genre formation. At the same time, the existence and wide circulation of Hollywood genres gives rise to imitations and fragmentary appropriations by Hindi film-makers: the dacoit film was combined with elements from the Hollywood western in films like *Khotey Sikkay* and *Sholay* and 'horror films' combined *mantravadis* and white-clad ghost-beauties from folk narratives with hairy monsters from a western repertoire.[20]

In the midst of such forays, the portmanteau 'social' has remained the dominant, and during certain periods, the sole genre with a contemporary signified. The only element that is exclusive to the social and thus critical to its identification as a genre is its contemporary reference. Its dominance attests to a certain ideological imperative that is peculiar to the modernizing Indian state.

With a few exceptions, these socials are usually musicals. The musical, which is an intermediate form in which cinema's links with the stage are worked out, and in which pre-and extra-cinematic skills and languages are put on display, has become a marginal form in Hollywood, whereas in the Hindi cinema the continuing dominance of the musical-social is a symptom of the continued dependence of the cinema on the resources of other cultural forms.

This is not to be read simply as a question of a gradual technological advancement which will eventually lead us out of a dependence on music. The problem of what Rajadhyaksha (*Framework*, 1987) calls the 'neo-traditionalism' of Indian popular film culture is a political, not a technological, issue. The social does not occur as a transitional form marking the non-completion of some technological journey. Its function, on the other hand, is to *resist* genre formation of any kind, particularly of the type constituted by the segmentation of the contemporary. This ideological function is imposed on it by the nature of political power in the modernizing state. The segmentation or disaggregation of the 'social' is prevented by the very mode of combination of the aesthetic of the signifier (music, choreographed fights, parallel narrative tracks, etc.) with that of the signified (or realism, which requires continuity, a serial track and subordination of music to a narrative function).

[20]Steve Neale (1980) provides a good introduction to the theoretical significance of the genre question in film studies. See also Jane Feuer (1982) and the essays in Grant (1986).

In the period of crisis, we encounter a moment when a genre formation based on political differentiation is forced on the industry as a solution to the delegitimation of its dominant formal strategies. Here it is necessary to free ourselves from the spontaneous association of genre formation with the specific form it has taken in the case of Hollywood cinema. While differentiation does manifest itself in the Indian case, it does not follow the Hollywood pattern. The new cinema, the middle-class cinema and the reformed social emerge as three strong generic identities whose necessity derives from the same political pressures that led to a transformation of the national consensus from which the Indian state derived its legitimacy.

In the three chapters to follow, I take up each of the three generic tendencies identified above for discussion, in order to bring to light their substantive identity, to investigate their strategies of representation and their ideological projects.

6

The Aesthetic of Mobilization

The recuperation of the commercial film industry from the crisis of the Indira Gandhi era required a reconstruction of its cultural base and a reform of its mode of address. In the past its composite textual form had been capable of including a variety of pleasures. The protocols of darsanic spectacle had been sustained by the deployment of narratives of familial splendour. With the disaggregation of the socio-political order, however, the middle class became amenable to the seductions of a new identity based on disidentification with the 'socialist' programme in the national project. The dominant textual form's consensus-effect broke down and a search was launched for new modes and targets of address.

Amitabh Bachchan's star personality has to be understood in this context. Bachchan came to be identified with the dominated, a figure of resistance who appeared to speak for the working classes and other marginalized groups. However, the effectivity of the Bachchan persona must be investigated not only at the level of a shift to proletarian themes but more importantly, in its function as a rallying point for the industry as a whole, a magnetic point around which the industry reconstituted itself. The ingredients of this persona, go beyond the personal 'charisma' of the individual and include political, aesthetic and institutional values. Bachchan thus became an 'industrial hero' (Valicha 1988) not only in the sense that he played working class characters but also because he was the hero *of* the industry.

Bachchan's emergence as the main source of value for the industry was preceded by parallel attempts to achieve autonomy of the production sector through an emphasis on narrative.[1] Further developments contributing to this end were the experimentation with a novel approach to screen writing in which the indivisibility of the story and dialogue departments was maintained.[2]

Rajesh Khanna was the reigning male star during the years in which the Bachchan persona was being constructed. Sippy Films, Shakti Samanta and other commercial film-makers had tried to make films with an emphasis on narrative. Shakti Samanta's *Aradhana*, based on an old Hollywood melodrama, *To Each His Own*, proved a tremendous success, with its message of patriotism and a little boost from the rumoured 'controversy' over Sharmila Tagore's appearance in a bath-towel. G.P. Sippy's *Andaz* was also a 'script film' with a borrowed French narrative. It was successful, but the brief appearance of Rajesh Khanna in a flashback, singing the immensely popular *'Zindagi ek safar hai suhana'* became the highpoint of the film, obscuring the somewhat unorthodox plot involving widow remarriage. Thus, there were signs that commercial cinema was itself experimenting with a gradual reform of the dominant textual form that could preserve the star as the industry's main source of value while asserting the autonomy of the production sector with an emphasis on narrative. Other successes of the period like *Bobby, Jawani Diwani, Imtihan, Hare Rama Hare Krishna* addressed the student/youth segment of the audience. Of the star

[1]See interview with G.P. Sippy in *Screen*, 21 February 1969. Combining arguments for national reconstruction with promises of economic benefit, Sippy remarked that films depicting social and political problems that could raise awareness were necessary to 'revive the declining patronage' of the industry's products. The immediate evidence for this was the failure of some big-budget productions. The industry wanted freedom from censorship to tackle themes that would help 'the crystallisation of political, social and religious outlook of the country and restoration of communication between the generations.'

[2]*Filmfare*, 13 December 1974. See also, interview with Javed Akhtar in Kak (1980). *Filmfare*, in the spirit of its leadership role in reforming the commercial industry, had in 1969 renamed the award for the best dialogue as a screenplay award, to give importance to 'the blueprint which incorporates the total vision of the projected film' (3 January 1969, p. 3). While the reformist impulse of the magazine may have had some impact, the problem it was supposed to attack was not caused by the incompetence of individuals but by the conditions prevailing in the industry (discussed in Part I). The peak of Salim-Javed's fame, moreover, was reached with the enormous popularity of the dialogues of *Sholay*. While the story and dialogue departments were indeed fused into one in the sense that they were both written by the same people, the autonomous force of the dialogue within the film text remained unaffected.

figures involved in these films, only Zeenat Aman and Rishi Kapoor developed lasting careers. Dimple Kapadia, who might have had greater success than any of the others, left the industry to get married. While many stars succeeded in developing star-images of minor significance, only Bachchan evolved into a national figure. His role is thus to be understood trans-textually, as a figure of cohesion in the industry as a whole.

Bachchan's star-image was constructed through two different points of entry. After an initial period in which he failed to secure any significant acting roles, Bachchan found a hospitable climate in Hrishikesh Mukherji's middle-class films where he appeared as a cultured, concerned doctor (*Anand*), angry son of an industrialist (*Namak Haram*), a singer who rebels against his orthodox father (*Aalap*), etc. In this early period he also worked as a hero of the old style in films like *Pyar ki Kahani* and *Bombay to Goa*, while taking on roles in some low-budget films as well which might well have led him the way of minor stars like Navin Nischal and Vinod Mehra. The turning point came with the scripts written by Salim-Javed. Of these the most significant were *Zanjeer* (1973), *Deewar* (1974), and *Sholay* (1975). Bachchan came to be associated so strongly with the latter that his early films, even the successful ones made by Mukherji, have been almost forgotten.[3] This is despite the fact that it was Mukherjee's casting of Bachchan in the 'brooding' roles of *Anand* and *Namak Haram* that disclosed the potential that would be exploited on a gigantic scale by the commercial industry.[4]

[3]Sumita Chakravarty, who mentions some of Bachchan's early films, nevertheless makes the surprising observation that *Chupke Chupke* was 'the only film in which Bachchan appears as a "gentleman" ' (1993: 231). This perhaps demonstrates the retroactive power of the evolved Bachchan image. Chakravarty does not dwell on the process of production of the Bachchan persona, attributing his success instead to his 'haunting and haunted eyes' (ibid: 231) and other 'innate' sources of charm.

[4]Thus *Filmfare*, looking back in 1989, commented: 'They called him the One Man Industry and for sixteen years he churned out hits with assembly-line regularity. *Zanjeer, Deewar, Don, Amar Akbar Anthony, Muqaddar Ka Sikandar, Trishul, Kasme Vaade, Kaala Patthar, Mr. Natwarlal, Laawaris, Kaalia, Naseeb, Namak Halal, Andha Kanoon, Coolie, Mard, Geraftaar* . . . It seemed as if the sun would never set on the reign of Blockbuster Bachchan. Never before had a star seen this kind of success, and for so long. The distance between him and his rivals was so vast that in the number game, they'd allotted the numbers 1 to 10 to him, the competition really took place way down there and it never affected the big man at the top' (*Filmfare*, 6 June 1989, p. 38), cited in Sumita S. Chakravarty (1993: 230). Not a single Mukherji film is named in the list, although *Abhiman* was a big success and other films like *Chupke Chupke* cashed in on his star status.

The difference between Mukherji's films and those that built up Bachchan as a star persona was that in the former, the star represented only an infusion of additional value into a narrative which retained its primacy. (In a film like *Abhiman*, the conflicting trajectories of narrative and spectacle were sought to be resolved through the narrativization of the star figure.) In the Salim-Javed led project, however, the star remained a semantic excess of the narrative process, available for future exploitation.

The value deriving from a star persona is part rent and part profit. From the star's perspective, his/her body is a source of rent, since its principal quality, charisma, is coded as a possession that he/she is 'born with', notwithstanding the work that goes into producing it. From the perspective of the film-makers, the payment of rent enables the exploitation of this 'ground' in profit-making ventures. The star's persona thus accumulates within itself attributes that are specific to various instances of performance, as well as various value-laden associations deriving from personal history. Thus, as an example of the latter, we may cite Bachchan's literary and political affiliations. His father, Harvansh Rai Bachchan, is a well-known Hindi poet and his mother Teji Bachchan, a distinguished member of the social élite. (Mukherjee's *Aalap* showed Amitabh singing one of his father's poems.) The Bachchans were also close friends of the Indira Gandhi family. Amitabh would later enter politics as a Congress candidate for parliament and remain Rajiv Gandhi's close ally for many years. These bits of information were stirred into the star persona by the press.

The persona also absorbed the characteristics of several characters played by Amitabh in the early part of his career. Anger, self-absorption, rebelliousness, devotion to mother, proletarian identity were some of the attributes of the roles that came to be absorbed into the star persona. While the power derived from élite affiliations served to legitimate the persona for the middle class, the personality derived from the subaltern roles was the basis for a new mode of address, which spoke to the proletariat and other marginal sections and mobilized the spectator behind the star. The rest of this chapter will be devoted to a discussion of the first three Salim-Javed films, *Zanjeer, Deewar* and *Sholay*. The primary aim will be to identify the strategies through which these films constructed the mobilized (and mobilizing) subaltern hero as an agent of national reconciliation and social reform.

Zanjeer (Prakash Mehra, 1973)

This was one of the first independent successes of the writer-duo Salim-Javed, whose star status is intimately tied up with the three films we are concerned with. Employed for a period in the G.P. Sippy Films Writing Department, where they participated singly or together in the writing of *Andaz* (based on *A Man and a Woman*), and *Seeta aur Geeta* (based on *Ram Aur Shyam*), Salim-Javed struck out on their own with Nasir Husain's *Yadon ki Barat* (based on an idea that Husain had already tried out in *Pyar ka Mausam*) and Prakash Mehra's *Hath ki Safai* and *Zanjeer*. While all of these films were big earners, *Zanjeer* was the film that launched Salim-Javed into stardom. Bachchan was chosen for the role of Inspector Vijay when Dev Anand, enjoying a resurgence of popularity after the success of *Johny Mera Naam* and *Hare Rama Hare Krishna*, rejected the offer. As Salim-Javed recollect it, the final form of Zanjeer owed much to their insistence on strict adherence to a tightly-composed screenplay. (Prakash Mehra, the producer/director, had wanted to make room for a plane hijack half-way through the shooting.) Indeed, by their own reading, it was a novel approach to screen-writing which insisted on the indivisibility of the 'story' and 'dialogue' departments (traditionally regarded as separate skills in the industry) that makes their films distinct.

The institutionalization of the subaltern as mobilized subject, however, was effected through narrative mechanisms to which we now turn. In *Zanjeer*, the Bachchan persona came to be identified with a subaltern anger and an affiliation with the masses symbolized by an alliance with a figure representing the Muslim minority. The hero of *Zanjeer* is an honest police officer who uses extra-legal methods to bring criminals to justice and in the process antagonizes his colleagues and incurs the wrath of the criminal underworld. Tormented by the memory of his parents' assassination by a criminal, Inspector Vijay (Amitabh Bachchan) has a recurring dream of a masked figure on horseback. The image is traced back to a bracelet worn by the killer. The dream and the hero's inability to understand it signal his possession by an elemental force which drives him to act in unorthodox ways but always towards honest ends. In the course of an investigation, he becomes friendly with a female knife-sharpener (Jaya Bhaduri) whom he rescues from the street after persuading her to give evidence against some criminals. Next he confronts Sher Khan (Pran), a Pathan who runs a gambling den in a *mohalla* notorious for criminal activities. This confrontation has a symbolic dimension because it pits Vijay, as a representative of the law against Sher Khan, who is a law unto himself. Agreeing to Sher Khan's challenge to meet him on his own ground, Vijay goes to his mohalla after duty. In the ensuing duel neither is able to defeat the other. Sher Khan, acknowledging his rival's strength, abandons his illegal activities and pledges to assist Vijay in his fight against crime and injustice. Thereafter, dismissed from the force on a false bribery charge, Vijay, assisted by Sher Khan and a Christian old man (Om Prakash) confronts the city's big crime gang, discovers that the gang boss is his parents' killer, and has his revenge. The novelty of the narrative is the combined result of two elements.

1) *The revenge of the orphan:* The orphan is a figure of marginality, deprived of the normal familial pleasures by the intrusion of evil. The orphan's actions are attributed to a force beyond his control, haunting his dreams and driving him to act in ways that conflict with the procedural protocols of the law. He lacks the personal stability that would enable him to function as a normal law-enforcing agent. He is a loner and a stranger to his colleagues, a narcissistic personality. His personal need for revenge is not recognized by the law that he serves. The law draws upon his strength to implement its will but refuses to loan him any part of its strength so that he may extract his revenge. This figure exists in a space between the law and illegality, a figure whose ability to fulfil his role as a citizen is obstructed by the pathological history of the subject, which demands a cure that is extra-legal by definition. It represents the unfinished character of the bourgeois revolution, the failed reconstruction of the social in accordance with a new philosophy.

At the same time, the figure of the inspector with an unreconciled history stands for the existence, within the field of the law, of a fund of transformative will. It heralds the possibility of a reform of law to make it serve the needs of the dispossessed and the marginalized. The law displays its humanity by revealing its pathological side: it too is haunted by unfinished projects of retribution and redistribution. Through the in-between figure, the law maintains its position of impersonal power, while allowing a part of itself to respond to the demands of those who are its victims.

2) *The mobilization of the dispossessed:* Whether it is a question of the suspension of the law for the duration of a retributional narrative or the re-awakening of the law to its unfinished historical project, the solution has to be backed by the will of the people. In *Zanjeer* the hero's mission is aided by a series of 'donors' (to use V.I. Propp's term somewhat loosely), who stand for different segments of the dispossessed. There is first of all the female knife-sharpener,

who represents women on the margins of respectable society, abandoned by the patriarchal network to fend for themselves. Second, there is Sher Khan, who represents a criminalized but essentially honest Muslim proletariat. And third, the Christian old man, drinking to forget his son's death at the hands of the criminals, who comes to Vijay's aid with information about smuggling operations. These poor/gendered victims of society and marginalized minorities gift their combined strength to Vijay, giving his mission a significance beyond his need for personal revenge. It is through their active involvement in the mission that Vijay comes to be identified as a hero of the masses. He acts with their support but also on their behalf, as their voluntarily chosen representative. Their support endows his personal mission of revenge with a social purpose.

The Amitabh persona is a 'proletarian hero' who is at the same time a representative of the state. It is the act of switching sides, positioning himself on the side of the 'illegal' (but morally upright) margin, that gives the figure its power.

Deewar (Yash Chopra, 1974)

In *Deewar*, however, this double identity of the hero is split into two separate figures, resulting in a powerful drama of epic conflict,

Vijay (Amitabh Bachchan) listens to a Muslim co-worker explaining the significance of the number on his badge in *Deewar* (Yash Chopra 1974). Courtesy National Film Archive of India, Pune.

a civil war between state and community. The film begins with a traumatic childhood event, the humiliation of the father and his disappearance, and the flight of the mother with two children to the city to escape the community's insults. The father (Satyendra Kappu) is an upright trade union leader who is forced to sign an agreement detrimental to the workers' interests when the mine-owners threaten to destroy his family. Unable to bear the opprobrium, he disappears. The mother and two children go to Bombay and become part of the unorganized working class, living on the streets. As the children grow up, a field of conflict is established in which the state/citizen confronts the community/subject. Inspector Vijay of *Zanjeer*, who embodied the combination of citizen and pathological subject, is split into two separate figures in *Deewar*: Inspector Ravi (Shashi Kapoor) and criminal Vijay (Amitabh Bachchan). Educated with the earnings of both his mother, who works at a construction site, and his elder brother, who works as a shoeshine, Ravi grows up to be an exemplary citizen, passing all his exams with high marks and after a futile search for employment, trains as a police officer. Meanwhile, Vijay grows up to be a dock worker and defends his fellow workers against gangsters who take away a part of the workers' weekly earnings. Picked up by a gang leader (whose rivals run the extortion racket at the dock), Vijay soon becomes the second in command. The gang leader Davar (Iftikhar) becomes Vijay's surrogate father. Meanwhile, Ravi completes his training and is posted in Bombay, to tackle the smuggling menace. When he realizes what his brother does for a living, Ravi tries to back out of the case but, inspired by a visit to the house of a poor schoolmaster, he resolves to put aside all personal considerations in the fight against injustice. The mother Sumitra Devi (Nirupa Roy) who loves Vijay more than Ravi, nevertheless opposes Vijay's criminal activities and goes to live with Ravi. Vijay, for whom his mother's love was the sole justification for living, despairs. Meeting Ravi near a bridge where they had spent their childhood, Vijay reminds his brother of bygone days and tries to persuade him to take a transfer out of Bombay. Ravi refuses and steps up the anti-smuggling operations. Vijay is pursued on the other side by the rival gang. Resolving to marry his girlfriend Anita (Parveen Babi), a call-girl, and then give himself up, Vijay sends word to his mother to meet him at the temple. Meanwhile, Samant (Madan Puri), boss of the rival gang, returns to take his revenge. He kills Anita as she is getting dressed for the wedding. Giving up all hopes of a return to normal life, Vijay kills Samant and

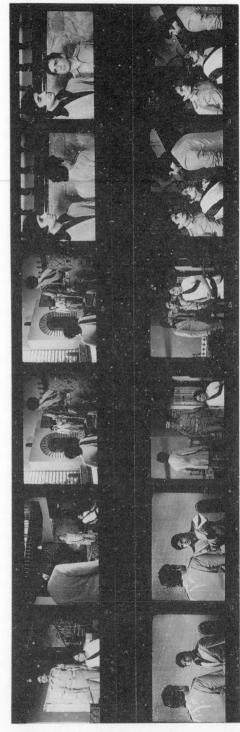

The sequence shows Vijay's exclusion from the Oedipal enclosure, as brother Ravi (Shashi Kapoor) occupies the place of the father, beside the mother (Nirupa Roy). The mother goes

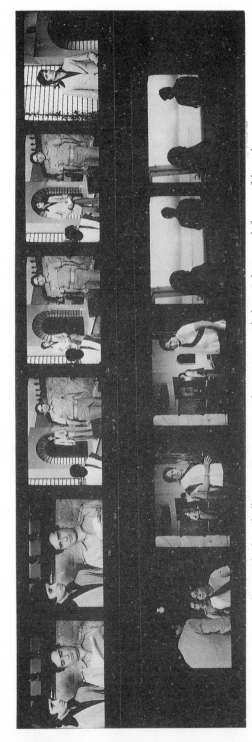

alongwith the phallic imperative, punishing Vijay with her righteous defence of law, but when alone with Vijay, she is racked by guilt. Courtesy National Film Archive of India, Pune.

his gang members. Ravi, informed about Vijay's killing spree, sets out to catch him. His mother hands Ravi his gun and wishes him success in his mission. She then proceeds to the temple to await the arrival of Vijay. Fatally wounded by Ravi and pursued, Vijay arrives at the temple and dies in his mother's arms.

The narrative is framed by an awards ceremony at which Ravi is receiving a medal for bravery. In his speech Ravi invokes those who stand behind the nation's heroes but are never acknowledged in the official record. He asks his mother to receive the medal on his behalf. The mother, escorted to the dais, receives the medal but is distracted by a memory. Her gaze, directed at a point outside the frame, prompts the 'flashback' which tells the entire story. Thus the story of Vijay is presented as doubly erased, confined to the depths of a mother's memory, remaining her secret, not to be recounted in the public space of the awards ceremony. The flashback structure codes the narrative as a mother's memory hidden from public view, evoking a powerful sense that the film will tell an 'unofficial' history, one which the audience can share in, although no official record will include it. It evokes the community of the 'pre-historic', the solidarity of the mother's world against the world of the father, the Law. It imbues the tragedy of Vijay with a secrecy, a subterranean quality. The 'flashback' concludes with Vijay's death and we return to the official assembly where the mother is still standing on the dais and the hall resounds with applause. The applause, officially intended for the brave police officer, has now been partially re-allocated to the rebellious son. The enactment of masochistic fantasy takes place in the shadow of the triumphal march of the patriarchal order.

Thus the text stages an imaginary and unofficial elevation of the resistant subject to a place of honour in the community's informal memory. Sumitra Devi serves as the link between the world of the citizen, of law and the rule of merit, and that of the poor, the victimized and the unreconciled. As a 'woman', she is firm in her submission to the law, she takes Ravi's side and leaves Vijay when his smuggling activities are disclosed. As a 'mother', she is equally firm in her love for Vijay, the elder son, the one who has borne the permanent mark of his father's dishonour. By thus splitting the woman into two functions, the film offers the spectator the pleasure of a secret liaison with the mother as a surrender to the political power of matriarchy. The martyred rebel has achieved a reunion with the mother's body suggested not only by the concealment of Vijay's story in the mother's memory but also by the image of Vijay resting his head in her lap at the end and asking her to put him to sleep. Vijay's tragic destiny is ensured by his attempt to place his mother in the position of the Father, as the authority whose desires he seeks to fulfil. After joining the gang, Vijay buys a skyscraper as a gift for his mother, who had worked as a coolie when it was being constructed. This phallic offering, an invitation to occupy the position of dominance, is rejected by the mother.[5] Instead she punishes him by serving as the vehicle of the Father's law. Before the final confrontation, handing Ravi his gun, she gives him her blessing: 'May your hand not tremble when you shoot.' After his departure, she declares, 'The woman has done her duty, now the mother will go and await her son.'

Deewar dramatizes the relations between the contractual, law-abiding society and its subterranean, criminal obverse, through a masochistic scenario in which the hero's movement towards death becomes a fantasy resolution of the impossible desire for reunion with the mother's body. This dramatization points to the political uses of masochistic fantasy as an ideological disavowal (which amounts to an acceptance) of the legal order. *Deewar* can be usefully read as an example of cinema as masochistic fantasy as defined, for instance, by Gaylyn Studlar, following Gilles Deleuze. 'The masochistic fantasy may be viewed as a situation in which the subject (male or female) assumes the position of the child who desires to be controlled *within* the dynamics of the fantasy' (Studlar 1992: 778). According to Deleuze, masochism is an enactment, 'above all formal and dramatic', determined by 'a specific story' (cited in Studlar 1992: 774). It is the enactment of mythical reunion with the oral mother. The subject desires such a reunion, a return to the state of infancy, but '[t]he promise of blissful reincorporation into the mother's body and re-fusion of the child's narcissistic ego with the mother as ideal ego is also a threat. Only death can hold the final mystical solution to the expiation of the father and symbiotic reunion with the idealized maternal rule. The masochist imagines the final triumph of a parthenogenetic rebirth from the mother' (ibid: 780).

This theory locates the origins of masochistic fantasy in the experience of the child and by extension, defines the cinematic experience itself as being continuous with that experience. However,

---

[5]By contrast, the mother in the British gangster film *The Krays* submits entirely to the criminal splendour of her sons' world. In return she is worshipped by one of them and elevated to a position of familial power.

Deewar is more accurately described as an allegorization of the history of the nation-state itself through the masochistic fantasy. The film text deploys the fantasy politically, as a mechanism of provisional counter-identification. In doing so it draws from the power of masochism to produce a resolution of the internal conflicts of the nation-state which is pleasurable and acceptable to the dominated. In *Deewar* the masochistic subject elevates the mother to the position of the all-powerful ruler and enacts death as the means of mystical reunion. In the context of a patriarchal order, whose triumph cannot be disavowed and to which all must submit, the fantasy serves as a pleasurable staging of surrender coded as masked victory. The masochistic fantasy enacted in *Deewar* is subterranean by definition in that it must be staged in the shadow of the patriarchal order's triumph. In its political dimension, the fantasy becomes possible only in a relation of subordination to the dominant patriarchal order. The masochistic fantasy in *Deewar* is fully determined by the dominatedness of its scenario, by the fact that the fantasy cannot be represented in the public domain except in the shadow of the dominant, although it offers itself as a subversive alternative to the dominant.

The conferral of power on the female serves to allegorize the problem of the internal schism of the modern state, the co-existence of the law and the community as conflicting *terrains*. The 'ideal' configuration would have the law fully enveloping the community, of reconstructing the individual as citizen-subject. But the crisis of the state derives from the fact that the law, in its drive to desacralize and colonize the space of the community,[6] faces a number of hurdles and rival political formations. The mother-figure serves as a narrative surrogate for all such rival formations: the traditional family, the criminal underworld, the community of the devout. She represents the border between the law and these rival formations. But she is not the 'prize' for which the two realms are fighting, because only one of them has the discursive ability to reduce the mother to the status of a possession. She is thus a liminal figure who represents the resistance of the community to a reorganization of social space according to the laws of private property. (This does not mean that the resistance represents a collective consciousness. In its resistance to reorganization along individualistic lines, the past comes to be

[6]See Jameson's (1988) essay 'Cognitive Mapping' for a discussion of the capitalist reorganization of space.

embodied as 'community'.) One of the turning points in the film is the scene of the meeting at the bridge where Vijay tries to persuade Ravi to take a transfer to another police station. The entire scene is constructed to highlight the difference between Ravi, whose memory has been erased by his emancipation to the position of a representative of the law, and Vijay who remains a victim of his past. The scene opens with Ravi waiting at the bridge. On the soundtrack the patriotic song *'Sare jahan se achcha'* is playing, reminding us (but not Ravi) of an event from the past: One morning, finding Ravi missing, Vijay and his mother go in search of him. They find him standing at the gates of a school, listening to the uniformed children singing the song. Up to that point, the mother's earnings had been too meagre to send either boy to school. On that day, Vijay decides to take up a job himself so that with the additional income Ravi could be sent to school. The spectator recalls this earlier scene, but Ravi has no memories of the bridge under which he had slept as a child. For Vijay this bridge of memory is the only remaining link between him and Ravi, and he wants to reactivate it. Ravi does not yield to the unifying power of memory. Frustrated, Vijay boasts of his achievements, his worldly possessions, beside which Ravi's sub-inspector's salary is a pittance. 'I have all this, but what do you have?' he asks, to which Ravi replies, 'I have mother.' This scene prefigures Vijay's tragic destiny. It is here that we learn the difference between the new figure, that is representative of the law, and the old one. One is possessed by the past and seeks to be possessed and dominated by the mother, who is a figure from that past. The other, emancipated from the past, is able to 'have the mother', to possess her as a part of his familial affective realm.

Through the metonymic link to the world provided by the narcissistic son, the mother also comes to stand for the marginalized, the working classes, as well as the minorities. Vijay's rebellious spirit is aroused when a fellow dockworker gets killed after refusing to pay the extortionists who run the protection racket. The next week he too refuses to pay and takes on the whole gang single-handedly. His victory makes him the workers' hero. An old dockworker, Rahim Chacha, advises him to hold on to his badge because it bears the number 786, which is sacred to Muslims. Like Sher Khan in *Zanjeer*, Rahim Chacha functions as a donor, bestowing on the hero the beneficent powers of his religion and at the same time nominating him as a representative of the minorities and the marginalized. This is another instance of the scenes of election and nomination that we have already noted in *Zanjeer* in which the Muslim minority symbolically adopts the hero as its own leader. The badge saves his life twice. The third time, pursued by Ravi, Vijay drops the badge and cannot retrieve it, ending his good luck.

Deewar is one of the few film epics produced by the Bombay industry. It is the most powerful of all Salim-Javed screenplays, combining tried narrative devices, a new mode of address, and new iconic material in a displaced enactment of the hopes and disaffections of modern India. Two films from the past provided the primary narrative material. *Mother India* (Mehboob 1957) was the source for the thematics of the mother-son relationship. There the mother herself killed the rebellious son, who had turned into a bandit, and was rewarded with a symbolic role at the opening of a dam. Her sacrifice thus made her a contributor to the progress of modern India. From Dilip Kumar's *Gunga Jumna* (Nitin Bose 1961) Salim-Javed took the theme of confrontation between two brothers, one representing the law and the other an honest and hard-working farmer forced into a life of crime by feudal exploiters. Combining the two, Salim-Javed added to an already powerful mix, a third element, the spectacle of nomination whereby the hero becomes a point of counter-identification for the spectator, assuring a pleasurable 'subversion' without undermining the supremacy of the law. Amitabh is at once Birju, the rebellious son of 'Mother India', whom the mother must sacrifice in order to establish the rule of law, and Gunga, the honest man forced into crime by a feudal system which the law is unable to smash. Gunga also represents the consequences of the failure of the legal system of the modern state. Where the law does not fulfil its role as destroyer of feudal oppression, an alternative system of justice arises. At the same time both *Gunga Jumna* and *Deewar* emphasize the element of primitive accumulation through which the modern state itself is established. Both Gunga and Vijay work to send their brothers to school, their sweat has gone into the making of the exemplary citizens, Jumna and Ravi. Thus, the law is presented as a product of the labour of the poor which turns against the poor, the dead labour of the proletariat, alienated from it and turned hostile.

Gunga Jumna and *Mother India* portrayed the rebels as dacoits, rural bandits who belonged to the world of popular criminality celebrated in folklore. Their criminality was a direct result of feudal oppression and had the additional dimension of Robin Hood style altruism. In *Deewar*, however, the hero does not start an enterprise of popular criminality. He joins an existing smuggling ring and rises to the top. The initial elaboration of the confrontation between exploiters and exploited is displaced onto a more traditional plot-line of police versus criminals. Within the world of crime, Vijay's gang is depicted as being more ethical in its criminality than the others and the audience is invited to applaud Vijay as he tricks the rival gang. Haji Mastan, the real life smuggler and slumlord of Bombay, is reputed to have been the model for Vijay's role. (Mastan and other smugglers were arrested after the film was made, under the new laws of Indira Gandhi government.) Although Mastan, like other urban gangsters, enjoyed popularity in the slums where he ruled and dispensed charity, as a point of counter-identification the smuggler did not have the same power that the rural dacoit had. This is why Davar's gang had to be endowed with a vague ethical status and Vijay himself to be isolated from the gang into a figure of brooding inwardness. It is through this isolation that it becomes possible to return the spectator to the 'psychic' pleasures of a masochistic fantasy.

Sholay (Ramesh Sippy, 1975)

Sholay was the third high point in the formative phase of the aesthetic of mobilization. Here again Amitabh Bachchan's star-image was combined with Salim-Javed's narrative of the epic confrontation between the state and an internal rival political power. The setting is a village where a ruthless dacoit, Gabbar Singh (Amjad Khan), is terrorizing the villagers and extorting payments in the form of seasonal gifts of farm produce. The biggest landlord in the village, Thakur (Sanjeev Kumar), is also a police officer who captures Gabbar Singh and has him sent to jail. Swearing revenge, Gabbar escapes from prison and kills everyone in the Thakur's family, except his daughter-in-law who was not at home. The Thakur goes to Gabbar's camp and is captured. Gabbar cuts off both his arms and sends him back to the village. During his tenure as police officer, the Thakur had had occasion to observe the valour of two petty criminals, Jai (Amitabh Bachchan) and Veeru (Dharmendra), who helped him when the train they were travelling in, was ambushed by dacoits. The Thakur tracks them down and offers them money to help him capture Gabbar alive. They arrive in the village and decide to run away after raiding the Thakur's safe. The Thakur's widowed daughter-in-law (Jaya Bhaduri) arrives as they are trying to break open the safe and offers them the keys. Shamed, they give up the plan and decide to stay. The first opportunity for a confrontation arises when three of Gabbar's men arrive to collect grain from the villagers. The Thakur intervenes, and with Jai and Veeru demonstrating their bravery, the three dacoits have to return to camp empty-handed. All three are killed by Gabbar. On the day of Holi (a spring festival of colours), Gabbar leads his men in an attack on the village. Jai and Veeru are disarmed but manage to trick Gabbar, leading to a fight in which Gabbar's men are defeated. Jai and Veeru make another attempt to capture Gabbar as he meets with an arms dealer, but fail. Meanwhile Veeru falls in love with Basanti (Hema Malini), who drives a tonga and Jai is attracted to the mysterious widowed daughter-in-law of the Thakur.

Ahmed (Sachin), son of the blind Imam (A.K. Hangal), who has secured employment in the city, is on his way to the railway station when he is captured by Gabbar's men. Gabbar kills Ahmed and sends the body back to the village. The villagers turn against Jai and Veeru for inviting Gabbar's wrath upon the village but the Imam stands by them, declaring that he would sacrifice more sons for the honour of the village. Jai and Veeru kill a few of Gabbar's men in retaliation. The Thakur persuades the widow's father to agree to her marriage to Jai. The final movement begins when some dacoits come upon Basanti waiting for Veeru near a pond. After a long chase, she is caught and so is Veeru who went in search of her. Gabbar makes her dance on broken glass to save Veeru's life. Jai arrives and frees Veeru and Basanti and the three make their way back to the village. When they lose a horse, Jai stays back and sends the other two away to fetch help. He blows up the bridge but is fatally wounded. Veeru, returning with the villagers, vows revenge, rides into Gabbar's camp, and captures Gabbar. The Thakur arrives and asks Veeru to keep his promise and hand over Gabbar to him. He then proceeds to take his revenge but the police arrive just in time to prevent him from murdering Gabbar. Veeru, mission accomplished but minus his friend, boards the train out and finds Basanti waiting for him.

Like most of Salim-Javed's other films, *Sholay* is also a reworking of elements borrowed from various sources. However, unlike *Zanjeer* and *Deewar*, *Sholay* transformed the epic formula and its borrowed ingredients into an explicit narrative affirmation of the feudal order and the subordination of the counter-identified spectator's pleasure to the restoration of that order. The central narrative device in this project is the figure of the Thakur, who embodies the unity of the interests of the state and the feudal order. The Thakur is a landlord who became a police officer, as he puts it, for the sake of the thrills the job promised. His role as representative of the law is thus coded as disinterested but at the same time, tied up with the drama of rural conflict. The Thakur's dismemberment has two conflicting but equally significant meanings: On the one hand, it represents the disabling of the apparatus of law and order, its debilitation in the confrontation with criminality. On the other hand, it also signifies a temporary breach of the coalition between the rural rich and the state: the Thakur remains but loses his hands, which he had himself described as 'the hangman's noose', i.e. the law. Both of these scenarios make possible and necessary the infusion of new energy from a source outside the coalition. The petty criminals, who provide this supplement of energy and serve as replacements for the lost limbs of the Thakur, are the infra-legal, but not irredeemably criminal, figures with whom the new proletarian and ,other disaffected audiences could identify. One of the truly astonishing features of the developing cinema culture of this period is the success with which criminality could be deployed as a metaphor for all forms of rebellion and disidentification.

The liminal figure in this narrative, the one that straddles the border between two realms is itself doubled. The petty criminals, already doubled, provide the link across one border, between legality and criminality. They are criminals who function on the side of the law. But there is another border, which previously coincided with the first one, but now stands separate: this is the border between the state and one of its former representatives, undertaking an infra-legal mission of vengeance. Here the border figure is the Thakur himself, who temporarily sets aside the legal protocols in order to effect a justice which the law cannot bring about. The Thakur initiates the suspension of legality, thereby breaching the border, but his plan has to be implemented by the production of another border internal to the criminal order. This doubling is implicit in both *Zanjeer* and *Deewar*: in *Zanjeer*, Sher Khan is the figure of the second border, the good criminal, and in *Deewar*, the mother's role as the figure in-between the law and the community is doubled by Vijay himself when he allies with the 'good criminal' Davar against the bad Samant. But in *Sholay*, the doubling takes on an added significance for two reasons: one, the figure who demands our sympathy at the first border is a landlord; by sharing in his desire for vengeance, we are also seduced into participating in a reaffirmation of the feudal order. Secondly, the political address to the audience through which Vijay (of *Zanjeer* and *Deewar*) wins a constituency in the cinema hall as well as among the diegetic co-workers, is eliminated in *Sholay* by the fact that the two men are hired as mercenaries. The film begins with the Thakur's attempt to track down the two men with the help of a jailor, as part of his plan for revenge. Of course, there is an attempt to provide a certain amount of political support through the mobilization of the village. But the villagers appear as the prize for which the Thakur is fighting the dacoits. It is a rivalry for the rights to political power over the villagers. The protection of the villagers is only a subsidiary effect of the primary plot to defeat Gabbar and restore the Thakur's honour. This is why, although they are hired to go out and capture Gabbar, Jai and Veeru function more as hired protectors of the village. Protecting the village is the form taken by the action initiated to restore the Thakur's honour.

The spaghetti westerns were the principal source of narrative material for *Sholay*. In this period the Terence Hill/ Bud Spencer adventures and Sergio Leone's films starring Clint Eastwood, *The Good, the Bad and the Ugly, For a Few Dollars More*, etc. were extremely popular in India. Indio, the mad laughing villain of *For a Few Dollars More* was the model for Gabbar Singh, India's most popular screen villain. Throughout the seventies, indigenous filmmakers cashed in on the popularity of this genre by making 'westerns' in local settings, with local themes. The most significant phenomenon arising from this transfer of cowboy iconography and revenge themes was the Tamil/Telugu 'western' (the English press referred to it as the 'idli western'). A series of cheaply made films were released in the seventies in which male stars like Krishna and two 'cabaret dancers' Jyothilakshmi and Vijayalalitha, starred in avenger roles. It was a sub-cultural phenomenon which re-duplicated the cultural status of the spaghetti western (and the indigenous stunt films of an earlier era) not only in its choice of themes of revenge but also in the construction of an alternative star system which survived in the interstices of mainstream culture on the enthusiasm of proletarian audiences.

In Hindi, a similar tendency was manifesting itself just before *Sholay* arrived on the scene. An emblematic film of this sub-genre is *Khotey Sikkay*, released in 1974. The main character in this film was played by Feroze Khan, who until then had been a star in another long-standing sub-culture supported by a predominantly Muslim lower-class audience. (Sheikh Mukhtar, Dara Singh, Ansari were some of the other stars in this subterranean constellation. Others like

Mumtaz began their careers there and moved up into the mainstream.)
Feroze Khan's role in *Khotey Sikkay* was a blend of elements from
Clint Eastwood, Zorro, and perhaps also the Lone Ranger comics.
He was a man in search of a dacoit who had killed his parents. He
roams the countryside, protects the weak and punishes the wicked
in the course of his search for his parents' killer. Meanwhile, the son
of a farmer who was killed by the dacoit's men brings a gang of five
people (echoes of *The Five-Man Army*, a popular foreign film of the
period) from the town to help him protect the village. Helping each
other but acting separately, the gang of six and the Zorro character
together enact a narrative similar to that of *Sholay*, at the end of
which the dacoit is vanquished and order restored to the rural
landscape. The title, which literally means 'counterfeit coins' is a
metaphor for the gang of five: they are urban petty criminals who
are persuaded to give up their disorderly life in order to help a
village. They give up their counterfeit lives for the authenticity of
village life.

In *Sholay*, the same term is employed to describe Jai and Veeru.
When the Thakur tells the jailor to find the two men, he explains
that although they were criminals, they had a good side. The jailor
responds by saying that a counterfeit coin is bad on both sides. The
Thakur, however, asserts that there is a difference between coins
and human beings. *Khotey Sikkay* was released the year before *Sholay*
and it is difficult to say whether Salim-Javed had made use of its
narrative material. However, the westerns in circulation at the time
(in particular Sergio Leone's *For a Few Dollars More*) provided most
of the material that these two films shared. Like the southern
'westerns', *Khotey Sikkay* was a sub-cultural text in which marginal
figures and 'villains' like Narendranath, Ranjit and Danny became
heroes.

Sholay, on the other hand, is one of the most expensive Indian
films ever made, with a long list of top stars, spectacular fight scenes
and other potlatch features. It was a successful appropriation of a
sub-cultural form for mainstream exploitation. Like *Sangam*, which
a decade earlier had annexed the fledgling genre of women's
melodrama to the 'national' textual form (see Chapter 3), *Sholay*
annexed a marginal B-film genre to a mainstream big-budget
extravaganza. It supplemented the structure of the revenge film with
a frame that incorporated other interests into the motivations for the
narrative.

Sholay adopts a mode of othering that follows the urban/rural divide. In films like *Gunga Jumna, Jis Desh mein Ganga Behti Hai and Kachche Dhage* the dacoit is portrayed as a rational subject, i.e. one whose criminality has a social motivation. In *Sholay* the dacoit figure is evacuated of all social content, has no personal history. Pitted against the legitimate rule of the landlord, his political ambitions are not supported by any manifesto, whether personal or social. The film stages the triumph of the Law over the intransigent political order of the countryside which threatens the dominant coalition's rural partner, the landed bourgeoisie.

As we have seen, the narratives of these three films were drawn from other sources. The originality of the textual form derives primarily from the mobilization effect which accompanies the narration. The scenes of nomination, in which the hero is elected to lead workers and minorities, function to extend the relationship of leader and led to the audience as well. The figure who commands the audience in this way is the star. The star's function is mobilization, the rallying of forces behind a narrative exposition. This elevation compensates for the loss of the hero's traditional authority, and enacts a transition from feudal to populist power. Through the production of a supplemental charisma, the industry overcomes the problems posed by a shift of narrative focus to the realm of the ordinary. The star-image restores the heteronomy of the text.

Although unprecedented in the history of the Hindi cinema, the extra-cinematic authority of the star as mobilizer was already a feature of Tamil cinema, in the star-image of MGR. Amitabh Bachchan did not enter politics until much later in his career but even in the formative stage his star-image had a political dimension that paralleled MGR's. A populist political culture, elaborated through the cinema, developed very early in Tamil Nadu as a supplement to the Dravidian movement.[7] The spread of populism led to similar developments in the neighbouring states of Karnataka and Andhra Pradesh, where Rajkumar and N.T. Rama Rao, respectively, became the focal points of a political-cultural formation. The Amitabh Bachchan phenomenon can be said to represent the arrival of populism on the national arena. Populism, employing the supplement of charisma produced in the scenes of election and nomination, enables the control of the text's meaning-production from a point outside it. Through this

[7]M.S.S. Pandian's *The Image Trap* is the best available study of the politics of Tamil cinema and the persona of MGR (M.G. Ramachandran). See also S.T. Baskaran's *The Message Bearers* for a history of Tamil cinema's role in the national movement.

supplement the heteronomous condition of the text as a *darsanic occasion* is maintained. The industry favours a situation in which its profits depend on the rent-earning star body, rather than one in which the ability of a narrative to interest audiences is the decisive factor in making or marring a production. In response to the pressures for a transformation of the textual form, the industry thus managed to produce a populist aesthetic of mobilization designed to contain the centrifugal tendencies to segmentation.

7

Middle-Class Cinema

The FFC project was defined by a commitment to realism, but this was by no means the first attempt in that direction. There already existed a progressive realist tendency of which K.A. Abbas's *Dharti Ke Lal* (1946) and Bimal Roy's *Do Bigha Zameen* (1953) are the best known examples. Italian neo-realist cinema, seen in India for the first time in 1952, is said to have inspired some realist ventures, including *Do Bigha Zameen*, the story of a small peasant family driven to the city in an unsuccessful effort to save their little piece of land from the landlord's greed. While *Dharti Ke Lal*, made under the left-wing Indian People's Theatre Association (IPTA) banner, ended with the vision of a brighter future modelled on Soviet collective farming, *Do Bigha Zameen* ends without the slightest hint of hope for the peasant. Realism here signified a thematic shift, focusing attention on the poor and the exploited but continued to feature a melodramatic narrative.

Satyajit Ray's work represented the other great strand of realism. In an influential essay, Satish Bahadur hailed *Pather Panchali* as 'a film which reflected the Indian reality as no other film had done before' (Bahadur 1982: 13). Ray was the exemplar of realism as an artistic form which Bahadur in another essay defined as:

> an organic form in which all elements are in a state of interdependence; it has no extraneous elements in its structure. The technique of composition used in creating the form derives its logic from the themes which the work expresses; in other words, what is being said is achieved through the way it is said . . . . (Bahadur 1985: 71).

While progressive realism was political in its choice of themes, the aesthetic project associated with Ray was political in the sense that it was related to the project of nation-building. The Nehruvian theme of the 'discovery of India' was seen to have found its cultural expression in a realist portrayal of the nation in cinema (ibid: 70).

The FFC project drew from both these strands in defining its realist programme. However, in 1969 the possibilities for a realist aesthetic were determined not only by the available models but also by the political imperatives of the moment. In the event two broad tendencies began to emerge within the single programme of realist cinema. The beginning of the shift is usually identified with two films, *Bhuvan Shome* and *Sara Akash*. In a comment on the latter, we find this version of a frequently encountered statement: 'A simple story, told with touching realism, *Sara Akash* was made the same year that Mrinal Sen's *Bhuvan Shome* ushered in the "new Indian cinema".' Part of the same genre, both films have realistic locales, new faces, and an unglamorous setting' (Banerjee and Srivastava 1988: 162).[1] Five years later, a new round of national enthusiasm was focused on two privately-financed films, *Ankur* and *Rajnigandha*. The first named in the two sets (*Bhuvan Shome* and *Ankur*) represent a continuation of the political realist tendency while *Sara Akash* and *Rajnigandha* belong to the genre of the middle-class cinema. The movement from Sen's film to Benegal's is paralleled by the movement from Basu Chatterji's first film to his first major commercial success. These continuities are reinforced by another feature: while Sen and Benegal set their narratives in rural India, Chatterji's films were about the urban middle class. One invoked the image of the nation, while the other addressed itself to a class. One invited the urban spectator to witness a world other than its own but falling within the same political unit, while the other promised to create a world which the spectator could recognize as his/her own.

While these two tendencies within the realist programme thus seemed to diverge in their thematic concerns and seemed to posit two different spectator positions, they were addressed to the same audience. The audience is an empirical category, referring to the actual individuals who frequent the cinema whereas the spectator is

[1]It is also characteristic of the standard critical explanation that *Sara Akash* and the middle-class cinema that it prefigured should be defined in relation to the other realist enterprise. In the comment cited, the authors place *Sara Akash* in the exalted neighbourhood of *Bhuvan Shome*. The latter is said to have 'ushered in' the new cinema, thus suggesting that it was the more important historical landmark. The very next sentence refers to both as belonging to 'the same genre'. This ambiguity is symptomatic of the fact that middle-class realism had a subordinate position in the project as a whole. The same authors, in their comment on *Bhuvan Shome* make no attempt to highlight its kinship with *Sara Akash*.

a theoretical concept that stands for the viewing position arising from the text's strategies of representation.[2] As spectators the audience of citizen-subjects were called upon to occupy two different positions. One corresponded to the citizen side of the entity and involved a frame of reading that included the perspective of the nation-state while the other was addressed to the subject, the individual in society, faced with the struggle for existence, the locus of desires, fears and hopes. This chapter deals with the realist cinema of the subject, or what is commonly known as the middle-class cinema.

In *Sara Akash* ('The Whole Sky', 1969) the urban middle-class world is treated with a solicitous detachment that was to disappear with the further development of the middle-class cinema. This mild trace of ethnographic objectification is a sign that Chatterji had not as yet recognized the possibilities of a cinema of identification based on realist principles. The interventionist agenda of the FFC project and the freedom from considerations of marketability no doubt contributed to this. The objectification effect in *Sara Akash* is achieved through an emphasis on the characters' immersion in a feudal culture, although the joint family home in which the story unfolds is located in an urban milieu. The potential for a cinema of identification was still concealed by the burden of ethnographic distancing which the FFC's realist programme placed on the film-maker. As in Avtar Kaul's *27 Down*, the story deals with the problem of modern individuals still caught up in a network of feudal customs and mental habits. A university student marries an educated woman but both are in the grip of family traditions which determine their lives. The marriage is arranged by the family. Unhappy with a relationship brought about in this manner, the hero rejects the woman, while his family burdens her with all the housework. When she goes away to her parental home, the hero finds himself missing her company. A reconciliation is brought about when, after her return the wife becomes more assertive and rejects him.

While employing the imagery of feudalism to effect an ethnographic distancing, the film does not undertake a critique of feudalism. Instead, it attributes the failure of the couple's union to their shyness and immaturity. The film tries to produce a nuclear couple within the confines of an extended family. Since both members are educated, there is a possibility of their overcoming the initial extraneous compulsion that brought them together and of

---

[2]See Kuhn (1987) for a discussion of the significance of this distinction.

establishing intimacy. In their ability to do so lies the value of the aesthetic: to wrest from the feudal space a couple who can be relocated in the space of modernity. In this task it is equally necessary to distance the feudal structure of the extended family as well as foreground the couple as the object of our sympathy. A visit to the cinema is an important moment in the film: the scene where the couple walk to the theatre, with the wife walking several steps behind the husband, heightens the pleasures of realism. On the one hand, the ethnographic interest is aroused by the recognition of the image: who has not seen such a phenomenon? (The answer of course is: those who walk like that, in single file; but the pleasure of recognition that realism offers us is not diluted by such reminders of realism's institutional/class determination.) On the other hand, the narrative proceeds to 'demonstrate' that the possibility of closing the gap between husband and wife depends on a process of psychic, rather than social, reform.

The middle-class cinema is predominantly characterized by an emphasis on the extended familial network as the proper site of production of nuclear couples. Even when, as in *Rajnigandha*, no such common ground of kinship is suggested, the idea of *endogamy* is strongly inscribed in the narrative delineation of the class. This is because middle-class narratives are confined to the world of the upper castes. These castes find themselves dispersed in an urban world, and define themselves as the middle class in the language of the modern state, while maintaining their endogamous identities. In deference to the semiotic prohibition which inaugurates the modern state, the caste identity of this urban society is generally concealed behind the term 'middle class'. It is thus that the paradoxical thematics of 'class endogamy' emerge as a narrative element in films like *Guddi* and *Rajnigandha*.

The middle class, however, also carries the burden of national identity on its shoulders. While one sector of the middle-class cinema represents a community hemmed in by the larger society and devoted to its own reproduction, there is another that presents the class's national profile, its reformist role in the drama of class and religious conflicts within the nation-state. Here the realist aesthetic draws upon the tradition of Gandhian melodrama, including Bimal Roy's *Sujata* and *Bandini,* and the films of his pupil Hrishikesh Mukherjee from before the FFC era, such as *Ashirwad* and *Satyakam.*

Thus, there are two broad sectors of the middle-class cinema, of which one is oriented towards asserting the national role of the class while the other is committed to the construction of an exclusive space of class identity. While the first sector enjoyed a strong pre-FFC history, in the post-FFC era it was redefined around the political pressures of the moment. Three significant films of this type are *Anand, Namak Haram* (both by Hrishikesh Mukherjee) and *Mere Apne* (Gulzar). All three take up the question of national and class reconciliation in a period of political crisis.

The second·sector, concerned with the consolidation of middle-class (upper caste) identity, can be further divided into three sub-types based on thematic differences. The first sub-type would include films like *Guddi* and *Rajnigandha*, both of which raise the question of the threat to class identity posed by the lures of the outside world, to which women in particular are susceptible. The second sub-type includes *Abhiman, Kora Kagaz* and *Aandhi* where the post-marital tensions of the middle-class family arise from the ambitions and individualistic tendencies of one or both the partners. Films of the first sub-type differ from the second mainly in that they resolve the conflicts prior to marital union. The third sub-type includes films which take up the question of the space for middle-class existence, the dependence of middle-class life on·the possibility of privacy. While *Piya ka Ghar* deals with the problem of private space in a humorous fashion, *Anubhav* and in particular *Dastak*, in a complex mode uncharacteristic of the middle-class cinema in general, employs the thematic of private space to explore questions related to the institution of cinema itself as well as the transition to class society. *Aandhi*, included in the second sub-type, can also be discussed in terms of the third sub-type.

The Dissemination of Bengal

The middle-class cinema is marked by an overwhelming dependence on Bengali culture for its narrative and iconographic material as well as film-making talent. This cinema was founded on the twin distinctions of primacy of narrative and the ordinariness and authenticity of the world represented. Bengali literature and cinema provided a ready source of such narrative material. Even a commercial film-maker like Shakti Samanta, after making films like *An Evening in Paris, Pagla Kahin ka*, and the deftly plagiarized *Aradhana*, turned, for *Amar Prem*, to a Bengali middle-class narrative set (without too much emphasis on realist detail) in the nineteenth or early twentieth-century Bengal.[3] It would be wrong to conclude, on this basis, that there was a demand for Bengali middle-class narratives. It would be more accurate to say that the industry found in those narratives a ready supply of 'difference' which could be re-presented. Examples of films directly based on and iconographically faithful to Bengali narratives were *Balika Badhu*, *Uphaar*, *Amar Prem*, *Chhoti Bahu* and *Swami*. Others like *Guddi*, *Anand* and *Kora Kagaz* derived part of their claim to difference from the fact that the characters had Bengali names and dressed like the Bengali middle class. In *Kora Kagaz*, the final scene at the railway station, like a similar one in *Swami*, has Bengali literary resonances. Yet others, like *Rajnigandha* (based on a Hindi story), *Abhiman* and *Aandhi* were less specific in their cultural allusions but reinforced the popular association of good middle-class culture with Bengal if only because they were either directed by Bengalis or had Bengali actors in principal roles. (It is difficult to think of *Aandhi* without being reminded of the historic 'return' of Suchitra Sen to the Hindi screen.) Of course, Bengali narratives had been used in the Hindi film industry before, but in the seventies they served as the resource for a major thrust towards product differentiation and market segmentation. The FFC-sponsored films of 1969 played no small part in provoking this change. Let us now turn to a discussion of the sub-types of the middle-class cinema.

Narratives of National Reconciliation

National reconciliation acquired urgency in the context of the disaggregation of the social already discussed. Martyrdom is the cleansing event which produces the possibilities of reconciliation in all the three films in this category. In *Mere Apne,* the martyr is an old peasant woman. In *Anand* and *Namak Haram*, he is a middle-class individual (played by Rajesh Khanna) who rises above the conflicts that surround him and reunites a divided world by dying.

In *Mere Apne* ('My Dear Ones', Gulzar, 1971), based on the Bengali film *Apanjan*) an old woman is brought to the city by her relative who needs household help, while he and his wife go out to work.

---

[3]Some of the narrative elements of *Amar Prem* can be recognized in the sociology of prostitution in nineteenth-century Calcutta. See, for instance, Sumanta Banerjee (1993).

The woman is thrown out when she questions the exploitative motive behind the altruistic gesture, and finds refuge in an old ruined building where two orphans live. A student gang leader, estranged from his family, also spends his nights there. In the midst of daily confrontations between two rival youth gangs, the woman's motherly affection and innocent and upright behaviour wins the hearts of the gang members. At election time the two gangs are hired by rival candidates. In the explosion of campaign violence, the woman is killed by a police bullet as she tries to stop the street fighting between the gangs.

During a conversation with the gang members, the old widow recounts an event from her past which identifies her as a patriotic woman along the lines of the heroines of *Bandini, Mother India* and the Tamil film *Anda Naal* (1954). Set in pre-independence India, the flashback recounts the events of a night when the woman and her husband hid a freedom fighter, who was being pursued by the police, in their bedroom. This scene serves as a reminder of the sacrifices made in the past to produce the community which is now breaking apart.

A conversation between some gang members at the beginning establishes the film's reading of the contemporary world. Socialism has become a mere collection of empty slogans which all parties, including communal ones, use indiscriminately. On the other hand, the blood ties which united people in the past have become an excuse for exploitation. The well-to-do extract free labour by using the rhetoric of kinship while the poor and the young find themselves helpless in a world in which parents and college principals do not understand their idealism or the frustrations of the unemployed. The woman functions as the agent of an infusion of binding affect into a world divided by class and generational conflict.

While the peasant woman is the textual agent of resolution, the affect deployed in the movement towards resolution is a complex one, combining values drawn from several sources. One such source is the village, which figures in the text as an 'elsewhere', untouched by the conflicts that are tearing the urban community apart. Another source is the past, the history of nationalist struggle, of which the woman serves as a reminder. Thirdly, there is the maternal element that the peasant woman brings to the urban scene. The hero's disaffection with the world is partly attributed to the fact that his mother died early. The only urban mother in the film is the wife of the peasant woman's relative. She is a working woman with a character that is completely negative. She colludes with the husband in exploiting relatives as unpaid servants and readily abandons her child to the servant's care in order to enjoy the pleasures of the city. Finally, part of the affect is also drawn from the star system. The legendary actress Meena Kumari is cast as the peasant woman while young trainees of the Film Institute play the roles of the gang members. The nostalgia evoked by the presence of Meena Kumari, combined with the emerging star identities of actors like Vinod Khanna and Shatrughna Sinha, enabled a textual compromise between old and new which reinforced the narrative drive towards a resolution of present conflicts through the restoration of links with the past and the far away.

In *Anand* and *Namak Haram,* the martyr figure is male and clearly identified as belonging to the urban middle class. Nevertheless, Anand, the eponymous hero of the first film, is closer to the woman in *Mere Apne* in being a figure of national reconciliation whereas *Namak Haram* directly takes up the question of class struggle. The story of *Anand* (Hrishikesh Mukherjee, 1970) is narrated by a doctor. The film opens in a literary gathering where Dr Banerji (Amitabh Bachchan), is being honoured for a novel based on his diary entries about a man who defied death by living life to the full and spreading happiness wherever he went. In his address to the assembly, the doctor recalls his own state of mind at the point of time when Anand (Rajesh Khanna) first came into his life. An idealist, Banerji had devoted himself to treating the poor who could not afford to pay for his treatment or buy the medicines they needed to recover from their illnesses. His helplessness against the social 'diseases' of poverty and unemployment had driven him to a state of utter despondency. At this point a fellow doctor and friend who runs a small hospital informs him of the imminent arrival from Delhi of a patient with a fatal illness. Anand arrives, a day early, and with his charming ways, endears himself to all. He becomes a living enigma for everyone around him. He knows that he does not have long to live but will not let that spoil his fun. Doctor Banerji feels angry with himself for being unable to cure him. Moving into Banerji's house, Anand hides his own private anguish and involves himself in good deeds. He reunites the doctor with his girlfriend (Sumita Sanyal), whom he had neglected in his idealist pursuits. He adopts doctor Prakash's wife as his sister, the matron in the hospital, Sister D'Souza (Lalita Pawar), as his mother, and a theatre owner, Isabhai (Johny Walker), as a friend. Hindu, Christian and Muslim pray to their respective gods for the health of Anand. On his death-bed Anand asks for a tape of Banerji's poetry reading to be played and he dies as the poem ends. When Banerji, who was away, returns with some medicine, Anand's and his laughter, taped inadvertently, bursts forth to break the spell of grief. The last words in the film, spoken by Banerji, are 'Anand is not dead, anand (joy) does not die'.

In *Anand* as in *Mere Apne*, the central character comes from elsewhere and brings purpose and meaning into the lives of those who were drifting apart and sinking into despondency. Anand functions as a focus for the scattered, free-floating affect of his acquaintances. Failing in their commitment to social causes, they take him up as a surrogate cause. He is an exemplary figure who teaches the despondent to value all that life offers. In contrast, Dr. Banerji's clear and unambiguous perception of the evils of society makes him despair. As a doctor he rejects the path taken by his friend Prakash (Ramesh Deo) who thrives on the anxieties of his rich patients. On the other hand, he perceives that society is plagued by evils that are for the most part beyond the healing power of medicine. His clarity of vision makes him anxious. The arrival of Anand serves as a distraction from this anxiety. Anand is an enigma. In a world whose reality had seemed so transparent to Banerji a

Amitabh Bachchan and Rajesh Khanna in *Anand* (Hrishikesh Mukherjee 1972). Courtesy National Film Archives of India, Pune.

moment ago, there now appears a mystery. The paralysing effect of intellectual clarity is reduced as the enigma re-activates the emotions. The centripetal force of the enigma effects a displacement so that the spectator can participate in a surrogate resolution for the world's problems.

In *Namak Haram* ('Traitor', Hrishikesh Mukherjee 1973), the martyr is explicitly named as a member of the middle class. The film is roughly modelled on the Richard Burton and Peter O'Toole starrer *Beckett*. Somu (Rajesh Khanna), a middle-class youth, and Vijay (Amitabh Bachchan), a big industrialist's son, are close friends. When Vijay takes over the running of a factory, he refuses to concede a legitimate demand for compensation and abuses the trade union leader (A.K. Hangal). Faced with a strike, he is forced to apologize to the union leader. Swearing vengeance, he recounts the whole affair to Somu. The latter offers to help him. Joining the factory as a worker, Somu (now called Chander), with the help of Vijay, scores a couple of successes as a self-proclaimed workers' leader. His popularity grows as the workers find that his confrontationist ways pay quicker dividends than the old union leader's slow, rule-bound methods. He defeats the old leader in the union elections. Having had his revenge, Vijay wants Somu to leave the job and go back to his old life. But Somu, having lived in the workers' colony and become acquainted with their misery, has had a change of heart. Vijay's father (Om Shivpuri), who believes in the policy of divide and rule, realizes the threat posed by a middle-class man whose conscience has been awakened. He deliberately exposes Somu's real identity before the workers. When the workers turn against him, it is the old trade union leader, who has recognized Somu's change of heart, who defends him. Vijay goes to the slum to bring his friend back but Somu declares his intention of staying on with the workers. Rejected, Vijay prepares to fly to another part of the country where his father is setting up a factory. In his absence, the father hires some criminals to get rid of Somu. Vijay misses his flight, and on returning home, learns about the plot. He arrives too late to save his friend, who is run over by a lorry. Knowing that his father is too powerful to be convicted of a crime, Vijay takes the blame for the murder on himself and goes to prison. On his release from prison, he is met by the old trade union leader, his girlfriend (Simi), and the mother and sister of Somu.

At the heart of the film is a long speech by the industrialist who tells his son about the unreliability of the middle class. They are usually pliable and can be useful, but every now and then, when their conscience is aroused, one of them decides to aspire for greatness. Somu, fulfilling this prophecy, becomes a martyr to the cause of working-class rights. But in the process he also unites the classes: Vijay rejects his father's divide-and-rule strategy as anti-national and pledges to continue Somu's struggle. In terms of the film this does not mean Vijay's transformation into a trade union leader but a process of reform whereby capitalists abandon their loyalty to British values and enter into a mutually beneficial pact with workers. The virtues of socialism are proclaimed in the film by Vijay's girlfriend, daughter of another industrialist. The camp of capitalists is thus shown to be internally divided and containing the seeds of a self-transformation. The middle-class martyr functions as a catalyst of reform, cleansing the capitalist class of its colonial habits.

In these narratives political conflicts are resolved by aesthetic and affective infusions mediated by disinterested subjects whose power lies in their ability to serve as distractions. Gandhi is the prototype for this magnetic point, whose charismatic power draws the spectator into the fiction of a surrogate resolution and liberates her/him temporarily from the obligation of decisive action imposed by intellectual clarity. These narratives thus propose a non-political resolution of political conflicts as the middle class's contribution to national cohesion. They assert the role of the middle class as a depoliticizing influence, as a repository of affect that absorbs and neutralizes class conflict.

The second type of middle-class narrative, on the other hand, attempts to represent the class as struggling to maintain its unity and identity in the face of disruptive intrusions and external pressures. Hrishikesh Mukherjee bridges these two segments. Firmly committed initially to Gandhian melodrama, which portrayed the middle class as the force of national reconciliation and reform, Mukherjee turned, with *Guddi*, to the new aesthetic of identity in which middle-class isolationism was the primary theme. The two forces that threaten middle-class identity in these films are sexuality and politics.

The Middle Class as Endogamous Unit

In *Guddi* (Hrishikesh Mukherjee 1971), the sexual economy of a middle class upper caste extended family is disrupted by the lure of the cinema. Guddi is the pet name of Kusum (Jaya Bhaduri), a charming school girl who is obsessed with the film star Dharmendra, who plays himself in the film. A chance meeting with the star turns this fan's admiration into a serious sublimated love for him which is modelled on the medieval saint Meera's love for the god Krishna, a love that is unrequitable but eternal. The change is registered by means of a linguistic shift, with Kusum adopting the grandiose prose of popular film dialogue. This love threatens the endogamous network within which she has been marked out as the future wife of Navin (Samit Bhanja), her brother-in-law, an engineer from Bombay who is in search of a job. A visit to Bombay provides an opportunity for visiting the studios, where her uncle (Utpal Dutt), entering into a secret pact with the star, introduces Kusum to the 'reality' behind the images seen on the screen: the lowpaid workers, the screen villains who are kind souls in real life, the stuntmen who substitute for the stars in fight sequences, etc. She also discovers her friend's brother (Asrani), who had run away to Bombay to be a film star, working as an extra and struggling to stay alive. These revelations apart, the star and the uncle, in a patriarchal plot to direct the girl's desire towards the legitimate object, provide opportunities for Navin's courage and masculinity to be revealed in a dramatic form. Kusum's education, a two-pronged process of demystification of the cinematic image and a remystification of the legitimate male's image and the patriarchal system, is complete when she expresses her love for Navin of her own will.

Hrishikesh Mukherjee, the maker of *Guddi*, was one of the people involved in the implementation of the new FFC policy. He also played an important role in transferring the realist aesthetic to the commercial sector. In this context, *Guddi* can be read as an ingenious allegorical representation of the construction of a constituency for the realist sub-sector of the commercial cinema. The subject who is liberated from the spell of commercial cinema in the film, is also the subject who is addressed by the film. As we watch Guddi maturing into responsible middle-class womanhood, we too go through a process of maturation at the end of which we, and Guddi with us, become rational, intelligent film-goers. Through our privileged access to the machinations of the well-intentioned men who undertake to educate Guddi, we become partners in an operation to reclaim the middle-class woman from her captivity to an irrational obsession.

The film deploys images of authenticity and realism as a point of contrast to the illusions of popular cinema. Here it would be appropriate to mention the role of the press in promoting the aesthetic value of authenticity and narrative integrity. *Filmfare* played a pioneering role in this regard. In its pages the necessity of short, integrated, linear narratives was emphasized relentlessly. Read primarily by the English-speaking middle class, the magazine served as a vehicle for the creation of a demand for a realist cinema.

One of the most popular columns in the magazine was called 'Readers Don't Digest', under which were printed entries from readers pointing out errors and inconsistencies in popular films. In *Budtameez*, a reader pointed out, the hero and heroine covered 'four miles on foot in the space of a three-minute song'.[4] Here the objection is to what more charitable critics have described as a non-linear conception of time that is characteristic of Hindi film narratives. Another reader observed the Hindi film-maker's indifference to historical accuracy: in *Baharen Phir Bhi Ayengi*, the Chinese war of 1962 is shown but a character refers to the narrative present as 1965. Sociological accuracy was also demanded: 'Funny that Dharmendra becomes a News Editor and still stays in a hut.'[5] Other readers pointed out formal inconsistencies: in *Vaasna*, 'Surprising that Padmini, narrating the past to her son, remembers the comedy sequences in which she didn't figure.'[6] More commonly, failures of continuity like a character's clothes changing within the same scene were detected by the dozen. As a pedagogical tool, this column was instrumental in training the readership to anticipate a Hollywood-style realism. It also provided opportunities for a kind of disdainful engagement with the popular which sustained the existing industry by making available the supplementary pleasures of readerly superiority.[7]

Guddi combines both these pleasures in its representational strategy. It offers a narrative suffused with iconic and situational

[4]*Filmfare*, 5 August 1966, p. 45.

[5]Both in *Filmfare*, 19 August 1966, p. 45.

[6]*Filmfare*, 28 February 1969, p. 33.

[7]Another feature that enhanced the pleasures of disdainful engagement was the film review. Baburao Patel, editor of *Filmindia* and later *Mother India*, was a pioneer in this regard but it was S.J. Banaji of *Filmfare* who liberated the review from the referential relation that it bore to the film. Banaji, whose byline began to appear in 1969, developed the review into an independent prose form which quickly abandoned the responsibility of commentary. Although the stories of the films were recounted, the main source of enjoyment was the style, which was copied by reviewers everywhere. When *Filmfare* started a column for readers' reviews, it was the Banaji-clones who won the prizes for best reviews.

Guddi swallows her disappointment at not being able to go to the cinema and sings a 'classical' song for her suitor's benefit, surrounded by India's artistic heritage. Jaya Bhaduri and Samit Bhanja in *Guddi* (Hrishikesh Mukherjee 1971). Courtesy National Film Archive of India, Pune.

authenticity, inviting spectator identification. At the same time it softens the critique of popular cinema through a 'disclosure' of the human world behind the illusion. The film industry emerges from the process unscathed, with the stars absolved of any blame for the fantasies the industry puts into circulation. One of the devices employed to produce a 'realist' effect in the film is that of 'not going to the cinema'. Guddi and Navin set out to go to the cinema but Navin changes plans and takes her to an archaeological site. This deflection or re-routing of the characters gives what follows a realist significance. Taking shelter from the rain in a cave at the site, Guddi offers to sing a film song but is persuaded to sing a 'classical' song instead, reinforcing the withdrawal from cinematic fantasy. At this stage in the film, Guddi's obsession with films is contrasted with Navin's complete dislike for them. In the concluding segment, at a party to celebrate her birthday, Guddi sings a film song. But this time the song, *'Aa ja re pardesi'* has been wrested from the fantasy world of film and redeployed as an external aid to the resolution of a 'real' narrative (Its difference is also guaranteed by the fact that it is from a film—*Madhumati*—made by Bimal Roy, one of the revered precursors of the middle-class cinema.) The song, whose meaning is appropriate to the context (while Guddi is singing, Navin is absent and thus becomes the addressee of the song), serves as an illustration of the ideal attitude to adopt towards cinema. This attitude consists of a detached indulgence, a knowing and provisional surrender to its pleasures. The subject must be able to draw affective material from the cinema for the narratives of real life without being sucked into its illusory world. The middle-class cinema thus provokes a disidentification with the mainstream only to open up the possibility of a reidentification based on a compromise.

The carefully produced authenticity-effect is the source of the positive counter-popular valence that is assigned to this cinema. Its ideological function differs from that of the New Cinema in that its site of intervention is not only a 'real' in which new subject positions, allied to a shared political anxiety need to be produced; further, rather than a representation of an alternative reality in its distinction from the reality represented in the popular cinema, the middle-class cinema confronts the popular cinematic image and exposes its falsehood, its unworthiness as an object of emulation. At the same time, by means of the very cinematic devices which conceal the realities of the industry, it renders the 'real' world of the endogamous petty bourgeoisie desirable in itself. The new screen image is not a fantasy creation with no basis in reality, it is coded as the spectator's own image reflected back to him/herself. The mirror is adjusted to remove the look of surprise from its face.

In this world, endogamy—the signifier of class solidarity—has to be enforced in order to maintain that solidarity, which rests on the affirmation of patriarchal authority. Meera Bai, the *bhakti* poet and devotee of the god Krishna, whose example Kusum wishes to emulate, is an instance of the disruptive power of a love that transgresses the rules of endogamy: Meera was a princess who abandoned her royal family for a life of spiritual love and devotion. Woman is the displaced site of the struggle over the re-integration and re-identification of the class which hitherto shared the spectatorship of the popular cinema with the lower classes. If Kusum is not cured of her spiritual love, Navin would have to go to his new posting alone, increasing the potential for the breakdown of the network. The reconciliation between the cured Kusum and the engineer takes place in the nick of time, a few hours before his departure to his posting.

The film rescues the popular cinema from its own critique in another way too: Navin, the man who never goes to the movies, however finds a good friend in Dharmendra. The industry, as an economic enterprise, is thus represented as redeemable even as its product, the screen image, is rejected. The logic of this is not difficult to see. In the first place, the rejection is only partial: cinema as a source of discursive devices for use in the real world is approved. What is criticized is the absorption of real subjects into the screen image, the displacing, ungrounding of the spectator from his/her true being. Besides, by endorsing the industry and the entrepreneurial spirit behind it, the film is more firmly restricting its audience membership, for it does not dispute the suitability of the fantasy screen image for another kind of person, another class of people. It situates its audience on the other side of the camera as potential participants in the economy of film-making, which effectively renders the top strata of film personnel the class allies of the real world characters as well as the implied audience, thus distancing itself from those whose only access to the film world is through the image on the screen.

Basu Chatterji's *Rajnigandha* ('Tuberoses', 1974) also includes, at the very beginning, a scene of not going to the cinema. The scene begins with the heroine waiting in front of a theatre. Her boyfriend arrives, but has forgotten to bring the tickets. She is disappointed but agrees to go to a restaurant. This initial turn away from the cinema, which in *Guddi* occurred a little way into the narrative, is even more effective in establishing the authenticity of the rest of the narrative as a representation of the real world. The story centres round Deepa (Vidya Sinha), who is writing her Ph.D. thesis and looking for a teaching position, and her boyfriend Sanjay (Amol Palekar), who is a clerk awaiting a promotion as officer. Sanjay's initial indifference to the movies is a character trait—when he does go, he eats constantly, disturbs his neighbours and goes out for a stroll whenever a song begins. His eyes are never fixed on the screen like the others' in the theatre.

Sanjay's promotion faces two hurdles—one, a rival in the office who has the advantage of being from the same region as the boss, a strain of mild social satire which provides some gentle humour. The second hurdle is Deepa herself and her conflicting desires: the impending Ph.D. which signifies her independent ambition, her job search, which threatens to take her away from Delhi (where they live), and Navin, a college boyfriend whom she has almost, but not quite, forgotten. The possible negative outcome of her transgressive desires is prefigured in a nightmare, with which the film opens. An

Waiting to go to the movies: Vidya Sinha in *Rajnigandha* (Basu Chatterji 1974). Courtesy National Film Archive of India, Pune.

interview call from a college in Bombay is the occasion for the surfacing of the anxieties over these potential threats to their stable life. Sanjay jokes about the imbalance that her Ph.D. will cause and the equalizing potential of his promotion. He does not object to Deepa's desire to go to Bombay for a job, and even talks of taking a transfer in order to be with her. In response to her anxieties about getting around in Bombay, Sanjay jokingly drops the name of Navin, which Deepa has forbidden. Bombay itself (as in *Guddi*) is a possible threat, the city of disruptive fantasies.

Arriving in Bombay alone, Deepa is met by Navin (Dinesh Thakur), who has been sent by Ira, Deepa's host and former college friend who couldn't come herself. Navin is wearing sunglasses and khadi clothes—the sole mark of continuity between his college days, when he was a student radical, and his current life as an ad film-maker with high connections. In a flashback that followed Sanjay's mention of Navin we have already seen him and Deepa as students, at the moment when they break up because of a difference of opinion over a strike. Deepa insists on breaking the strike and going to classes, which leads to an argument and Navin's words of rejection. Deepa's apolitical subjectivity is shown on one more occasion when, trying to persuade Sanjay to leave his urgent office work and meet her, she suggests, 'Why don't you start a strike?' Her indifference to the strikes that preoccupy the young Navin and the promotion-hungry Sanjay is a repudiation of politics. But while Navin's radical politics is as threatening to middle-class integrity as his later ad-world life-style, Sanjay's trade-unionism, restricted to economic demands, is not subjected to any critique—it is presented with humour and equanimity as an unavoidable means to upward mobility.

Deepa's forgotten fascination for Navin resurfaces almost instantly. Ira tries to encourage her and Navin to rediscover their old passion. Navin, taking a keen interest in her job search, makes phone calls to fix a favourable impression prior to the interview while Deepa wonders expectantly about the significance of his interest in her welfare. Deepa faces the interview board and spends her free time going around Bombay with Navin.

On one of these outings Navin takes her to see his ad film unit in action, filming a beach scene. Watching the two models come running out of the water, Deepa fantasizes herself and Navin in the same roles. This fantasy transforms her revived emotions into a consuming desire to hear Navin speak the words of love that she is sure are on the tip of his tongue.

The recurring image of Navin with sunglasses (Deepa too begins to wear them in the course of her outings with Navin), like the images of the cinema, is irresistible. Sometimes the image is interrupted by that of Sanjay, but reasserts itself. The transgression, thus, is located in the obsessive return of a cinematic image of Navin which, like Kusum's absorption in the screen image, is a form of possession, a capture by an alien force which portends a ruinous loss for the endogamous sexual economy. Navin is not blamed (any more than the film-makers are in *Guddi*) for causing this obsession. On the other hand, Navin's use of his connections to fix Deepa's interview is presented with no moral overlays. At once (economically) useful and (sexually) dangerous, the figure of Navin is invested with both the fears and desires of the class.

Returning to Delhi and awaiting news of her interview results, Deepa continues to be haunted by Navin's image. Sanjay, who has meanwhile been regularly bringing a bunch of tuberoses to replace the old ones in the vase, has had to go away on duty and is absent in this period of continued fascination with the screen image. When Navin's letter arrives, it proves to be quite formal, informing her of her success in the interview, wishing her well, but with no hint of any other emotion. The image finally fades and at that very instant, as she is still holding the letter in her hand, Sanjay reappears at the door with a bunch of tuberoses, smiling—the image is repeated, lingered over, till it suffuses her lately evacuated being. Sanjay has got his promotion, Deepa decides (on the spot) not to take the job in Bombay.

While in *Guddi* the endogamous group was still represented as a natural (blood-related) one, *Rajnigandha* takes the logical step forward by introducing a stranger into Deepa's life—a stranger who is familiar, instantly recognizable, trustworthy. They meet one rainy day when Sanjay invites her to share his umbrella on the way to college. He quickly becomes a member of the family and endears himself to all with his wit and charm. He talks non-stop about his job, the union, his rival for promotion, the coming strike, and cannot be persuaded to act romantically. The familiar grammar of romance which everybody has learnt from the movies is foreign to Sanjay but we are assured that a more genuine love lurks behind the clerical facade, signified by the constant supply of tuberoses that he brings to Deepa. The title song, which is heard as Deepa paces her home and arranges the flowers, speaks of her longing for the man's love to flourish in her heart as the flowers do in the vase. When the song exclaims 'How enjoyable is this bondage', it speaks of the flowers uncomplainingly standing in the vase in a corner as well as the woman who stays at home. Another song, played against Deepa and Navin's wanderings in Bombay, tells of the mind's (natural) boundaries which it breaks on occasion and goes in search of 'unfamiliar desires'.

In moments of crisis, thus, the spotlight is turned on woman, locating all threats to class identity in the transgressive nature of female desire, a desire that takes its own undiscriminating route to fulfilment, threatening to establish undesirable contact with the lower classes (through the cinema) and disruptive political movements (through declassed individuals like the student radical turned ad film-maker). The polymorphous sexuality of the Bombay woman, Ira, who whispers in Deepa's ear on her departure, that she will 'miss her in bed' provides a glimpse into the future in store for Deepa if she were to abandon the security of Sanjay's love for the exhilaration of a renewed affair with Navin.

The third set of middle-class films deal with post-marital conflicts arising from a variety of factors. In *Abhiman* and *Kora Kagaz*, the couples are torn apart by envy and pride. Of these *Abhiman* ('Pride', Hrishikesh Mukherjee 1973) is the more significant film from our point of view because its narrative of domestic conflict is intermeshed with certain cultural questions important to the middle-class cinema's identity. Subir Kumar (Amitabh Bachchan), a popular singer, marries Uma (Jaya Bhaduri), daughter of a traditional brahmanical scholar and herself a singer in the classical style, although she only sings for her own pleasure. After marriage they decide to sing together (and only together) in public. Her popularity soars and recording companies ask her to sing solos. She resists but Subir persuades her to break their pledge and accept the offer. Subir is consumed by envy and the suspicion that she is a better singer. In an attempt to save the marriage Uma gives up her career, but as the relationship deteriorates, she goes back to her father's house. She has a miscarriage and enters into a state of deep shock. Subir, now repentant and trying to save his wife, agrees to a plan that is aimed at making her cry and break out of the state of shock. At a public gathering, Subir sings a song which he had written in happier days, expressing their longing for a child. Uma breaks down and sings with him.

The contrast between the ordinariness of popular music and the superior skills required for classical singing is deployed in *Abhiman* to provide the affective aura within which domestic conflict is staged. The 'light classical' song was reinvented for the middle-class cinema with Vani Jayaram's *'Bol re papihara'* in *Guddi*. *Abhiman* includes some songs of this type. Unlike the popular song that Subir sings at the beginning of the film, the 'classical' song is not presented as a spectacle, with the singer dancing on stage. Popular music is meant for others' pleasure, whereas Uma's singing is not addressed to any audience. Parallel to this theme of musical traditions in conflict, the film also touches upon the question of the conflict between narrative and spectacle. Domestic harmony is broken when, in his desire to display Uma's talent to the world, Subir urges her to sing with him in public. Her singing thus acquires an addressee other than herself and the members of her family.[8] In *Abhiman* the classical aura is maintained by making Jaya a reluctant public singer. The disruptive effect of her popularity is not her own fault because she did not want to sing in public.

Gulzar's *Aandhi* ('The Storm', 1975) however, does not 'protect' its heroine in this way. Political ambition is the factor that disturbs

---

[8]The story of *Abhiman* has echoes of the real-life story of its leading actors, Amitabh Bachchan and Jaya Bhaduri (as does *Silsila*, a later film). Jaya Bhaduri gave up acting after her marriage to Amitabh in a realization of the moral of the story of *Abhiman*.

domestic harmony in *Aandhi*. Arati Devi (Suchitra Sen), a popular politician, goes to a town for campaigning and stays in the only hotel there. It is owned by her husband (Sanjeev Kumar), from whom she has been estranged for many years. The husband lives in the hotel with his trusted servant. After their encounter at the hotel, a series of flashbacks cover the previous history of their relationship. Arati's father (Rehman) is a man with great political ambitions for his daughter and is impatient with her for wasting time in romantic frolic instead of pursuing a political career. For a while Arati tries to balance the two lives but ultimately decides to sacrifice family life for her political career. In the narrative present, Arati Devi's election campaign is jeopardized by gossip about her relationship with the hotel owner. At a public meeting where her rival is exploiting the gossip for political gains, she makes a confession of her true relationship with the hotel owner. After winning the election, she decides to subordinate her political career to her renewed domestic life.

Indira Gandhi may have been a possible model for the character of Arati Devi. Mainly for this reason, *Aandhi* was banned and then allowed to be re-released with changes. There are references within the film to Nehru and Indira Gandhi which leave us in no doubt as to the parallels being suggested. However, it is not a 'biopic' that purports to be based on Indira Gandhi's life. The protagonist emulates Indira Gandhi and brings suffering upon herself as a result. Arati feels suffocated by the dullness of domestic life and longs to return to public life. The husband contributes to her rebellion against domesticity by his authoritarian ways. In the movement towards resolution, both have to acknowledge and atone for their sins.

Arati Devi's political career serves as a narrative device to symbolize a threat to the middle-class family. Arati is an idealist in politics, and is oblivious to the shady dealings of her own supporters. She is thus represented as a pawn in the hands of male politicians, who exploit her sincerity and honesty. The cinema, the world of glamour and advertising, politics: all these have the same function, in the middle-class cinema to signify a threat to the integrity of the family. With the change in enemies, however, there is also a change in the protected object itself. The family unit in these films is nuclear while its field of existence is the class. This is a significant step away from the narratives of pre-crisis popular cinema, in which the threat was directed at the *khandan's* property and honour, and where the couple's sexual and affective energies remained harnessed to the furtherance of the khandan's splendour and enjoyment. In middle-class cinema the class continues to be identified with an enlarged and more diffuse traditional unit, the kinship network or the caste, but the couple emerges into relative autonomy. The sources of conflict shift from the economic and moral domains to the realm of the psychic, where envy, ambition, pride and other disruptive emotions reside. With the middle-class cinema, women's subjectivity becomes a cultural issue.

This brings us to the last sub-type of the middle-class cinema, which takes up the construction of a class space as a condition for the emergence of bourgeois subjectivity. (*Anubhav*, one of the films in this category, has already been discussed in Chapter 3.) *Piya ka Ghar* (Basu Chatterji 1972) narrates in a humorous mode a couple's trials in the city of Bombay as they search for a place to have sex. In Rajinder Singh Bedi's *Dastak* (1970), the housing question is combined with the thematics of conjugal intimacy in a complex narrative that foregrounds some of the central preoccupations of the middle-class cinema.

When it was first released, *Dastak* ('The Knock') achieved notoriety for a single shot lasting no more than a couple of seconds in which Rehana Sultan appears in the nude. This 'displacement' of audience attention, which in any case was encouraged by the publicity, points to one of the central contradictions of middle-class ideology that the film tries to deal with but itself ultimately succumbs to. Hamid and Salma, a newly married couple, find an apartment in Bombay after a long search. After moving in, they realize that the previous tenant had been a *tawaif* (courtesan) called Shamshad Begum. Her customers, unaware that she has moved, come and knock on the door and disturb the young couple. The *panwala* in front, who owns the apartment, expects to persuade or force the young woman to become a tawaif. Two youth living in an opposite apartment watch Salma as she bathes and dresses. As if all these signs of scrutiny motivated by voyeuristic interest were not enough, Hamid finds a framed photograph of a stranger lying in the house and hangs it up on the wall. (This man is later discovered to have been a client of Shamshad Begum.) The *mis-en-scéne* functions to foreground a lack in the conjugal relationship. At first sight it appears to signify the absence of privacy, the difficulty of maintaining a zone of intimacy impervious to the prying eyes of the world. Soon we learn that there is more to it. When Hamid goes away to work, Salma is alone, and unaware that she is being watched by the men across the street, enacts her fantasies. She plays cards with an imaginary partner, smokes a cigarette and dresses up as a man. Her subjectivity is expressed in these enactments but it is only the intrusive eyes of the voyeurs (and, by extension, the spectator) that witness her self-expression. Hamid protects her from the world, and orders her to stay indoors. A caged bird which he brings home for her symbolizes her condition. When Salma tells Hamid that it is a crime to keep a bird in a cage, Hamid replies that the alternative is worse, because the bird would be devoured by animals if it were set free.

Thus for Salma, the attention of the outside world, while distasteful at one level, is also a reminder of an aspect of herself that the protocols of domestic space prohibit. Listening to a song being sung by a tawaif in the neighbourhood, Salma sings the same song to a different tune, thereby indicating that the tawaif is also a part of her being, a part that Hamid will not acknowledge. When she finishes singing, Hamid appreciates the performance for its elevating artistic qualities but does not hear the expression of desire.

The middle-class home, whose boundaries are penetrated by the voyeuristic gaze of strange men, will achieve its closure only when the woman's desire is acknowledged by the husband. The porousness of the domestic boundaries represents the failure of bourgeois subjectivity, whose closure must be achieved not by the forcible confinement of woman within the walls of the harem or behind the veil but by an inter-subjective bond. By confining her in the apartment, Hamid, like the strange men, treats Salma as essentially a sexual object. He stands between her and the would-be clients. The problem of the narrative is to constitute the bourgeois couple by achieving an adequation between the two spaces in which a woman's sexuality is distributed: the home and the brothel. On the one hand, a woman's sexuality is reduced to its reproductive function and the repression of excess is achieved by the erection of impenetrable walls. On the other, a woman is pure sexuality, her quarters open to all comers, but she is also an independent subject, capable of self-expression. This arrangement of sexual relations corresponds to a despotic political structure. The nuclear couple, disengaged from the reproductive sexual economy of the feudal home, has yet to find the erotic substance that will cement the relationship and secure it against the feudal public space. (The feudal public sphere is out of bounds for an honourable woman, which is why any woman who shows herself in this space is automatically identified as a prostitute.) The couple must produce its own habitat through a struggle for domestic space. For Hamid this battle is a repetition of the feudal one: in the new neighbourhood, he tries to erect a barrier between the world and his own domestic space. But he does not realize initially that the intrusion is not purely external. The photograph of the previous tenant's client, which he himself hangs up in the apartment, clearly indicates that the voyeurs who look in from outside are only external embodiments of a gaze that is inside, haunting the domestic space. When a group of angry men gathered outside try to force their way in and attack the couple, Hamid, in the midst of the panic, turns to Salma and asks, 'Who are you Salma?' This question marks the beginning of the process of internal scaffolding by which domestic unity will ultimately come to be secured. It is by going through the role of a tawaif that Salma returns to Hamid as a wife. The film ends with a scene in which a former client of Shamshad Begum enters and before Hamid can send him away, Salma takes up the *tanpura* and begins to sing. The man stops to listen to the song. Hamid resolves to kill Salma and positions himself behind her with a knife. At the end of the song, however, Salma throws the tanpura at the man and turning to Hamid, asks for his forgiveness. Hamid declares that he too had 'fallen', and vows to stay on in the house and fight to protect their home. Salma whispers in his ear that she is pregnant.

On a visit to Salma's parental home in the middle of the film, we witness a feudal family in decline. Salma's sister, whom the impoverished family is unable to marry off, soon runs away from home. The sister thus falls into the gap between feudal honour and bourgeois domesticity, a gap created by the decline of the feudal order and the fragmentariness of the new bourgeois patriarchal order. In Hamid's office, the Christian typist Maria represents another example of female subjectivity. Maria once types out a little love note and leaves it in front of Hamid. When he looks up, she does not return the look. She remains a sympathetic but silent colleague, coming to his aid but making no demands. For Hamid she represents female subjectivity, a person whose actions and words are not always reactive or response-seeking. It is precisely what he does not see in Salma that reveals itself in the form of the mysterious Maria.

Dastak deals with the middle-class Muslim family, whose difficulties are doubled by the minority status of Muslims. The film's conclusion reveals Hamid's resolve to fight for the transformation of Muslim society to produce a habitat for the middle-class family. Another option, however, is explored only to expose the compromises it necessitates: at first the realization that they are living in a red-light

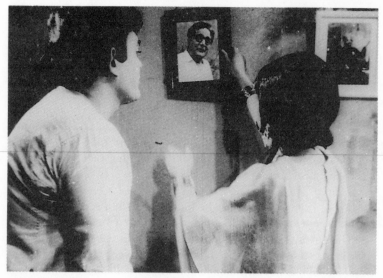

Symbolizing the lack of closure in the domestic scene, Hamid hangs up a picture of a stranger found in the house. Sanjeev Kumar and Rehana Sultan in *Dastak* (Rajendra Singh Bedi 1971). Courtesy National Film Archive of India, Pune.

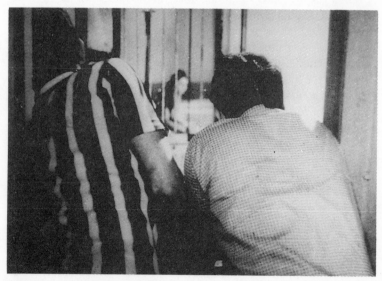

The voyeurs can see Salma (Rehana Sultan) talking to someone . . .

. . . but try as they might, they cannot see the other person

. . . when the camera moves into the house, *we* see that the Other is imaginary. Courtesy National Film Archive of India, Pune.

district makes the couple decide to move to a better place. Hamid struggles to find money to pay for an apartment under construction. When asked for his name, he hesitates and comes up with a Hindu name. The option thus translates into a fugitive existence in the midst of a Hindu middle class. However, the problem of the divided woman whose re-integration is one of the conditions of bourgeois subjectivity, is not exclusive to Muslim society but also affects Hindus, as the other films in this category demonstrate. The message of *Dastak*, however, is that Muslim society must be reformed from within by its educated members, instead of running in search of neutral spaces in which they can only survive by adopting a Hindu identity.

The middle-class film foregrounds the problem of bourgeois subjectivity through the exploration of the contradictions and conflicts of conjugality. Sometimes the continued hold of the parental family over the conjugal scene is the source of the conflict, as in *Kora Kagaz* where the wife's rich family tries to compensate for the husband's meagre salary by providing modern amenities. In all cases, however, the woman is at the centre of bourgeois narrative, the journey towards the recognition of woman's subjectivity stands as proof of the arrival of bourgeois conjugality.

For middle-class cinema as an institution, the thematics of female subjectivity and the problem of domestic space form the basis of a new aesthetic. Homologous to the problem of the domestic space and its unresolved conflicts, the middle-class segment of the industry, in its products, confronted the problem of its own cultural space. In the populist/socialist political climate, the middle class, whose class identity was intimately tied up with an upper-caste status, was more amenable to the exclusivist aesthetic enclosure produced by the narratives of domestic conflict than the national integrationist role delineated in the narratives of martyrdom.

The structure of the narrative of *Dastak* can be read in this context as an allegory of the middle-class cinema's aesthetic aspirations. The gaze mobilized by the popular cinema is a national gaze which reads the woman-in-public as a 'public woman' and thus denies her subjectivity. The unity of middle-class cinema as an institution however, depended on an ability to create an audience whose gaze is responsive to the subjectivity of the protagonists, especially women. As such the task that the film-makers undertook was not a confrontation with the popular cinema but an education of their audience in a narrative form which could retain its integrity while absorbing the libidinal excess of the polymorphous popular film text. From the contracted voyeurism of the popular film text (and the brothel), the middle-class cinema turned its audience towards a 'realist' voyeurism in which sexuality occurred in the depths of screen space, as an attribute of subjectivity.

In one of the most intriguing sequences in *Dastak*, the two voyeurs on the balcony opposite the apartment are seen looking through the window at Salma. From where they stand, they can see her only, holding a bunch of playing cards, but her actions suggest that she has company. The two men try to look from various angles but cannot catch sight of Salma's companion. Leaving them behind with their frustrations, the camera takes the spectator into the room to disclose the truth: Salma is alone and is playing with an imaginary Hamid. She follows up the card game with more play acting; she lights up a cigarette, chokes on it and then dresses up as a man. The importance of this scene lies in its representation of *the imaginary* which startlingly draws our attention to the naive materialism of the spectatorial gaze in the popular cinema. As long as we persist, like the spectator of the popular film and the voyeurs on the balcony, in reading the image as a (partial) representation of objective reality, our attention is fixed, with intense curiosity, on the point outside the frame where Salma's gaze is directed. By means of a leap through the window, however, the camera rallies the spectator behind another strategy, which permits us to see that the other resides in Salma and is an expression of her subjectivity. The spectator is separated from the communal voyeurism of the men on the balcony (such voyeurism is always collective), placed inside the room and made intensely aware that he/she is alone with Salma and her fantasies. The bourgeois spectator is invented as a support for the institution of the middle-class cinema.

Dastak and *Phir Bhi* (1971) belonged to a sub-genre which explored sexuality and the question of bourgeois (female) subjectivity. But *Dastak* in particular came to be identified with the sex films, which briefly ruled the film scene in India. They were supplemented by the sex education films, another brief eruption in the early seventies, which represented cinema's taking over of certain developmental functions, particularly the more lucrative ones. In any case, *Dastak's* attempt to forge an aesthetic predicated on individualized voyeurism was negated by the reigning logic of collective voyeurism. The bourgeois cultural revolution had to be postponed yet again.

8

The Developmental Aesthetic

The FFC's policy shift, as we have seen, is usually traced to 1969, when Mrinal Sen's *Bhuvan Shome* was released, heralding a new aesthetic turn. But it was initiated much earlier, for it was in 1964 that Indira Gandhi, as Information and Broadcasting Minister, prompted a change in policy that was carried out by B.K. Karanjia. From 1964 until 1968, when Sen got the loan for *Bhuvan Shome*, though the new policy of encouraging low-budget 'art' films had benefited Satyajit Ray and a few others, it had not gathered momentum as a national aesthetic programme (Vasudev 1986: 33–4). The conditions for such a momentum emerged in the late sixties, mainly in the form of a small, politicized audience, the arrival of new directors and actors from the Film Institute, and the rise of a re-invigorated Congress socialism. In such conditions, what had until then been an isolated policy decision suddenly became the rallying point for a cultural movement, reminiscent of an earlier national cultural initiative by the left, the Indian People's Theatre Association.

The list of films made in the first few years after *Bhuvan Shome* demonstrates the diversity of formal and thematic concerns, techniques and political positions that were emerging at the time: Basu Chatterji's *Sara Akash*, Kantilal Rathod's *Kanku*, Shivendra Sinha's *Phir Bhi*, Mani Kaul's *Uski Roti*, Kumar Shahani's *Maya Darpan*, Avtar Kaul's *27 Down*, Basu Bhattacharya's *Anubhav*, Chidanand Das Gupta's *Bilet Pherat*, Satyadev Dubey's *Shantata, Court Chalu Ahe*, Pattabhi Rama Reddy's *Samskara*, Girish Karnad and B.V. Karanth's *Vamsa Vriksha*, Karnad's *Kaadu*, Adoor Gopalakrishnan's *Swayamvaram*, M.T. Vasudevan Nair's *Nirmalyam*, Mrinal Sen's *Interview, Calcutta 71, Chorus*. The travails of the urban middle-class, questions of women's agency and sexuality, social satire, agit-prop, critiques of feudal power structures, conflicts of modernity and tradition, realism and formal experimentation: a multiplicity of directions were being explored.

Nevertheless, about five years after *Bhuvan Shome*, when Shaym Benegal's first film was released, it seemed to many that a 'New Cinema' had just then arrived. Aruna Vasudev, for instance, explains that before *Ankur*, 'new modes of perception and technique for both film-makers and audience were still hazy and barely formulated. In the context of its time, *Ankur* was a major step' (Vasudev 1986: 40) While Sen, Chatterji, Mani Kaul, Shahani, and others are hailed as major figures of the New Cinema, there is also a teleological perspective on the era which settles on Benegal as the moment of arrival, after a preliminary phase of experimentation. It is as if his films contained the essence of the New Cinema.

Benegal was the first major figure not financed by the FFC to be identified with this movement. His first two films were financed by Blaze Advertising, the company for which he had been making commercials. The third, *Manthan*, was financed by collections from the members of a milk co-operative in Gujarat. Vasudev regards the entry of private financing as 'the signs of a widening of the base of the means of production' (ibid: 40). Like many others who write on Indian cinema, Vasudev regards the New Cinema as a long-gestating, aesthetic propensity nourished by the FFC project and coming into its own with the entry of private finance. From the early 'gropings' of K.A. Abbas, Bimal Roy and others, the 'genesis' in Ray, to the FFC project and its adoption by private finance, what Vasudev presents is an evolutionary history culminating in the emergence of the 'good film'. The changing conditions of production are thus explained as external constraints and contexts. As such, with the expansion of the 'base of the means of production' the aesthetic undergoes maturation and expands its sphere of influence but remains essentially the same.

I am less interested in disputing the claim made on behalf of *Ankur* than in investigating the reasons for the success of this aesthetic re-formulation in redrawing the map of the New Cinema movement so as to place itself at the centre. It is equally important to return to the texts of other film-makers and track the exploration of other significant aesthetic choices which may have had limited popular success but which demonstrate that the triumph of the 'realist' aesthetic was not a foregone conclusion. My concern here, however, is less with an alternative Indian film history and more with the investigation of the cultural politics of the cinema and the dominant ideological tendencies.

Apart from the entry of private finance, the availability of exhibition time in the foreign film theatres was an important institutional factor in the growth of the New Cinema. The industry, faced with scarcity and high cost of theatre rentals, had for some time been demanding that the foreign film theatres should be made to reserve part of their exhibition time for Indian films. The FFC programme increased the pressure for such reservation. In 1971, when the five-year contract for import of Hollywood films came up for reconsideration, the government decided not to renew it. This decision resulted in part from the United States' aggressive posturing on behalf of Pakistan during the recently-ended Bangladesh war. The decision was also justified by making a case for more imports from other film producing countries and breaking the monopoly of Hollywood. This did happen to some extent. It was as a result of this policy that Indian audiences got to see films from France, Germany, Japan, Poland and other countries in commercial theatres. However, since these imports were canalized through a government body, exhibition time was not monopolized by foreign distributors and remained available for the local product. But exhibition space is not value-neutral. Only a certain kind of Indian cinema could be exhibited in theatres which were associated in the public mind with the aesthetic modes of Hollywood.

Benegal forged a distinct aesthetic with elements drawn from various sources to fill this gap. While the realist tendency represented by Ray was important to the formulation of the Benegal aesthetic, the more proximate sources were the realist films made under the FFC aegis, in particular the energetic regional cinemas of Karnataka and Kerala. Ray's had been a humanist realism, akin to the 'documentary humanism' of the photographer Cartier-Bresson and perhaps to the cinema of Jean Renoir. Ray's Apu trilogy had already inaugurated the project of representing the nation, and charting the emergence of India. However, his work retained an aura of individual artistic achievement. This is why critics referred to the FFC project rather than to the work of Ray as the beginning of the New Cinema movement in India. Under the FFC aegis, realism became a national political project. *Bhuvan Shome* represents this dimension of the project. It was a realism devoted to the mapping of the land, producing the nation for the state, capturing the substance of the state's boundaries.

The State and the Nation

The basic structure of this realist mode of representation can be traced to *Bhuvan Shome*, a fact which is somewhat obscured by its comic narrative. Shome, a stern and unbending bureaucrat, goes on a holiday to the western state of Gujarat after ordering the dismissal of a ticket collector accused of taking a bribe. In the course of this holiday he is transformed into a more caring, slightly insane, human being who sheds his stiff demeanour and even reinstates the ticket collector. The main agent of this transformation is a charming rustic woman who, it turns out, is the wife of the ticket collector. She breaks through his tough exterior and humanizes him with her innocence and exuberance. The visual dimension of the transformation is the shaking up and softening of the bureaucrat's body through subjection to a series of unfamiliar movements. Utpal Dutt's brilliant acting is thus of vital importance to the effects of the film. (Sen has acknowledged Jacques Tati as an inspiration.) The buffalo chase is one of the highlights of the film, where the comedy derives from the contrast between the bureaucrat's customary stiffness and the transforming power of fear, helplessness and speed.

Sen has said that the details of the narrative were made up on the spot, and has even attributed some of the episodes to Utpal Dutt's imagination. The basic structure, however, consists of a relation between centre and margin, state and nation. Quite literally, here the bureaucrat encounters the nation in a remote corner of the state and is humanized by the experience. Set in the late forties, this basic structure can be described as a national allegory, enacting the realization of independence through a transformation of the relations between state and nation. It is the narrative of a bureaucracy, previously serving the colonial project of domination, which must now establish a more intimate relation with the world over which it rules. It is the allegory of transition from colonial domination to independence, in which the object of transformation appears to be the bureaucracy, which represents the continuity between the colonial state and the independent one. This link with the past, which condemns it to a position of external domination, is broken by an immersion in the awkwardnesses of Indian everyday life. The film thus enacts the submission of the inherited and overarching power of the state to a reworking that must go through the people.

While developing the basic structure of the realist mode, Sen's politically radical move was to suggest that the consolidation of the nation-state's democratic structure could only come through a subjection of the metalanguage of the state to a process of 'corruption' by the languages of the indigenous population. The body's conventional, 'standardized' language is corrupted by the strange 'dialects' that it has never before spoken—running, twitching, jumping, etc. *Bhuvan Shome* erects the realist edifice only to subvert it through a narrative that critically comments upon the politics of realism. The celebration of the 'simple, charming and authentic' story by commentators misses the complexity of Sen's political vision. If the bureaucrat's body represents the metalanguage of realism, Sen's narrative undermines its position of eminence in relation to the 'object language' of the nation's regional extremities and makes it go through a reconstruction from below. The congealed definition of corruption in the language of the bureaucracy is subjected to change. It is not a question here of 'condoning' corruption but of making visible the gap between the language of the state and the realities of everyday life, the contradictions arising from the formulation of legal codes without the participation of the people in the process. A film made under the aegis of an institution serving the project of passive revolution, *Bhuvan Shome* inverts the relations between state and nation assumed in that project and submits the state to a transformative process.

The result of this process of subversion of the realist hierarchy of discourses is a conclusion in which the bureaucrat's craziness is matched by an editing pattern that Sen himself described as 'all erratic and illogical' (Sen 1977: 40), disrupting the realist conventions and leaving the spectator with a sense of a world devoid of rationality. Sen's own commentary on the film seems to suggest his embarassment at how it concludes, as it dwells too much on the 'mad kick' of the final sequence and detracts from its critical force by tracing it to his own and Utpal Dutt's 'private experiences'. Perhaps Sen is putting in an 'insanity plea' to escape charges of abetting corruption! The corruption episode, however, is a critical challenge to those who regard a top-down enforcement of the constitution as the way to achieve a socialist democracy.

The subsequent development of the realist aesthetic retained the basic structure of the relation between state and nation but discarded the subversive commentary on it that distinguished *Bhuvan Shome*. The regional cinemas of Kerala and Karnataka further elaborated the realist mode. M.T. Vasudevan Nair's *Nirmalyam* and Karnad's

Kaadu (both 1973) are the best examples of this tendency. A village temple is the site of the conflict in *Nirmalyam*, offering opportunities for spectacle such as the temple festival and the oracle's final frenzied dance and public suicide. With the erosion of the feudal system which sustained the temple, the villagers including the oracle's family adapt to the changing situation while the oracle makes a defiant exit, rejecting both the new order, as well as the one which betrayed him. The fascination of the feudal order in decline was also the source of the power of *Kaadu*. The climax of this film also features a village festival at which the tensions between two neighbouring villages explode in a violent finale. The feudal landlord, played by Amrish Puri, exudes a power that cast a spell on urban audiences and led to a series of similar roles for Puri. The landlord's wife tries to win her husband back from a lover in the neighbouring village by recourse to black magic while the entire narrative is anchored in the innocent curiosity of the young son, who acts as a surrogate intra-textual point of relay for the urban spectator's voyeuristic pleasure in the contemplation of the 'distant' feudal order.

In dealing with such feudal narratives it is tempting to regard the use of a figure of relay, like the child in *Kaadu,* as a device to bring a distant and strange world closer to the audience. However, the realist project of representing feudalism in a society like India does not face the problem of a gap that must be bridged as much as a proximity which requires to be negated by a process of distancing. This gives to the mediating figures a wholly different function. The feudal world is *not* already distant, and needs to be made distant by the narrative. The familiarity of the feudal world and its proximity to the everyday world of the urban audience is a mark of the composite nature of the postcolonial society. The consolidation of the nation-state thus requires the production of a distance and a hierarchy, not the bridging of an already existing gap. True, there is an already existing hierarchy, but it is the continuing power of this existing order that must be counteracted by the establishment of a new hierarchy in which the old order is distanced in its entirety, *as a world*. This process of institution of a new hierarchy based in the pre-eminence of the modern state is a continuation of the process by which, during British colonial rule, a clarification of the existing social order resulted in the production of a new patriarchal order as the point of departure for Indian nationalism. In pre-British India the social order was a horizontal web in which patriarchally organized communities existed side by side with matrilineal ones, as well as other patriarchal orders conflicting with each other. British rule, through the identification of Brahminical Hinduism and Islam as the two patriarchal orders with nation-wide validity, inaugurated a process of the construction of that validity. This internal distancing effect was crucial to the emergence of a national movement.

A similar strategy of internal distancing is at work in the realist aesthetic of these representations of feudalism. Thus, the child who relays the spectatorial gaze in *Kaadu* serves two functions: (1) the more obvious function of serving as a diegetic motivation for the voyeuristic gaze, a rationalization of the spectator's vantage; (2) the production of a distance, a virtual, pan-textual depth-effect which is different from the cumulative effect of the employment of depth of field in the representation of profilmic space. The effectivity of this distancing strategy is not to be gauged by the nature of the images deriving from it but by the spectatorial position that is produced as a consequence. This position is the manifestation within the field of cinema of the citizen/state as a medium of cultural intelligibility.

The use of sexuality as a site of exploration of the fascinations of feudal power is another recurring feature of the realist aesthetic that is prefigured in *Kaadu*. The tension arising from the conflict between the two villages is heightened by the sense of danger and adventure involved in the narrative detail of the feudal lord's mistress being a resident of the other village. The boy's curiosity about sex and the wife's frustrations add to the centrality of the sexual thematics to the feudal narrative. The film encodes the sexual scenes with suggestions of savagery, primal physicality, innocence and erotic wilfulness. Right up to Govind Nihalani's *Aakrosh* (1980), the power and fascination of the feudal world was linked in realist cinema with images of the untamed sexuality of feudal lords, their mistresses and peasants.

Although the regional cinema's strategies of distanciation produced a realist spectatorial position coinciding with that of the state, its regional-ness was still a hindrance to its national effectivity. This is why the realist cinema of the regions, which arose at the same time as its Hindi counterpart, is still relegated to a subordinate role in the histories of the New Cinema. These films belonged to specific regional and linguistic formations whose cultural difference conflicted with their ability to communicate the distancing effect outside the regions where they were produced. In a multi-lingual state, this distancing effect needed a supplementary articulation that would provide the aesthetic with a national ground for its operation, otherwise there was a risk that the citizen-function, wrested from the undifferentiated social by a process of hierarchization, would be re-absorbed into a regional cultural formation. In India, regionalism is still associated with feudalism. The citizen-function could only achieve stability (and function as the distinguishing mark of an aesthetic) if it could be inscribed in a more tangibly hierarchical discursive order. The regional cinema's realist efforts, in other words, could not sustain the metalanguage of realism because their languages were themselves region-specific. The solution was to deploy Hindi as the metalanguage in relation to which the regions, their languages and cultures would automatically fall into place as the objective *substance*.

Benegal's central importance to the realist programme derives from his successful construction of just this classic realist hierarchy. A minor event in the career of the Benegal aesthetic helps explain the nature of the discursive hierarchy and its significance. Soon after the release of *Ankur, Screen* published a letter from Aziz Qaisi of Hyderabad, who complained that his contribution to the film had not been properly acknowledged in the credits. He claimed that although he had written the dialogue for the film, Satyadev Dubey had been given credit for it, and his own name had appeared in a subordinate function. (Qaisi is credited with 'dialect' and his name is placed below that of Dubey, in smaller type.) In his reply, Benegal explained that Dubey had written both the script and the dialogue for the film. But since the film was set in rural Andhra Pradesh, it was decided to use the Dakhani Urdu spoken in that region in order to heighten the realism. Qaisi had been commissioned to 'translate' the dialogue written by Dubey into this regional dialect. As such it was proper to give primary credit to Dubey and not to the letter writer.[1]

We need not concern ourselves with the justness of this rationale. What interests us is the conception of the relations between metalanguage and object language that lies at the heart of the formulation. For Benegal, the regional specificity achieved through the use of a 'dialect' amounted to the enrichment of an already complete text. Qaisi's complaint is based on the perception that the specificity of the film text derives from its regional setting and therefore cannot be detached from its use of the regional language. But for the 'central producer', the abstract text of the realist narrative can be potentially filled by any regional content. Its meaning, for

[1] See *Screen*, 17 January 1975, p. 2.

the national spectator, is not 'Andhra' or 'Dakhani'. The regional element is there simply to signify 'regional' as a means of establishing the centre-margin relation as a frame of cultural intelligibility. If the authentic representation of the regional were at issue, *Ankur* would be a bad example of it. The fact that the characters speak Dakhani makes the spectacle authentic only from the point of view of the subject who speaks a standardized Hindi/Hindustani. In reality, the people of Andhra speak both Dakhani and Telugu and most of the characters in *Ankur* and *Nishant* could be expected to speak Telugu 'in real life'. Since 'region' in general (paradoxical as that may seem) and not 'Andhra' in particular is the real signified of the representation, this relation reminds us once again that the most important product of this representational strategy is the viewer, not the viewed. By inventing 'regionality' as a grid of intelligibility, the new cinema was able to forge a new aesthetic of statist realism.

Benegal's first three films do not deploy the realist mode of representation in the same way. It is therefore necessary to examine each of them in some detail to trace both the unique achievements of each one and to assess their cumulative cultural significance. On the latter question it can be said at the outset, in the form of a hypothesis, that the movement through the three films in question is a movement towards the consolidation of a developmental aesthetic allied to the contemporaneous stage of the passive revolution.

Spectacles of Rebellion

In *Ankur* and *Nishant,* the narratives of feudalism are set in the past, that too in a past doubly distanced from the present by the rupture of independence. The pastness of feudalism is a necessary protocol of realist representation. Realism, as argued earlier, is a mode of cultural production that is tied to the fiction of the social contract. The legal citizen-subject of the modern capitalist state is its only possible addressee. In the post-colonial Indian state, the proclamation of the social contract in 1950 did not put an end to the feudal order. In the early seventies, the audience for the New Cinema's narratives of feudalism were well aware that the immediate provocation for this aesthetic venture was the post-independence peasant struggles against feudalism, especially the rise of Naxalism. But to admit the contemporaneity of feudalism would be to place the citizen-subject addressee of realism at the hypothetical end-point of a still ongoing

A periscopic relay of the look from the zamindar to the poor village woman passes through the spectator: Shabana Azmi and Anant Nag in *Ankur* (Shyam Benegal 1974). Courtesy National Film Archive of India, Pune.

revolution, to admit, in other words, that the nation-state is not yet governed by contract. Thus the pastness of feudalism is a representational protocol which retroactively 'proves' the post-feudal, contractual nature of the present. No other purpose is served, for instance, by setting the narrative of *Nishant* in '1945', and 'in a feudal state'. The narrative itself contains little by way of historical detail which substantiates and justifies the precise dating. The date is simply a device of distanciation that enables the spectator to gain access to the fascination and power of the spectacle of feudal oppression and rebellion without being reminded of its proximity in time and space, without undermining the realist spectatorial position.

Ankur (1974) tells the story of an absentee zamindar's son Surya (Anant Nag), who having failed his examinations, is despatched to the village to look after the land. In a hut close to the zamindar's house lives a woman Lakshmi (Shabana Azmi), who is employed in the house as a servant with her mute husband Kishtayya (Sadhu Meher), who drives a cart and does other odd jobs for the master. Accused of theft and shamed before the community by the zamindar's son, the husband runs away. Surya seduces Lakshmi and she begins to live in the house as his mistress. After some time, the young zamindar's wife, who had remained in her parents' home, comes to join him in the village, putting an end to the relationship with Lakshmi. The father arrives and restores water rights to his mistress's family which the son had taken away. Kishtayya also returns one night and is pleased to see his wife pregnant. The next morning, telling Lakshmi that he will go and ask the zamindar for work, Kishtayya sets out with a stick in hand. Striding purposefully, he walks along the ridges of the paddy field, with his arms stretched across the stick resting on his shoulders. The young zamindar, watching him approach, grows anxious, suspecting that the man is coming to confront him. As his fear mounts, he runs into the house and comes back with a stick and when the smiling man approaches, starts beating him. People gather, Kishtayya takes the blows without retaliating and Lakshmi comes running to save her husband. She curses the young zamindar, who goes back into the house and shuts the door. A young boy, who had witnessed the beating, stands staring at the house. The film ends as he picks up a stone and throws it at the house.

Ankur's ending generally evoked positive responses. It was seen as a powerful moment which captured in miniscule the awakened consciousness of the innocent oppressed peasant. 'The years had not dulled the pain nor blunted the power of *Ankur's* climax', remarked the critic Maithili Rao in 1991, 17 years after its release. While this was the general opinion, Satyajit Ray, in his comments on the film soon after its release, raised the question of the credibility of the conclusion from a realist point of view. 'The whole denouement has the air of being conceived as a forced rounding-off of a story whose normal course would have led to an impasse' (Ray 1992: 103). Ray's reading betrays his unfamiliarity with the context in which Benegal's film was made. Missing the strong evocation of 'feudalism' in the film, he regards the hero as 'a rather trite symbol of urban pollution invading the pure air of the country' (ibid: 102–3).[2]

As a film promoted and received as an example of 'political cinema', the abrupt ending of *Ankur* was more important to the effectivity of the text than a conclusion deriving from the 'natural' propensities of the narrative. Indeed, it can be said that it is the narrative preceding the denouement that had to be contrived as a

[2]Ray was later to try his hand at the New Cinema style of realism in *Sadgati* (1981), a film made for television. In 1974, however, he refused to see anything new in the FFC-inspired aesthetic or Benegal's reworking of it.

way of leading up to the climax. The motivation for the ending derives from the representational dynamics of the preceding narrative and the extra-textual 'demand' for the spectacle of peasant revolt that the film promised to satisfy.[3] There was no question, then, of not including in the text a glimpse of the violence of feudal oppression and revolt. The question was how to prepare the ground for it, how to frame it in such a way as to contain its potential for challenging the citizen-figure's own position. It was not a question of building a naturalist case for the spectacle but of erecting a structure within which rebellion could be produced as spectacle. The possibilities of manipulation lay not in the details of the narrative but the dynamic in which the spectator was engaged with the figures of the represented.

Upto the point when the denouement begins to unfold, the text functions through the deployment of two structures of relay, one intellectual, the other libidinal. The three figures who form the three points of these paths of relay are the spectator, the urbanized zamindar and the object world of the feudal social order, represented by the figure of the servant woman. Their positions in the two relational paths can be represented as follows:

1. The intellectual relay:
   Spectator $\longrightarrow$ Zamindar $\longleftrightarrow$ Servant woman.
2. The libidinal relay:
   Zamindar $\longrightarrow$ Spectator $\longleftrightarrow$ Servant woman.

The first path belongs to the ethnographic dimension of the representation. The spectator's relation to the represented image here is one of curiosity about the inner workings of feudal society, the desire to gain knowledge about the 'unfamiliar' world of the feudal other. In realizing this wish, the zamindar's son functions as an intermediary. By having been a town-dweller, himself not very familiar with the village, he goes through a process of learning that makes him an unwitting 'native informant'. At the same time, he is not urbanized enough to *consciously* adopt an ethnographic approach to the field which would place him more in our space than in the space of the represented. It is important for him to be an *unwitting*

---

[3]Benegal himself attributed the success of the New Cinema to the existence of a demand. 'Political cinema will only emerge when there is a need for such a cinema,' he observed. 'We have to realise that whatever films are made can only be shown if there is a need for such films—a latent demand that is tapped' (Rizvi and Amlad 1980: 7–8).

point of relay of our desire for knowledge. In one of the scenes at the beginning, when we are still in the process of being led around the place to familiarize ourselves with it, the zamindar's son asks the servant woman if she has ever seen a film. She says yes and names the Telugu film *Balanagamma*. This popular film from the early forties helps to date the narrative or to indicate the distance between the film-literate spectator and Lakshmi. But the scene is also meant to enact the intermediary role of the zamindar's son. He has no particular use for the bit of information which he has extracted but we do. The zamindar's relay function must be 'unsolicited' because otherwise he would be the conscious agent of our investigation. Our detachment from him, on the other hand, assures us a position of non-complicity with the feudal power and the objectivity of the knowledge produced, while sustaining our sympathy with the oppressed peasant as the overt justification of the exercise.

In the shadow of the intellectual relay structure, which provides one logic of representation, and as a supplement to it, there functions another, the libidinal relay structure. Here the spectator becomes the 'unwitting'—though not unwilling—point of relay for the zamindar's gaze directed towards the servant woman as well as her desire for him. The material evidence for this lies both in the narrative ordering, as well as in a recurring shot composition in which the three points are arranged in such a way as to force the look to be relayed through the spectator. On the narrative plane, the spectator is first afforded a brief glimpse of Lakshmi, before cutting to Surya in the city. Lakshmi is praying for a child. Throughout the film, occasional glimpses of Lakshmi as she ponders her situation enable a veiled relation between the two points. In these moments of solitude, Lakshmi discloses her own desire, revealing to us an intention that Surya is not aware of. Visually, there is a supplementary strategy of shot composition which places the spectator at the node of a periscopic conveyance of the gaze. Thus, in one of the scenes which develop their love relation, Lakshmi is in the foreground, facing camera, while Surya is sitting up in bed in the background, and looking through the open doors into the room where Lakshmi is standing. As she is positioned to one side of the door, he cannot see her directly. His gaze is directed straight at the camera but is coded as directed at her. Her look is directed downwards and to the left, crossing the open door and settling on a point to screen right but outside the frame. Her look is thus directed out of the relay structure, although it is also coded as inclining towards the zamindar, since they are engaged in

'Tell me something about yourself. . . .' In an ethnographic relay, the spectator's curiosity about the oppressed is satisfied through the unwitting mediation of the young zamindar. A scene from *Ankur*. Courtesy National Film Archive of India, Pune.

conversation. The distribution of figures and spaces thus compels the spectator to function as the point of relay, as the empty conduit in a circuit, whose points of emanation and arrival are elsewhere. The mediated depth produced by the intellectual relay is here negated by the spectator's direct access to the other as sexual object by virtue of the unwitting function of relay. Another scene, when Surya encounters Lakshmi near the well in the backyard, shows the same relational structure in lateral inversion. The same positions of the two figures in the frame are maintained, woman in foreground and man in the background. The look and its object similarly cannot meet without mediation, although they are 'intended' for each other. In the process of serving as the point of relay, the spectator is afforded a direct access to the image of the woman.

Thus, during the film's middle segment in which the love relation between the two unfolds, an intimacy between the spectator and the woman is established by means of the libidinal relay structure. The middle section constitutes an interregnum, a restful pause in the linear narrative during which the libidinal theme unfolds. During this segment the spectator is drawn into an intimate complicity in the unfolding of the sexual relation between the zamindar and the servant woman.

After the erotics of feudalism, however, the spectator must confront the reality of the exploitative relation in which he/she has been seduced into participating. How is the spectator to extricate him/herself from this complicity so as to be able to identify with the oppressed? It is here that the dramatic climax of the film comes to the spectator's rescue. The film has enacted a voyeurism that captures the rural/primordial in its field. The breaking of the voyeuristic nexus, however, is so engineered as to spare the spectator and enable a last minute switch of loyalties. The spectator knows that the voyeuristic interregnum will have to come to an end but he/she does not anticipate the intensely pleasurable way in which this parting of ways with the zamindar will be staged. Our ability to switch loyalties at this point depends on a supplement of knowledge. This is provided by two scenes: in the first, Kishtayya, finding Lakshmi pregnant, is happy and takes her to the temple, demonstrating that he has no suspicions on that score; in the second, he indicates to his wife his intention of going to the zamindar to ask for work. Armed with this knowledge, we recognize that his aggressive stride as he

The revolt of the oppressed, shown here as a young boy throwing a stone at the zamindar's house, is coded as spontaneous and innocent. A frame from the last shot in *Ankur.* Courtesy National Film Archive of India, Pune.

walks towards the house is simply an expression of his innocent and energetic rural persona. The zamindar does not. This difference in knowledge for the first time liberates us from the compact in which we were bound to the zamindar and places us in a position of objective arbitration, as well as identification with the peasant. Had we not been in possession of this additional knowledge, our speculations about the approaching Kishtayya's intentions might have been closer to those of the zamindar, thus traumatically foregrounding our complicity and undermining our assumed position of objectivity. However, erotic exploitation, in which the spectator is complicit, goes 'unpunished'. Instead, we witness the zamindar's beating of Kishtayya with a consciousness of its wrongness. When the little boy throws a stone at the house at the end, we are grateful for it, we are able to stand with him because we know that the stone is not directed at the sexual exploitation in which we were complicit. Had the stone been motivated by a different revenge, we might have been at the receiving end of it.

The 'power' of *Ankur's* climax, which has provoked so much comment, thus derives from the sense of relief and pleasant surprise that we feel when we are rescued from the *ménage-a-trois* and placed on the side of the oppressed for the brief space of a stone-throwing incident. Responding to the 'demand' for a political cinema, *Ankur* provides the pleasures of voyeuristic contemplation of the feudal world as well as the opportunity to vicariously participate in the peasants' moment of awakening, without ever calling into question the spectator's own position.

Muteness and innocence are the primary attributes of the oppressed in this school of New Cinema. In *Ankur*, Kishtayya is literally mute. In *Nishant* (1975), Benegal's second film, the peasants suffer the landlord's injustices silently until they are awakened by two leaders. In *Ankur*, peasant rebellion was represented symbolically in the form of a child's act of protest. In *Nishant*, a full-scale peasant uprising, a spectacle of violence, explodes on the screen. While some of the representational strategies from *Ankur* are carried over, *Nishant* approaches a more explicit and direct representation of feudal violence and retaliation. Of the three films, *Nishant* is the least reassuring because in it the possibilities of a framed and distanced presentation of the spectacle of peasant violence are strained to the point of rupture. It is not surprising that *Nishant* was the least successful of the three films. All its representational strategies could not effectively contain the force of the spectacle of peasant violence. The struggle for narrative control over spectacle is clearly lost at the end. By its evocation of anarchy, the film hinted that the position of the sympathetic consumer that the spectator was able to occupy in *Ankur* was in fact not available, that peasant unrest was capable of breaking through the barriers erected by the leadership as well as the representational grids put in place by artists, and gathering a momentum all its own.

Nishant tells the story of a village ruled over by a family of brothers who exploit the villagers economically and sexually. The unmarried head of the family is Anna (it is only the Telugu word for 'brother' but this is how he is addressed) who rules over the village and his manor with a brutal hand. Of his three younger brothers, the first two (Anant Nag and Mohan Agashe) are brutal womanizers. The wife of one escaped to her parents' home and never returned while the other committed suicide. The youngest is the timid Viswam (Naseeruddin Shah) who disapproves of his brothers' activities but does not heed his wife's (Smita Patil) advice to stay away from them.

The film begins with the priest discovering early one morning that the temple jewels have been stolen. In the pit where the jewels were kept the priest finds a locket. With a close-up of Viswam's worried face, we enter the feudal manor and we learn, through the conversation between him and his wife as well as a later scene, that the brothers had stolen the jewels. Meanwhile Shamsuddin (Kulbhushan Kharbanda), the policeman stationed in the village, arrives to document the theft and the homeless man who was seen sleeping on the temple steps in the beginning is jokingly accused by another villager of having stolen the jewels. An oracle, dancing and singing, identifies the thief as a man of strength, unmarried and a drunkard. The homeless man, fearing that suspicion will fall on him, begins to retreat from the crowd and is caught and accused of the crime. Anna beats him with a stick and he is taken away by the police. Anna talks to the priest about renovating the temple and replacing the jewels and 'persuades' the priest to return Viswam's locket.

The new schoolmaster (Girish Karnad), his wife Susheela (Shabana Azmi) and their young son arrive in a horse-cart and take up residence in the small house allotted to them in the school compound. Their domestic life is settled and happy except for Susheela's longing for a big mirror which hints at a disruptive narcissism. Curious and free-spirited, she attracts the attention of Viswam who stares at her with a mysterious fascination. Catching him looking, one of the older brothers discovers his desire and together they kidnap Susheela and take her home. She is raped by the brothers and confined to a room in the house. The schoolmaster, having failed to mobilize the villagers behind him (although they had witnessed the kidnapping), bangs on the door of the manor but to no avail. The next day, he tries in vain to get the police, a lawyer and the district collector to help him fight the injustice. Meanwhile, Susheela becomes a part of the feudal household, living there as a mistress and attended by Pochamma, the maid. The schoolmaster, driven to extremes of despair and frustration, leaves his job and sits in the temple. Susheela, meanwhile, becomes more and more entrenched in the feudal household.

Meeting her husband at the temple one day, Susheela accuses him of lacking the manliness to confront the oppressor and liberate her from his clutches. Resolving to fight, the schoolmaster, with the assistance of the priest, begins to campaign among the villagers, urging them to rise up against the oppression. The mobilization of the villagers begins at a buffalo fight where the villagers are gathered and continues through a series of meetings and a final gathering for a street play based on the *Ramayana,* where the priest reminds the villagers that suffering oppression silently is as sinful as oppression itself. On the day of final confrontation, the residents of the feudal manor awake to find that none of the servants have come to work. As they cope with the situation, distant sounds announce the beginning of the temple procession. The procession stops before the manor and the eldest brother goes to the temple car to make his offerings. The schoolmaster makes the first move, and soon the landlord is beaten to death. The peasants enter the manor and a battle ensues. Meanwhile, Viswam grabs Susheela and leaving his wife Rukmini behind, escapes from the house to the hills. After killing the rest of the family, the peasants run towards the hills to capture the runaway couple, with the wounded schoolmaster running behind them. Entering the manor, a little boy surveys the devastation. He comes upon the priest, sitting on the floor, paralysed by the violent spectacle he has witnessed. As the boy runs away, the priest rises and covers the body of the dead Rukmini with his shawl. Outside, the boy is still running and in the last shot the rest of the children are seen huddled together in the safety of the temple.

Nishant offers the spectator a considerably less secure position of contemplation than *Ankur.* Vijay Tendulkar's script includes many brutal scenes of feudal violence and the fascinating power of the big brother is counteracted by the obscene, thoughtless viciousness of the brothers Anjaiah and Prasad. In the scene where these two brothers tell a poor peasant to send his wife to them at night, the camera shifts to a perspective from behind the woman, seeming for a disturbing moment to share in her mute suffering, unsettling the voyeuristic economy of feudalism-as-spectacle. There and later in the feudal manor, her mute submission is emphasized as the brothers refer to her and other women as cows. But at the same time the film is unable to ground the rebellion in the peasants' understanding of their condition. It is only through the intervention of a man motivated by his own need for revenge that they are mobilized for a battle with the oppressor.

Like the young zamindar in *Ankur*, the schoolmaster is an intermediary who is neither organically a part of the represented world not completely alienated from it. As a studious and responsible schoolmaster who comes from the town on a transfer, he brings values which are alien to the feudal order that reigns in the village. But at the same time he is not a conscious modernizer, and is himself mindful of feudal compulsions. His teaching is traditional and he expects his wife to stay indoors and away from the eyes of strangers. More importantly, we are not dependent on him as a point of intellectual relay because he arrives *after* we have been introduced to the village and its power relations. His function is to bring to the village a catalytic element which upsets the equilibrium of oppression and suffering. He is also an individual sufferer, who enables a narrative movement that the collective nature of peasant struggle cannot provide. The peasants have the experience of suffering but not a consciousness of it.

The film presents us with an image of feudalism in which the landlord stands all alone on one side while everyone else is ranged against him, except the policeman who vacillates between the two positions. The opening scene centred around the temple theft enables this demarcation. As the poor man is falsely accused and beaten up, the two figures who wield an independent authority in the village (deriving from the state and god) both submit to the might of the landlord. The priest meekly hands over the incriminating locket when the landlord asks for it. The policeman is more actively servile.

The schoolmaster observes the arrogant behaviour of the landlord's brothers but stays out of trouble. It is his wife Susheela's transgressions that generate the new conflict which culminates in the peasant uprising. Here the realist narrative is overlaid with an epic structure that enables the transformation of feudalism into spectacle. Her repeated demands for a big mirror and new clothes indicate a narcissistic preoccupation with looks. Soon after their arrival in the village, the schoolmaster stops to talk to the two brothers who have parked their car outside the school and are chatting with the policeman about filling up a pit in front of the school. Seeing his wife looking out at them through the window, he gestures to her surreptitiously to withdraw. She fails to understand. Back in the house, he rebukes her for not behaving as befits a schoolmaster's wife. A little later Susheela comes out of the house dressed carelessly and walks unselfconsciously to a shop where she is seen by Viswam who stares at her. A third scene follows in which her unwitting seduction of Viswam is carried a step further. Passing by a high wall behind which a peasant who did not pay his dues to the landlord is being evicted, she stops and peers over the wall at the scene. Viswam, who is standing there, stares at her again and is caught doing so by Prasad. That night, teasing him for keeping his desire a secret, they offer to bring her home for him. As the schoolmaster's family sit down to supper, there is a knock on the door and Susheela, who answers, is taken away.

The realist representation is thus channeled into an epic narrative. From the point when the schoolmaster's family arrives in the village, the film's narrative unfolds roughly along the lines of a part of the *Ramayana*. Beginning with the transfer to the remote village which Susheela resents and which parallels Rama's banishment to the forest, her abduction, like Sita's, results from a transgressive desire. Her confinement in the feudal manor, the mobilization of the peasant army and the assault on the manor to rescue her complete the parallels with the epic. This combination of a realist representation of a feudal structure and an epic narrative of one man's battle with the forces of evil gives rise to contradictions that the text is unable to deal with. The problem of the narrativization of feudal oppression is primarily a problem of the identification of the agencies of struggle and resistance. The statist realism of the Benegal aesthetic does not allow for the elaboration of the complex processes through which movements of resistance are organized by the peasants, nor can it explicitly represent a modern political force entering the peasant world and organizing them on the basis of a programme of resistance and opposition. Instead, it increases the temporal distance (the action is supposed to take place in 1945) by a few thousand years and inscribes peasant revolt in the timeless overarching epic narrative of conflict between élite groups.

As a result when the priest and the schoolmaster begin to mobilize the peasants, we only hear a few sentences about the need to fight oppression. The rest is elided as images of meetings with peasants are accompanied by loud music which drowns out the content of the conversations. In order to remain faithful to its *contemporary* project of depicting feudalism, the film must indicate that the peasants were mobilized on the basis of a manifesto. But this manifesto cannot be made explicit because the mobilization of peasants as an obedient army would be disrupted by it. Tellingly, in one of the few lines spoken in this sequence, a peasant declares that they would do exactly as the schoolmaster and the priest tell them to.

But, in the contradictory space determined by the conflicting co-presence of two aesthetic projects, the epic narrative cannot outrun the realist one without betraying itself. The epic's triumph is always the epic hero's triumph, the restoration of the epic couple. *Nishant* cannot afford to move towards such a denouement because it would negate the realist analysis at work in the understanding of feudal society. The spectacle of peasant violence would have to be subordinated to the restoration of some transcendent order. Abandoning the epic parallel before the utopian moment, *Nishant* suddenly turns around and leaves us with the vision of a terrible, uncontrollable, anarchic explosion of mass anger in the midst of which only the temple seems safe. Both the leaders of the rebellion are left behind in the avalanche of peasant revenge, the priest reduced to complete inertia, the schoolmaster running behind the crowd as they climb up the hill and begin assaulting Viswam and Susheela who are hiding behind a rock. After the epic interregnum, we have a traumatic return of the real, the spectacle of violence we are waiting for, but without the guarantees of a stable position from which to contemplate it. The scared faces of the children as they sit inside the temple, which is aglow with a warm light, may well reflect the position of the spectator, caught up in a whirlwind of destruction and deprived of all secular support.

While the rebellion must be provoked by the priest and the schoolmaster as an act of conscience, it cannot be controlled by them unless their leadership was based on a programme. In the absence of a critical realist approach to feudalism, rebellion can only be represented in voluntaristic terms as the result of an incitement. Once the rebellion transgresses the boundaries set by the leadership, it comes to be equated with feudal lawlessness.

In the end the tension between narrative and spectacle is resolved in favour of the latter. Rebellion can be staged as spectacle only in the absence of mediation, that is, in the absence of a purposive, goal-oriented programme. *Nishant* demonstrated that the game of observing the feudal spectacle from a distance was fraught with risks. Taken to its extremes, the spectacle of rebellion reminded the spectator that its consequence was an anarchy that would undermine his/her own position of objective contemplation. By representing the peasant in revolt as a figure of complete anarchy, it raised the question of leadership. The image of the schoolmaster running behind the crowd demonstrated the trauma of the loss of leadership. For the urban middle-class audience, lured by the promise of a safe, thrilling glimpse into the workings of feudalism, these were unexpected lessons. Consciously or not, *Nishant*, through its attempt to expand the spectacle of feudal violence, demonstrated the poverty and risks of the conception of 'political cinema' which consisted solely in a vicarious 'experience' of the political ferment in India's villages.

The unsaid of the text is the historical truth about peasant struggles in Telengana, where the film is set. In the late forties, Telengana was the site of a communist-led armed struggle against the feudal landlords and the Nizam. But the political cinema for which a demand was being created was not one which could explicitly define peasant revolt as a Communist programme. It was the peasant's 'instinctuality' that provided this cinema with its ideological armour. As such only a leadership that was 'national' in the sense of being derived from the consensual framework of national politics, could be acknowledged as legitimate. In 1974, Benegal's film was unable to identify such a leadership. Its bleak and terrifying vision of rural anarchy is a reminder of the break-up of the national consensus.

Unlike *Ankur* and *Nishant*, *Manthan* has a contemporary setting. It was noted earlier that the realist aesthetic, working through the figure of the citizen-subject, must represent feudalism as a thing of the past. How then does *Manthan* escape this rule?

The Bureaucracy in Arms

Manthan (1976) acknowledges the contemporaneity of feudalism because its narrative concerns the interventionist state. The citizen-figure here is mobilized in the service of a transformative politics.

The bureaucrat who undertakes a reformist social programme in *Manthan* is a mobilized intellectual, the citizen as revolutionary. This turn in the developmental aesthetic occurs in the context of a mobilized state apparatus which, during the Emergency, intensified the Congress programme of 'socialist' transformation. In her attempt to break the traditional chain of power in which the traditional ruling élites functioned as intermediaries, Indira Gandhi was aided by a mobilized bureaucracy which implemented her government's socialist programme. This combination of a Congress–left political alliance and a mobilized bureaucracy disrupted the old stabilities and made a bid to transform the social basis of the political order. The fight against feudalism was one of the highlights of the new agenda. The abolition of bonded labour and the cancellation of the privileges of the princes, who had continued to enjoy the special status bestowed on them by the British were two of the measures taken by the government which indicated its will to complete the bourgeois revolution. The actual achievements of this programme were of course limited and were cancelled out by the atrocities committed during the Emergency by the new ruling group and its implementation machinery. But the mobilization-effect was very strong and produced a sense of radical transformative possibilities.

Manthan is an Emergency film, a film about the transformative power of a mobilized bureaucracy. Emergency slogans are heard throughout the film, on the radio. The film begins with a scene epitomizing the changed circumstances of a nation in transition. The first shot is of a railway platform, where a train arrives and the bureaucrat who is sent to start a milk co-operative in a Gujarat village gets off the train. He is met by a few men who apologize for turning up late, saying 'Sorry, the train came on time'. This humorous incident establishes the mood of the film and places its narrative in the context of the Emergency period. One of the well-known achievements of the Emergency was the punctual operation of the railways. The rhetoric of efficiency, which was circulated throughout the country in the form of posters, radio announcements and slogans painted on lorries and buses ('Work more talk less', 'The nation is on the move', etc.) found its most visible illustration in the railways' punctuality. In the opening scene, this reference to the alert and responsive state also establishes the changed relationship between bureaucracy and hinterland. In the past, political leaders arriving in remote parts of the country would be welcomed by local leaders and people who sometimes gathered hours before the actual arrival.

'Maaf kijiye, gadi time par aa gayi' —The local representatives' apology to the bureaucrats for coming late to receive them, reminds us of the 'efficiency' of the Indira Gandhi government: A scene from *Manthan* (Shyam Benegal 1976). Courtesy National Film Archive of India, Pune.

With the bureaucracy taking on the mantle of leadership, the film suggests that there is a reversal, with the state representative arriving before the village has had time to prepare for his visit. The state is ahead of the nation: the condition of passive revolution.

The narrative can be divided into three segments, corresponding to the stages of exposition, intervention and resolution. The first segment, beginning with the arrival of the bureaucrat, consists of a process of getting familiarized with the situation on the ground. The existing power relations are mapped in a few deft strokes. The bureaucrat, Manohar Rao (Girish Karnad), is a veterinary doctor employed by the Dairy Board and sent to the village to start a milk co-operative with the help of two others from the board. He is brought to the village by a man (Sadhu Meher) who is used to old ways and contrasts his experience with the newcomer's lack of it. He is friendly with the local landlord, Ganganath Misra (Amrish Puri) to whom all the villagers sell their milk, and whose business is threatened by the efforts to start a co-operative. Together they represent the order which is traditional not in the 'timeless' sense in which that word is usually employed, but in that they represent the intermediate leadership through which the older Congress maintained the national coalition. The new socialist agenda is intended to replace this order. The two discuss the 'idealism' of youth and Misra, declaring that the country needs idealists, adds that idealism does not last very long. Rao, going round the village collecting milk samples, encounters the hostility of the poor villagers towards urban intruders. Meeting Misra, he reminds him of the changing situation. Acknowledging that in the past Misra's approach may have been useful, he asserts that now new methods were in order. The reformist goal is specified: not to merely transfer the control of the milk trade to a new agency but to ensure that the producers get their proper returns. Misra wants him to concentrate on health and family planning and leave the local economy, which he claims he built up, to him. At a public meeting where the co-operative idea is explained, further obstacles are revealed. The *sarpanch*, a traditional village leader, is opposed to the dilution of his authority by the introduction of elections and equal say to all members. The dalits support the co-operative only if they can get credit and one of them, Bhola (Naseeruddin Shah), is suspicious of all city folk.

The opportunity for an interventionist move comes when a

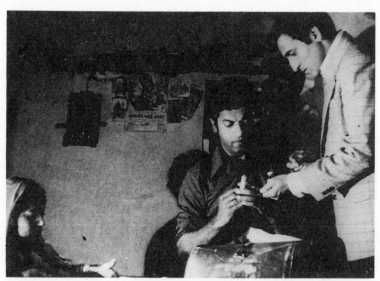

In a medical emergency, Dr. Rao (Girish Karnad), breaches professional ethics by treating a human patient, even as his colleague (Mohan Agashe) protests, in *Manthan*. Courtesy National Film Archive of India, Pune.

medical emergency arises in the village.[4] A villager asks Rao to save his child. Deshmukh, one of the other members of the team objects to Rao, a veterinarian, treating a human patient but in the absence of a doctor, Rao decides to take the risk. It is crucial for the interventionist narrative that the demand for such a radical step should arise from the field. This moment is decisive because it establishes the need for radical measures in a situation where a scrupulous adherence to the ethics of the professions is shown to be counterproductive. Deshmukh represents a conservative approach to the reformist work of the bureaucracy. While Deshmukh keeps reminding him that they must try to accomplish their task without upsetting the existing order, Rao extends his interventionist methods to the political structure of the village and actively campaigns among the dalits to raise their consciousness and make them active participants in the development project.

The poor villagers are won over by Rao's unorthodox intervention in the medical emergency and the co-operative gets going. When a film show on the milk co-operative movement is disrupted by stone-throwing, Bhola is arrested. Rao gets him released and realizing that Bhola is the key to getting untouchables to participate, gradually breaks through his hostility and gets him to become a supporter. Bindu (Smita Patil), a dalit woman who, after initial hostility, comes to appreciate the good intentions of the bureaucrats, helps in this task. Resisting the sarpanch's attempts to maintain caste divisions and traditional modes of power, Rao urges the dalits to contest the election. Emboldened, the dalits enter a nomination, and when the votes are equally divided between Moti, the dalit candidate and the sarpanch, Moti is elected by a draw of lots. Humiliated, the sarpanch transfers his loyalties to Misra, inaugurating the moment of conflict and resolution.

[4]The fact that *Khotey Sikkey*, an indigenized 'cowboy' film of the *Sholay* type, employs the same structure is no accident. In the Indira Gandhi era, the two armies of reform were the bureaucracy and the lumpen Youth Congress led by Sanjay Gandhi. The urban petty criminals who are recruited to protect the village in *Khotey Sikkay* are agents of reform but unlike the bureaucrats in *Manthan*, they do not hold the position of authority. They relate to the village as a place of their salvation. But otherwise the relations between the intervening urban team and the village unfold with remarkable similarity. Thus, in both *Khotey Sikkay* and *Manthan* the first opportunity for the intruders to demonstrate their usefulness comes in the form of a medical emergency, which requires the presence of a doctor. In *Khotey Sikkay*, the uneducated lumpen reformers hijack a bus and bring a doctor from the town to the village by force. In *Manthan*, Dr Rao, a veterinarian, transgresses the ethics of his profession by treating a human patient.

A bond of affection develops between Dr. Rao and a dalit woman (Smita Patil): A scene from *Manthan*. Courtesy National Film Archive of India, Pune.

The sarpanch and Misra plot to destroy the co-operative movement. While the sarpanch goes to the city to use his influence and get Rao transferred, Misra gets Bindu to sign a paper accusing Rao of molestation, which he uses to blackmail Rao. Misra and the sarpanch also set fire to the dalits' huts and Misra then wins them over with charity. He gets the dalits out on bail when they are arrested after the fire. While Bhola remains firm in his commitment to the co-operative, the others are lured by Misra's promise of restoration of the old ties of trust and paternal protection.

The resolution is marked by an escalation of class struggle on the one hand and the withdrawal of the interventionist bureaucrat, who is transferred out of the village. Rao's wife, who joined him half-way through the film, is bed-ridden with typhoid and wants to go back to the city. Her presence is represented as a private obstacle to Rao's political idealism. As he informs her of the transfer, a popular love song *'tum jo hue mere hamsafar raste badal gaye'* plays on the soundtrack, ironically commenting upon the anti-climactic end to his hopes. The song is followed by an Emergency slogan which declares that with courage and legislative initiative the nation is being transformed. Before this, we see Misra's lawyer attempting to bribe Rao, provoking the latter to explode in anger, vowing to destroy

Misra if it is the last thing he does. This anger is dissipated by the external agency of the transfer notice, but it stands as an expression of the resolve of the bureaucracy to crush the feudal order.

After his departure, the disappointed Bhola gathers a few people around him and revives the co-operative, determined to keep the development project going. The intervention thus has left behind an organic intellectual, who, fired by the developmental ideology, feels empowered to take charge. Thus, the film affirms the positive transformative power of the government's agenda.

The single most important difference between *Nishant* and *Manthan* is that in the former rebellion was a spectacle of anarchy, whereas the latter represents the rebellion of the oppressed as the result of a calculated intervention from above by a militant bureaucracy. The Indira Gandhi government's populist reprise of the momentum of peasant revolt results in a developmental aesthetic built around a reformist ideal. Unlike the traditional, 'mythical' leadership of the peasant revolt in *Nishant* who are left behind by the tide of vengeance they unleashed, the mobilized bureaucracy in *Manthan* produces an organic leadership which takes over the struggle and conducts it in a rational manner. The structure of the passive revolution remains intact.

Manthan is relatively free from the spectacle of feudal sexuality that was so important to *Ankur* and *Nishant,* as well as *Bhumika* which came after *Manthan*. Instead, an erotic supplement to the developmentalist project is included in the relationship between Rao and Bindu, the dalit woman. Hostile at first, Bindu soon becomes attracted to Rao and remains a reliable ally of the co-operative project. A song sung by a female voice, which recurs through the film, is first played when Rao arrives in the village, establishing the village's demand for a *'pardesi'* (outsider) reformer. This song comes to be associated in the course of the film with Bindu's unexpressed feelings for Rao. Rao's wife, who joins him in the village, represents the personal limitation which Rao has to overcome in order to function as a militant bureaucrat. When he is called out to the village at night when the huts are burning, Rao leaves his sick wife in bed and pleads with her to go to sleep. At this moment her presence is clearly coded as a hindrance. The film is unable to deal with the bureaucrat's private world except as a tool for narrative resolution. The middle-class cinema dealt with similar bureaucrats and professionals struggling with the difficulty of securing their domestic arrangements (*Guddi*). The bureaucrat-as-militant, however is constructed as a free-roaming figure who is lonely in his idealism and has to break his world up into two incommensurable segments. While the unspoken intimacy with Bindu makes the developmental aesthetic attractive to audiences (without it the film might have become indistinguishable from Films Division documentaries), the episode with Chandavarkar's (Anant Nag) sexual escapades emphasizes that the militant bureaucrat must put aside all emotional attachments in order to function effectively.

Thus, from *Ankur* to *Manthan* we move from a consumerist evocation of rebellion to a depiction of the initiation of class struggle by the mobilized state apparatus. The return of feudal sexuality, epic narratives and other features in Benegal's later films suggests that *Manthan's* difference owes a great deal to the pressures of the era in which it was made, as well as the modernizing ideology that the milk co-operatives stood for. V. Kurien, one of the architects of the 'white revolution', as the milk cooperative movement is known, is credited with the story idea for the film, along with Benegal. Govind Nihalani, Benegal's cinematographer, made a documentary on 'The White Revolution' during this period, no doubt a by-product of the *Manthan* venture. The film was thus something of a state project, meant to serve as propaganda for the developmentalist efforts of the Congress government. Critics have generally avoided comment on the emergency references of the film, no doubt because of the embarrassment it entails, although it is simplistic to equate the Indira Gandhi era as a whole with the atrocities committed during the emergency. After *Manthan* Benegal did return to the developmentalist aesthetic in films like *Susman* (1988), which was made with the assistance of a handloom co-operative. But such ventures were determined by their conditions of production and should not be submitted to a purely auteurist reading.

The reformist narrative of the film requires the removal of the bureaucrat from the scene. Any deeper involvement in the class struggle that he has contributed to intensifying, would cancel his bureaucratic identity and turn him into a revolutionary. The reformist bureaucracy whose worldview is represented in the film was committed to the passive revolution and not to a radical challenge to the political order itself. As such the brief vision of a reformist utopia at the end is a reassurance to the spectator that the reformist impulse has been communicated to the bottom rung and that a slow developmentalist trajectory has been put in place. The panic created by the vision of anarchy in *Nishant* is assuaged here by the assurance that everything is under control.

9

Towards Real Subsumption?: Signs of Ideological Reform in Two Recent Films

The present moment in the history of Indian cinema is, as suggested earlier, a moment of transformation. In the midst of the ongoing 'liberalization' campaign, cinema is acquiring new skills and technologies, new ideological tasks, and facing new challenges to its established modes of representation. Some cracks in the consensual ideology of the Bombay film are widening and new entrants into the field are bringing new skills and ambitions into play. One of the signs of this changing field of force is the sudden vanguard position achieved by one or two southern film-makers who, unlike their predecessors, have become nationally popular without making films directly in Hindi. A new capital base, the adoption of management techniques, Hollywood styles, and new aesthetic strategies have played a part in this transformation. This emerging segment of the industry (focussed around Mani Ratnam in Madras but also, nationally, consolidating its position slowly through the activities of the Amitabh Bachchan Corporation and other players) promises (or threatens, depending on your viewpoint) to establish the industry on a new basis. A nexus between directors of repute, cultural corporations, managers and other agents is emerging to shore up the achievements of the last few years.

Although behind the new developments, the vast majority of films continue to be made in the old style, the emerging formation is growing in strength and has achieved national visibility. It is bound to have a central role in shaping the future of the industry nationally.

From this complex, multi-faceted, changing field, two films from the early nineties are considered in this chapter, as instances of an ideological shift attempted by the emerging formation as a complement to its still evolving mode of production. They are subjected here to a symptomatic reading, to reveal processes of ideological reform underway in contemporary Indian cinema. The change in question is not in content, but in form, or the content *of* the form. The intention is not to suggest that the work of re-form in these two films is emblematic of the current transition. They represent only one of several different directions taken by the current flurry of experimentation in Indian commercial cinema.[1] However, they are of special interest in the context of the preceding analysis in that they try to constitute a new representational space which includes and overcomes the dominant form. As such they provide a glimpse into a process of transformation that, instead of coming in with *alternative* modes, and trying to establish parallel, competing segments, works on and appropriates the existing mode, bidding to replace the dominant rather than to wrest a space beside it.

We have noted (Chapter 4) how a redundancy of resolutions in the feudal family romance can be read as a symptom of the ideology of formal subsumption at work. To recapitulate, in the 'classical' Hindi film, two resolutions to the narrative crisis would follow in quick succession, one enforced by the traditionally given authority of the exemplary subject(s) of the narrative; the other, following immediately after, and comically redundant in appearance, enforced by the agents of modern law. The laughter evoked by this redundancy should not distract us from the ideological necessity of this doubling. If the first resolution was dictated by long-established narrative conventions, which emerged in a different social context than ours, the second one was necessary in order to assert the final (though not pre-eminent) authority of the law. Here the law has the 'last word' but this is as yet only a formality, an observance of form. The terms and relations of the preceding narrative are not reconstructed in anticipation of the finality of the word of the law; rather, the terms and relations and their modes of combination as already established are merely supplemented by the law's gesture of recognition.

This relationship of complicitous supplementarity was seriously disrupted in the early 1970s when, in the midst of a national crisis, the cultural economy of cinema underwent something of a

[1]Another significant trend has been discussed in Dhareshwar and Niranjana (*JAI* 1996).

transformation. After much groping and fumbling, a new dominant form emerged (Chapters 5 and 6), in which the law was no longer a supplement but the most important stake of narrative conflict and resolution. Whether as agents of the law or as its enemies, the characters around whom these narratives turned were initially defined by their expulsion from the familial utopia of the earlier dominant form. Disinherited, marginalized, and thrown into the world of law and criminality, their stories brought the state to the centre of the narrative, and while not eliminating the feudal family romance, relegated it to a subordinate status, where it sometimes served as an object of nostalgia, a lost object, the desire for whose repossession is the driving force behind the action. In spite of the dramatic entry and consolidation of this new form, however, there was no decisive turn away from the previous form. Rather, they co-existed as irreconcilable or very weakly reconciled forms.

We will have occasion to return to these instances later on, but for the time being the point of this brief recounting is to call attention to the existence of a problematic of form that is at least tendentially independent of the particular narrative content of individual texts. It is now time to turn to the two films in question, to see what kind of work of narrative re-formation they undertake. What follows is not meant to be taken as suggesting some kind of unique and irreversible turn. Indeed, it is possible to identify, throughout the history of post-independence cinema, similar instances of formal innovation which may or may not have proved to be significant. My purpose is to make a case for the existence of the formal problematic as a real and significant issue and to demonstrate that the critique of the ideology of form can give us insights into cultural processes that might otherwise go unnoticed.

Fredric Jameson and, more recently, Slavoj Zizek are among the few critics who have dealt with the question of the ideology of form. Jameson (1981), in his book on the 'political unconscious' has offered one of the most comprehensive accounts of the possibilities held out by Marxist cultural analysis. His theory of interpretation distinguishes between three related horizons or 'concentric frameworks' of textual analysis, each with its own specific object. These three horizons are identified by reference to their field of pertinence, the ground in which the interpretive act specific to these horizons places the textual object. The first, and narrowest, is the ground of political history, the yearly turnover of events; the second horizon is society, in its appearance as 'a constitutive tension and struggle between social classes'; and the third, and most comprehensive, is the ground of history, 'conceived in its vastest sense of the sequences of modes of production and the succession and destiny of the various human social formations' (Jameson 1981: 75). These semantic horizons are not just different contexts in which 'the same' textual object is to be placed—they differ from each other in the way they construe or reconstruct their object, the text.

Of these the third—historical—horizon, is where the idea of the content of the form is elaborated. Transcending the other two horizons, on the historical plane the analytical focus is on the historicity of the unity—the appearance of coherence—effected by a master code whose terms determine the discursive form taken by ideological conflict. It is the concept of mode of production that provides the 'organizing unity' of this horizon. Jameson does not employ this concept in order to develop a typology of cultural forms in which any text can be placed in one or another 'stage' of historical evolution. Such a permanent solution is ruled out by the fact that a mode of production is, strictly speaking, a theoretical rather than an empirical object. In other words, any social formation, as Poulantzas (1978: 22) has argued, is characterized by the structured co-existence in specific combinations, of several modes of production.

Thus, situating the textual object in the ground of mode of production need not result in a typology, since every social formation will have its own specific combination which will have to be discovered, and every text will be 'crisscrossed and intersected by a variety of impulses from contradictory modes of cultural production all at once' (Jameson 1981: 95). The same combination of modes also argues against the assumption of a homogeneous synchronicity or the permanence of the features of a social formation since the interaction of the elements of the combination is always open to change. This point finds support in the Althusserian argument against the empiricist notion of the synchronicity of the present and in favour of a structure where time is itself divided up into a combination of temporalities with a distinct and changeable character of its (the *combination's*) own.

What would be the object of study in such a horizon? In the second horizon, class contradiction was the object, understood in its relational aspect and not class as a group. Here, similarly, we cannot take any particular mode of production as the object. Jameson then proposes 'cultural revolution' as the object and defines it as 'that moment in which the co-existence of various modes of production becomes visibly antagonistic, their contradictions moving to the center of political, social, and historical life' (ibid: 95). However, the task of analysis under this programme will be the study not only of moments of crisis when contradictions attain visibility, but also the 'normal' time when such contradictions are dormant.

Having thus identified the horizon as consisting of the cultural revolution, the next step involves specification of the 'textual object', the equivalent, in this horizon, of the 'symbolic act' in the first and the 'ideologeme' in the second. The text here is conceived as 'a field of force in which the dynamics of sign systems of several distinct modes of production can be registered and apprehended' and this dynamics is termed 'the ideology of form' (ibid: 98). In this horizon, form itself undergoes a re-conceptualization, appearing not as the bearer of content but as itself content. The formal processes, when found in combination, can be understood as 'sedimented content'.

The primacy of form has also been asserted by Slavoj Zizek (1989) in his study of the discovery of the symptom by Marx and Freud. Parallel to the triple division of interpretive labour proposed by Jameson, we find in Freud the distinction between three elements of the dream: the manifest dream-text, the latent dream-content or thought, and unconscious desire. Of these, the third is the most difficult to discover because it is 'on the surface' rather than hidden from view, serving as the mode of articulation of the latent dream-content into the manifest text: the work of the unconscious lies in 'the *form* of the "dream" ', (Zizek 1989: 13). Similarly, Marx goes beyond the classical political economists when he focusses not on some 'secret' hidden behind the commodity form but on 'the secret of this form itself' (ibid: 15). However, Zizek's understanding of the relation between social reality and what he calls the 'ideological fantasy' differs from Jameson's in one important respect. On his reading, it is the fantasy that supports and organizes social reality and gives it coherence. Structured in this way by ideological fantasy, reality itself is a shield against any direct encounter with the Real—the antagonism that resists symbolization. The different social formations, the modes of production, etc. are on this reading, so many ways of organizing reality against the threat of the Real—the fundamental, irresolvable antagonism.

It is against this horizon that I propose to situate the following analysis of two recent films, Rajkumar Santoshi's *Damini* (1993) and Mani Ratnam's *Roja* (1992). It stands to reason that these texts can also be reconstituted as objects within the other two horizons, or even, indeed, approached through a combination of these and other theoretical tools. In fact one of them, *Roja*, has been the object of a number of interpretations which can be construed as employing, either separately or in conjunction, approaches specific to the first two horizons.[2] The ideological analysis I undertake here takes the 'content of the form' as its primary focus. The aim is to discover a new object, a different level of semiosis, with very different, and perhaps more durable, cultural consequences.

The reason for bringing together these films, from two traditions of film-making (Hindi and Tamil) which, while sharing a common history, have also developed along fairly independent trajectories, is simply that they both manifest the same global formal construction which can be represented as follows:

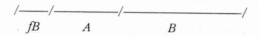

$$fB \qquad A \qquad B$$

where A and B represent the two principal narrative segments, and fB a fragment that is metonymically linked to B but separated from it by segment A; or, to put it differently, segment A is sandwiched between segment B and its brief, enigmatic premonition.

What are the effects produced by this formal organization of the text?

Let us note, first of all, that the transition from fB to A comes as a rupture, a sharp discursive break which leaves something unexplained until segment B retroactively absorbs the enigmatic fragment into its order of narration and thereby infuses it with meaning. Secondly, it is only because of the isolation of fragment B from its proper narrative habitat that we are at all able to identify a second break in the narrative, since the transition from A to B is *relatively* smoother. Thus the fragment serves, in the overall organization of narrative flow, as (1) an enigma which hovers over the action of segment A, a premonition of things to come, of which the figures of the narrative are themselves blissfully ignorant; and (2) a cue which enables us to identify the second break.

It should be obvious by now that this segmental analysis bears little resemblance to the more famous one that is associated with Christian Metz's construction of the 'grande syntagmatique' of the

---

[2]See Niranjana (1994), Chakravarthy and Pandian (1994), Bharucha (1994), and Vasudevan (1994).

units of film language in his search for the master code of cinematic narration, as well as its variants, notably that of Raymond Bellour (Bellour 1986). The Metzian segmentation is intended to provide a general table of all possible units of filmic narration. As such, beyond the basic filmic unit of the *shot* (recognized by the cut that separates one shot from another), the identification of syntagma depends upon the coincidence of shot changes with other indications of shifts in time, space, motif, theme, etc. that form part of the narrative content. As Metz himself put it, 'all the units I have isolated are located *in* the film but in *relation* to the plot' (Metz 1986: 58). In our examples, however, the segmentation is discovered not by scanning the units of narration from the smallest upwards or the other way round, but through a narrative device whose function is to signal the division. As such it has an ideological function that far exceeds its convenience as a way of breaking up the narrative. The segments discovered here signal a *formal* break, the insertion of an 'alien' body into the larger body of the film text, rather than a categorical separation or grammatical punctuation.

As mentioned above, the fragment serves as a warning about the future and enables us to identify the second break. But its narrative function is not limited to these two effects. This becomes clear if we speculate for a moment about the change that might come about if the initial fragment is removed altogether. In terms of narrative content, hardly anything is lost since in both cases, the informational content of the fragment is (i.e., will be) already contained in *B*. What will be lost, however, is the *masking effect* that conceals the break between two narrative trajectories that each have their own resolution. At the threshold that separates *A* from *B*, there is every possibility that the spectator will perceive, not the transition to a new stage of the same narrative, but the cessation of one plot and the beginning of another, entirely different one. Two stories instead of one, which would mean a fragmentation of the narrative. But the fragment, whose meaning remains a mystery until the beginning of *B*, has already served to re-define the action in segment *A* as a *prologue* to what will follow. It has already served to subordinate the action in segment *A* to that of segment *B*.

Thus (3), the organization of the textual sequence, while enabling the recognition of the break, also serves to mask the fragmentation that this would imply. It would then appear that *B* is the dominant segment, the main concern of these films (this is confirmed by the primacy accorded to segment *B* in discussions of *Roja*), but that

they are nevertheless dependent on the subordinate segment *A* for
. . . what? Why do these texts reject the easier solution for achieving
unity, that is to say the exclusive concentration on the action of
segment *B*, or even the subsumption of all narrative elements into
the spatio-temporal framework of narrative *B*? (Mani Ratnam has
been asked this question, in a slightly different form, by an
interviewer.) Why, instead, do they put the very possibility of narrative
unity at risk and *then* try to re-unify the text by deploying *fB* as a
sort of 'secret agent'?

On first glance this textual organization may seem no different
from other familiar instances where a part or all of the narrative is
recollected in flashback. But in those instances, continuity is
established by the flashback device itself, with an individual
character's memory serving as the link. In the two films in question,
the juxtaposition of segments, lacking any such diegetic motivation,
brings into play an authorial intention, an act of deliberate separation
and reorganization of segments that produces effects beyond those
deriving from the plot itself. This is important not because authorial
intention is itself new or unprecedented but because it makes visible
the absence of such a disjuncture, such a supplementary work of
signification, in the dominant narrative film. Not only does it bring
such absence into focus, it also indicates that that dominant form
cannot be re-formed internally, through the substitution or
supplementation of its content by a reflexive layer of meaning. Instead,
the method adopted here can be described as an act of laying siege
to the dominant form, of harnessing its pleasures to another narrative
project and staging, in the process, an ideological rehabilitation of
its narrative elements. The delegation of a fragment to an outer
zone, its separation from its proper metonymic chain, enables the
constitution of a syntagmatic chain marked by arbitrary juxtaposition,
which is its true function. Thus, the potentially metaphoric relation
between the two segments is pre-empted and the first segment is
integrated into a new syntagmatic order as a subordinate element.

Let us take a closer look at the segments themselves. In *Damini*,
the opening fragment shows a woman in a state of absolute terror,
in a nightmarish sequence in which we see her running away from
unseen pursuers and finding herself trapped. Her predicament is
highlighted by the interrogation that a doctor conducts. At first the
questions are hurled at her by a voice located somewhere behind
the camera—the voice of the Other—while the terror-stricken woman
is trapped in a paralysed state in front of the camera, as if by the

camera. For a moment it looks as if we in the audience are the collective Interrogator. The tension created by the invisibility of the interrogator approaches breaking point before we get relief in the form of a reverse shot of the doctor, who now looks benign, and appears to be doing no more than his duty. When the next cut brings the woman back into the frame, her terror has already been redefined as the result of her own unstable mental condition, a hallucination. Our spontaneous identification with her has been deprived of its rationality. The transition from this fragment to segment *A* is startling: from paranoid hallucination and terror we cut to a close-up of the same woman's face whence the camera pulls back to reveal a stage on which she is dancing. From madness to the innocence and romance of youth. The *mise-en-scène* in particular conveys a strong suggestion that the whole sequence *fB* is a nightmare, in which case it would fall within the diegetic framework of the narrative delineation of character psychology. Such an instance can be found in *Rajnigandha* where the heroine has a nightmare in which she dreams of being 'left behind'. However, the difference between these two sequences is that in the latter, we see the dreamer wake up and acknowledge the preceding sequence as an element of her own subjectivity, whereas in *Damini* the contrast between the woman's state of terror and the matter-of-fact look of the doctor and other indications argue against the reading of the sequence as a nightmare. And in any case, subsequent events prove that the fragment was not a representation of a psychic event. The change of scene also, in its abruptness, does not allow any scope for reading a subjective link, since in *A* the woman is introduced to us in a stylized space where her performance is emptied of subjectivity. In both these films, the psychic dimension is far removed from the 'psychological' approach of the middle-class cinema and is inscribed in the objective formal features of the text.

The same contrast between terror and innocence is conveyed by the parallel transition in *Roja*. Here, however, there is no scope for even the suspicion of a subjective link since the two scenes are completely different from each other in content, the only link between them being that they (presumably) succeed each other in time, since the dawn that breaks on the capture of the Kashmiri militant also illuminates the Tamilnad countryside. Fragment *B* in *Roja* shows the capture of the militant by troops combing the forests of Kashmir just before daybreak and cuts to the Tamilnad village, as the sun rises on a beautiful landscape and the heroine is introduced, singing a song about her 'small desires'.

Beginning thus, with a conventional representation of feminine innocence, suggestive of the anticipation of romance and conjugality, segment *A* reaches its own local (and of course, 'incomplete') resolution well before the midway point in the text. In *Damini*, the 'hero' Shekhar (played by Rishi Kapoor) watches the eponymous heroine performing a dance number with Aamir Khan (playing himself and serving as a reminder of the proximity of the 'romance' to follow to the conventions of the world of Bombay cinema) and falls in love, this event witnessed, again in keeping with conventions of film romance, by a male assistant/friend. He meets her again near her home, when she is out shopping, in order to pursue the romance. Here we get a glimpse into the distinction of Damini's character: she is a compulsive truth-teller. A quotation from Gandhi which serves as the epigraph has prepared us to expect an 'experimenter with truth' but at this point in the narrative, Damini, after publicly announcing the dishonesty of a merchant, is shown talking aloud to herself, as Shekhar follows her. This scene pathologizes the truth-telling subject, at least for the moment locating the origin of this compulsive honesty in her hysteria. This is because while in segment *B* her honesty will acquire a central role in the movement of the narrative, in segment *A* the independence of character that this implies would work against the requirements of the conventional family romance. As they walk together, they encounter Damini's father. On the spot, Shekhar asks him for permission to marry his daughter, and Damini expresses surprise but does not resist this abrupt turn. Shekhar leaves, to inform his family of his decision.

Damini's family, consisting of parents and an elder sister, is in crisis. Just before Shekhar's family arrives to 'see' Damini, her sister runs away with a boyfriend. In front of the guests, Damini, against her parents' wishes, reveals this incident and wins Shekhar's father's heart with her honesty. The wedding takes place quickly. In her husband's home, Damini resides in splendour, but as if in captivity until a reconciliation takes place between her and Shekhar. The segment concludes with the symbolic freeing of a caged bird, a present from Shekhar. What we get in segment *A* can be described as a highly compressed version of the feudal family romance which typically ends with the integration of the romantic pair into the politically autonomous order of the propertied joint family.

In *Roja*, the resolution of segment *A* is similar in so far as it also concerns the reconciliation of a couple bound together in matrimony in great haste, but the movement towards this conclusion takes a different route. Roja's marriage to Rishi Kumar (Arvind Swamy) in this segment occurs as a result of an unexpected hitch in an earlier plan by which Rishi was to marry Roja's sister. Rishi's declaration of his liking for Roja is received by the diegetic audience (except the sister) as a serious transgression and Roja is unforgiving even after she has moved to the city with her husband. But when he discloses the fact that it was her sister who rejected him because she wanted to marry another man in order to bring about a reconciliation between their feuding families, Roja is finally reconciled to her marriage.

To turn now briefly to the level of the 'latent content': In both films, the couple has already gone through two stages; first, a conventional union, legitimate in the eyes of society but as yet lacking its own internal unity; second, a moment of clearing of doubts and exchange of assurances which seems to fill the vacuum. But even after this second moment, in spite of the appearance of fullness and harmony, something is left over, an excess that provides the principal motivation for the continuation of the narrative drive. The movement into segment *B* and *its* specific resolution can be described as a movement from reconciliation (a local event) to *rehabilitation* or regrounding of the couple (a global change). To anticipate one of the conclusions of this analysis, the reconciliation is a sufficient resolution for the narrative movement of segment *A* but its 'insufficiency' has been ensured in advance by the arbitrary—and once introduced, compelling, unsettling—glimpse of another world, an alien threat, in fragment *B*.

As segment *B* unfolds, however, it becomes clear that the very self-sufficiency of the narrative of segment *A* is a threat to something else, to the existence of another ground. The closure that 'comes naturally' to the romance narrative cannot be breached, cannot be opened up to the experience of an alien reality (i.e. a reality alien to its conventions, to its congealed ideological discourse) except through the subterfuge of an unexpected juxtaposition which produces for the spectator the effect of incompleteness that will justify the prolongation of the narrative. The difficulty made visible here is a measure of how deeply the conventions and ideology of the dominant film form are entrenched in culture. At the same time, we should remember that the aesthetic project of these films does not simply encounter the resistance of the dominant form in the world at large but itself produces the (foreshortened) image of that resistance and, in the interior of its own body, stages a confrontation with it. This is important to note because it is perfectly possible—and there are many instances of films that try to realize this possibility—to produce a new aesthetic as an *alternative*, occupying another site, addressed to another audience, where the conflict with the dominant is staged, if at all, not inside the limits of the narrative but outside, in a segment of the industry. The desired result of this latter approach is a segmentation of audiences, since such films appeal to the audience's desire for distinction, and promise a pleasure that only the discerning can enjoy.

In *Damini,* it is the Holi celebration scene that clearly marks the beginning of segment *B*, while in *Roja* this is signalled by the transfer of the Kashmir assignment to Rishi in the hospital scene. During the Holi celebrations, the hero's brother and his friends rape the servant-maid Urmi. Damini and later Shekhar are both witnesses to the rape but as an autonomous political unit, the feudal family resolves to administer its own form of justice, which would consist of bailing out the family member by compensating the victim and her family for the loss. Shekhar, in spite of being a witness, goes along with this, but Damini refuses to hide the truth. She insists that the law of the Indian state alone has the legitimate power to render justice in the case. Although she goes along with the family's wishes for a while when they falsely assure her that Urmi is well and being looked after, this compromise is represented as a temporary suspension of her truth-telling character. Telling the truth thus acquires here a very precise definition. In the epigraph, Gandhi speaks of the conscience as an authority that transcends all human laws. The question underlying the truth-teller's dilemma is: tell the truth *to whom?* Who must listen in order for the truth *to have been told?* If honesty is merely a compulsion, then it would be satisfied by any telling, any declaration, anywhere, before anybody. The Gandhian dictum is that the conscience is the authority that insists on the telling of the truth. But who is the addressee of the truth? Unless the addressee is specified, the injunction loses all meaning. And if conscience itself (or God as its objective form, is the addressee, the truth need never be declared in public. For the truth involved in *Damini,* however, the issue is clear: it will not have been told until it is told to the state. Damini's honesty is a hysterical symptom because the problem that it represents for the narrative will not have been solved until the Other who listens to her truth and the demand implied in it, does not appear: 'what is hysteria if not precisely the effect and testimony of a failed interpellation?' (Zizek 1989: 113). It is through the invocation of this larger entity that the narrative succeeds in subverting and delegitimizing the moral-political authority of the state-within-the-state, the politically autonomous *khandaan*.[3] Within this framework, the process of rehabilitation of the nuclear couple is also set in motion, which ends with the couple's relation re-grounded in the state's range of vision, with Shekhar's public declaration of his love for his wife, under the aegis of the law. It is only now that the relation achieves full closure and permanence.

On the formal plane, this segment achieves its effects through a process of combination of filmic genres which ends in a new synthesis. In a Hegelian perspective, *Damini* can be read, on this level, as a synthesis that subsumes the feudal family romance and the post-70s narratives of disidentification with the state. Through the agency of the 'unhoused' female subject, the film breaks open the closed economy of the feudal romance and invokes the state as the sole legitimate authority. The state, however, is itself rotten, as the films of the seventies showed time and again. Like the innumerable rebels who walked out of the system, confronted it as criminals or militant transgressors of the code (in the service of the code), the lawyer Govind (Sunny Deol) lives as a recluse, having quit his profession after the law failed to render justice in a case relating to his wife's death. The casting also reflects the generic combination: Meenakshi Seshadri and Rishi Kapoor as the romantic couple and Sunny Deol (known for his action-hero roles in the genre inaugurated by the Bachchan films) as the disillusioned lawyer. In the seventies films, these heroes pursued their own desires, nostalgic for a lost harmony. Here Govind, who has abandoned all his own battles, enters the picture as a disinterested agent through whom the state will be reformed in order to produce the space where the romantic couple can be rehabilitated. As such on his very first appearance, there is a complete transfer of agency from Damini to Govind. Before this scene, Damini's honesty has led to a situation where she has been confined to a mental hospital by court order. Overhearing a plot to kill her, she runs from the hospital and is pursued by the group of killers. The entire scene conveys an overwhelming sense of helplessness, complete exhaustion, physical as well as subjective, before the relay of agency to Govind is accomplished (and visually represented) when Damini grabs him by the shoulder and pleads for help. (As if to compensate in advance

---

[3]See Pathak and Sundar Rajan (1989) for a discussion of the state-within-the-state as a structural feature of modern India.

for this impending loss of agency, the chase is preceded by a dance—again of ambiguous status: dream or extra-diegetic interpolation?—in which Damini is transformed into the all-powerful Kali.)

Having invoked the Hegelian dialectic, we should note that the synthesis accomplished here is not without remainder. At the end of the narrative, Govind remains excessive. At the same time this surplus leaves no trace of disruption in the closure achieved by the narrative. His role has been that of what Jameson calls the 'vanishing mediator' whose agency enables a transformation that destroys its own grounds for existence.

Turning to *Roja*, we find, not surprisingly, a similar narrative movement. This film has come to be received by the public as a film 'about Kashmiri separatism'. But this aspiration to 'about-ness', i.e. an aesthetic of topicality, is still only tendential, subordinated to the film's preoccupation with the allegory of transpatriarchal migration. One of the stakes of the struggle in which the film is engaged is precisely to wrest a space for staging the present, to break out of the timeless frame of conventional narrative.

Unlike *Damini, Roja* does not stage its narrative within the terms and terrain of the history of film genres, although it is possible to read the village segment as a reprise of narrative films set in the countryside, of which there is a steady output in the cinemas of the south, and which often reaffirm the autonomy and self-sufficiency of the village as a social unit.[4] As we have seen, the village segment ends with the reinforcement of the conventional union by a union of hearts made possible by the late revelation of Rishi's innocence in the matter of Roja's sister's 'betrayal'. That some obstacle nevertheless remains is made clear in the scene following the reconciliation when Rishi, as he prepares to leave for Kashmir, tells Roja to go back to her village even as she insists on accompanying him.

The story that unfolds subsequently is well-known: arriving in Kashmir, Rishi gets down to the work he has been sent there to do, deciphering the enemy's intercepted communications and, in his free time, showing Roja the sights of Kashmir. At the very moment when Roja is sending a message of thanks to her personal village deity through divine courier, her husband is kidnapped by militants. The plot then weaves together the parallel stories of Roja's encounter

[4]See Ravichandran (1997) for a discussion of this genre, known in the industry as 'nativity films'.

with the state and Rishi's with the militants. Finally, when the state agrees, at the risk of losing its advantage in the fight against secessionist militancy, to submit to Roja's demand that her husband's freedom should be purchased by releasing the arrested militant, Rishi, in a parallel move, saves the state's honour by escaping from captivity and, with the help of a reformed militant, returns to Roja, thus preventing the return of the captured leader.

At the conclusion of the second segment, the couple has been rehabilitated, rescued from a situation of terror and re-settled under the aegis of a new patriarchal authority, the state. In both the films, the couples move out of a pastoral world—the village and the genre of family romance—only to encounter terror. From the perspective of this overarching narrative, the perils of the outside world signify above all the acutely felt absence or suspension of Authority. In *Damini*, before the moment of transfer of narrative agency to Govind the lawyer, the terror of the moment derives precisely from the impending encounter with the trauma of what psychoanalysis terms the 'hole in the Symbolic' (Zizek, *For They Know Not* 1991), the terrifying encounter with the truth that there is no Other guaranteeing the consistency of the Symbolic order and the meaningfullness of the world. The image of the woman hounded by merciless killers intensifies the anticipation of the traumatic glimpse into the Real and then, at the very last moment of this intolerable tension, produces, (not out of nowhere but precisely from that one place where bodies have pre-assigned meaning: the star system) a male Rescuer whose provisional function is to fill the hole in the Symbolic until the law is ready to take over. Indeed, the entire scene of the chase can be read as a tendentially tableau-like representation of woman's state of in-betweenness, in a 'no-man's' land between the representatives of a discredited traditional phallic power and an emergent alternative, the patriarchal authority of the modern state. Now the scene of Damini's apotheosis, when she assumes the form of the phallic mother-goddess, which preceded the chase, can be retrospectively read, not only as a compensatory gesture to pave the way for the transfer of narrative agency, but also as a forewarning of the (terrifying) alternative prospect that might arise if the transfer of phallic authority from one patriarchy to another is not accomplished swiftly.

In *Roja*, such a glimpse into an unpleasant alternative to patriarchal authority is woven into the village segment itself. Apart from the hierarchical relation between two formally autonomous units of narrative that is common to both these films, *Roja* is distinguished by the repetition of key narrative and thematic features across the two segments. These two segments can in fact be read as mirror images of each other. A close reading of the first segment is required in order to reveal this parallelism. The comic episode of the man who wanders through the village in search of his lost goats and is ridiculed by a group of women is linked, by the metonymic relay of the goats' cries, to the scene in which, having commandeered the goats, Roja sets up an ambush at a spot that calls to mind similar scenes in dacoit films: a bend in the road, a cluster of rocks providing natural cover. The overt purpose of this trap is to catch a glimpse of the man who is arriving by car to 'see' Roja's sister. Roja's declared intentions are altruistic but for the spectator, the entire scene is so constructed as to invest her glance with a desire of which she herself is as yet unaware or which she is unwilling to acknowledge. The split here between conscious purpose and unconscious desire defines Roja too as a hysteric, creating the space for the narrative of re-interpellation to follow in segment *B*. It is not by coincidence that beginning with this incident, until the moment of his declaration of preference for Roja, Rishi finds himself besieged, a captive of the collective will of the village. Key elements of the second segment are prefigured in the first: abduction (by Roja), captivity, the 'exchange' proposal (Roja's sister wants Rishi to be an object of exchange in an operation that will restore to the family its greater unity by bringing an alienated branch back into the fold), the pre-emption of exchange by a counter-move: escape with another captive (Roja in the first segment, and the 'humanized' militant in the second). As for the last feature, there is, of course, a difference: what Rishi pre-empts is not the reunion desired by the sister, but his own neutralization as a pure object of exchange. His abrupt and scandalous declaration of interest in Roja makes possible the reunification of the family but at the same time successfully breaches its will to autonomy from another flank.

Through these parallels, the film establishes a strong connection between two kinds of resistance to the national-modern project: the anti-national and the pre-modern. The village's autonomy is not the result of a conscious disidentification with the modern state, unlike the separatism of the militants. Nevertheless, the modern state encounters both the pre-modern enclave and the separatist movement as challenges to its will to hegemony. The village threatens Rishi's and the modern state's project (his desire to marry a(ny) village woman symbolizes the state's need to subordinate the village/region/clan, in short the pre-modern, to itself) by imposing its own laws on him—first by attempting to absorb him into its independent social circuit, and again by trying to use him as an instrument for its own purposes. The women of the village are thus figured as castrating, as phallic mothers who jealously guard their domain. Roja demonstrates that she participates in this collective protection of phallic authority when she stages the ambush.

From the detour, this film 'about Kashmir' equips itself with a 'voice'. The autonomous village is a threat because it will not legitimize the state by demanding its existence. It is a structure that enforces its own laws on those who enter its domain. It is not in a dependent position *vis-a-vis* the state. The wedding and the second-stage reconciliation, however, change everything. Henceforth, the village figures as a voice, expressing a demand that only the state can respond to. Voices emerge from the ruins of a structure. This process is completed only when the demanding subject participates in elevating the state to absolute dominance by surrendering her own personal source of phallic power. In the case of *Damini*, this is accomplished when the Gandhian conscience is dissolved into the objective apparatuses of the state and truth-telling is equated with telling the truth to the state. For Roja, this shift involves a transfer of loyalties from her personal village deity (with whom she has a secret liaison, to whom she confesses and who grants her all her wishes) to the state: this is accomplished when she explicitly names the state as her saviour during her meeting with the central minister. This scandalous subordination of religious authority to the secular authority of the state is only one element of a long process: by making unreasonable demands, by fully assuming the position of a hysteric, Roja actively provokes the state to respond to her call. The state, figured as a neutral place of pure altruism, obliges and even indulges the demanding subject.

The gulf between two patriarchal zones is bridged in both films by the figure of the woman. It is through her agency that it becomes possible to allegorize historic transformations. The 'homeless' woman is the bearer of the phallus, which she must pass on to the emerging power. The doubling of the plot in *Roja* enables the allegorization by importing Roja from one domain into the other. The primary antinomy of the plot is subdivided into a series of oppositions, as shown below.

The call that Roja addresses to the state is its most important

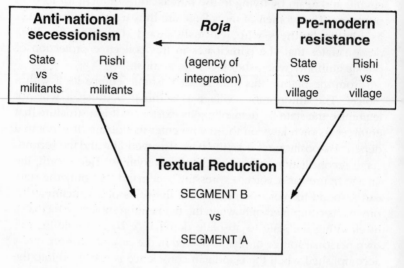

Master antinomy:
State vs autonomous segments

Anti-national secessionism	*Roja*	Pre-modern resistance
State vs militants Rishi vs militants	(agency of integration)	State vs village Rishi vs village

Textual Reduction

SEGMENT B

vs

SEGMENT A

source of legitimacy. As a demanding woman, her role is to provoke the state into existence, to free her of the unbearable narrative function of phallic authority. The relief attendant upon the transfer of this authority to an agent of the law is much more vividly represented in *Damini* but it is there in *Roja* too. In *Damini*, the split that we have noted in *Roja* is neither necessary nor possible. However, both texts manifest the anxiety created by the phallus-in-transit, and in both, the object of the female figures' crusade, not capable of narrative resolution in itself, is subsumed under the more manageable resolution by which their individual desires are fulfilled. Thus Damini's concern for justice, which seemed to exceed her personal interest, is redefined within the terms of her desire for conjugal rehabilitation. Whereas in *Roja* the hysteric's demands are deployed in another scenario of hegemony vs autonomy, in *Damini* the hysteric's demands focus back on the world she left behind. In one, the siege of the pastoral enables the invention of the topical film with a window to reality; in the other, the same assault on the pastoral romance leads to the invention of the modern women's melodrama.

The narrative process thus achieves its completion only when the subject *posits* the state as the external embodiment of its Self. Of course, the state in its objectivity pre-exists the subject's positing of it. But this state of affairs is intolerable, it provokes a movement of narrative resolution precisely because there is a gap between the subject and this external substance, a disjuncture which only arises when, having exited another structure and become 'voice', the subject comes face to face with what Zizek terms the 'pre-Symbolic reality'. The resolution of this crisis is arrived at when the subject 'posits the big Other, makes it exist' (Zizek 1989: 230). This positing is an empty gesture, a purely formal act which transforms what is already there, as external reality, into a subjectively posited, symbolized reality. It is this act that completes the subject's re-grounding: 'subjects are subjects only in so far as they presuppose that the social substance, opposed to them in the form of the State, is already in itself a subject (Monarch) to whom they are subjected' (ibid: 229).

One of the problems that the formal structure of these films brings to the fore is that of narrative enunciation. The fragment *B* causes unease in part by displacing the enunciative function of the narrative, putting this function into crisis precisely by emphasizing it, by foregrounding it as a problem through the conflicting and unexplained juxtaposition of sequences. The fragment hovers menacingly over the pastoral segment *A*, inscribing a lack at its centre, robbing it of its customary naturalness and self-identity. The spectator's attention is thus divided, so that it is impossible to fully identify with the pastoral narrative. In both films, the pastoral segment reinforces this distraction in scenes that demonstrate the split between the principal character's conscious assertions and unconscious desire: Roja directs an altruistic gaze at Rishi but we know that there is more to it; Damini always tells the truth but there is something else that speaks another truth: her hysteria. The narrative stages a 'war of position' (P. Chatterjee 1986: 48–9), robbing the pastoral discourse of its fullness and self-identity, creating the need and the space for another agency that will take on (indeed, has already taken on) the function of enunciation and narrative control. Segment *B* thus appropriates the position of subjective pre-eminence by demonstrating its capacity to commensurate the seemingly incommensurable content of fragment *B* and segment *A*. The resolution of the thematic conflicts—between the state and the militants, between Damini and a bunch of criminals—is secondary to the more important resolution that tackles the dissonance of incommensurate worlds co-existing in the same narrative/national space.

Everything depends on fragment *B*. What exactly does it do? We have seen how it helps to embed the feudal family romance in a new syntagmatic order, a symbolic register in which the principal figure of the romance enters and becomes Subject. Thus in both these films, the imaginary relation between husband and wife as represented at the end of segment *A* is subjected to a disruption in order to break the imaginary fullness and force the subject to enter the Symbolic network, where a final resolution will have to be achieved. This precise allegory of real subsumption has, however, proposed at the very beginning a solution to the disruption that it will enforce. The fragment *B*, as noted above, brings to the fore the question of narrative enunciation. Indeed, in a field (of popular cinema) where the enunciative function was non-existent as a problem, the wilful juxtaposition of *fB* and *A* abruptly produces the problem. In the process, it also posits an enunciator, invisible but not insignificant. The fragment that menaces the pastoral segment thus also contains the supreme ideological reassurance: that there is an Other who directs the unfolding of the new order. Not just the director, Santoshi or Mani Ratnam; nor even the efficient army which captures the terrorist in *Roja's fB* or the benign doctor of *Damini*—but one for whom they are all surrogates: the Other in whom we trust when we trust in capitalism.

It would be premature to say that a new popular film aesthetic is signalled by the work of ideological reform that these films manifest. Nevertheless, one can speculate on the significance of the strategic deployment of form, the struggle waged, within the framework of the text for enunciative pre-eminence: the imperative for this struggle arises from the ambition to occupy the same place that is now occupied by an older dominant form. In this effort, these films may deploy the resources of alternative/middle cinema, but they aspire, not to take the place of the alternative, but to conquer the larger market.

For a more comprehensive picture of the nature of ongoing transformations to emerge, we will need to examine several other dimensions of the process, such as the emergence of culture corporations, signs of monopolistic tendencies, the new bid by Hollywood to expand its market beyond Anglophone frontiers, etc. (Of these one of the most visible, and for speculations about the future of narrative film form, as also extremely important dimensions is that which concerns the film song as a sub-commodity. In this segment of the cultural market, the emergence of music video as an autonomous form, supported by a vast televisual system that is still expanding and experimenting with old and new materials and formats, can be expected to challenge the narrative film's role as the pre-eminent host of musical spectacle, forcing it towards new experiments as a means of survival.) This process can be defined as constituting a re-commodification, or re-invention of the cultural commodity.

Until these processes are clarified, we can only speculate on the significance of stray events like the coincidence of a formal structure in the two films we have chosen for analysis. One speculative proposition of this essay is that the formal structure of these texts is a trace of the work of the 'political unconscious'. In the moment of arrival of real subsumption (that we are living through), capital is breaking out of the impasse of the ruling coalition, emerging into complete dominance. It is no longer necessary to artificially prolong the life of 'tradition', that alleged entity which was modernity's own invention, its preferred rendering of the adversary's profile. The ideology of formal subsumption, which insisted on the difference between the modern and the traditional, and the need to protect that difference, resulted in the protection given to the feudal family romance as the appropriate form of entertainment for the masses. This difference and the apparatuses that are meant to preserve it are no longer sustainable. While the ideologues of formal subsumption stubbornly cling to their superannuated posts, the remaking of Indian ideology goes on apace.

It would nevertheless be a mistake to see these films as simply reflecting the changes that are under way, of being superstructural representations of what is happening in reality. These texts are works of ideology, not mirrors of reality. The changing realities are, no doubt, one of the conditions that make these films possible and necessary, not in order to reflect these conditions, but to construct ideological resolutions for the contradictions that accompany these changes.

Bibliography

Periodicals

Filmfare
India Today
Screen

Articles and Books

Alavi, Hamza. 'Structure of Colonial Formations'. In Utsa Patnaik ed. *Agrarian Relations and Accumulation: The 'Mode of Production' Debate in India*. Bombay: Oxford University Press, 1990.

Alston, A.J. (trans). *The Devotional Poems of Mirabai*. Delhi: Motilal Banarsidass, 1980.

Althusser, Louis. 'Ideology and Ideological State Apparatuses'. *Lenin and Philosophy*. New York: Monthly Review Press, 1971: 127–86.

Armes, Roy. *Patterns of Realism*. South Brunswick: A.B. Barnes and Co., 1971.

Aumont, Jacques. 'The Point of View'. *Quarterly Review of Film and Video* 11: 1–22.

Babb, Lawrence. 'Glancing: Visual Interaction in Hinduism'. *Journal of Anthropological Research* 37.4 (1981): 47–64.

Bahadur, Satish. 'The Context of Indian Film Culture'. Shampa Banerjee ed. *New Indian Cinema*. Delhi: Directorate of Film Festivals, 1982: 7–14.

———. 'The Nehru Years: Indian Film-makers 1945–65'. *Cinewave* 6 (1985): 62–71.

Balibar, Etienne. 'Citizen Subject'. Eduardo Cadava et al. (eds). *Who Comes After the Subject?* New York: Routledge, 1992.

Balibar, Etienne and Immanuel Wallerstein. *Race, Nation, Class: Ambiguous Identities*. London: Verso, 1991.

Banaji, Jairus 'Capitalist Domination and the Small Peasantry'. In Utsa Patnaik ed. *Agrarian Relations and Accumulation: The 'Mode of Production' Debate in India*. Bombay: Oxford University Press, 1990.

Bandhu, Pranjali. *Cinema in Focus: Black and White of Cinema in India*. Thiruvananthapuram: Odyssey, 1992.

Bandyopadhyay, Samik ed. *Indian Cinema: Contemporary Perceptions from the Thirties*. (Selected by Dhruba Gupta and Biren Das Sharma) Jamshedpur: Celluloid Chapter, 1993.

Banerjee, Shampa and Anil Srivastava. *One Hundred Indian Feature Films*. New York: Garland Publishing, 1988.

Banerjee, Sumanta. *In the Wake of Naxalbari*. Calcutta: Subarnarekha, 1980.

————'"Beshya" and the "Babu": Prostitute and Her Clientele in 19th century Bengal'. *Economic and Political Weekly*, 6 November 1993. Vol. 28, No. 45: 2461–7.

Bardhan, Pranab. *The Political Economy of Development in India*. Oxford: Basil Blackwell, 1984.

Barnouw, Erik and S. Krishnaswamy. *Indian Film*. 2nd edn. New York: Oxford University Press, 1980.

Barret, Michele and Mary Macintosh. *The Antisocial Family*. London: Verso, 1990.

Barthes, Roland. *Mythologies*. New York: Hill and Wang, 1973.

————. 'Upon Leaving a Movie Theatre'. Theresa Hak Kyung Cha (ed.). *Apparatus*. New York: Tanam Press, 1980.

Baskaran, S.T. *The Message Bearers: The Nationalist Politics and the Entertainment Media in South India 1880–1945*. Madras: Cre-A, 1981.

————. ed. *The Evans Report on Indian Cinema 1921*. Pune: National Film Archives, nd.

Basu, Shakti and Shuvendu Dasgupta eds. *Film Polemics*. Calcutta: Cine Club, 1992.

Bazin, André. *What is Cinema?* Vol.1. Berkeley: University of California Press, 1967.

Bellour, Raymond. 'Symboliques'. Bellour ed. *Le Cinema Americain: Analyse de Films*. Vol.1. Paris: Flammarion, 1980.

————. 'Segmenting/Analyzing'. Philip Rosen ed. *Narrative Apparatus Ideology*. New York: Columbia University Press, 1986.

Benjamin, Walter. 'The Work of Art in the Age of Mechanical Reproduction'. *Illuminations*. New York: Schocken, 1969: 217–52.

Bharucha, Rustom. 'On the Border of Fascism: Manufacture of Consent in *Roja*'. *Economic and Political Weekly*, 4 June 1994.

Bhowmik, Someswar. 'The State of the Indian Film Industry'. *Splice* 2 (July 1986): 31–7.

Bordieu, Pierre. *The Field of Cultural Production*. New York: Columbia University Press, 1993.

Bordwell, David, Janet Staiger and Kristin Thompson. *The Classical Hollywood Cinema: Film Style and Mode of Production to 1960*. New York: Columbia University Press, 1985.

Brooks, Peter. *The Melodramatic Imagination*. New Haven: Yale University Press, 1976.

Burch, Noel. *To the Distant Observer: Form and Meaning in the Japanese Cinema*. Berkeley: University of California Press, 1979.

Chakravarty, Sukhamoy. *Development Planning: The Indian Experience*. Oxford: Clarendon Press, 1987.

Chakravarty, Sumita.S. *National Identity in Indian Popular Cinema, 1947–1987*. Austin: University of Texas Press, 1993.

Chakravarthy, Venkatesh and M.S.S. Pandian. 'More on Roja'. *Economic and Political Weekly*, 12 March 1994.

Chatterjee, Partha. *Nationalist Thought and the Colonial World: A Derivative Discourse*. Delhi: Oxford University Press, 1986.

———. *The Nation and Its Fragments: Colonial and Postcolonial Histories*. Princeton: Princeton University Press, 1993.

Chatterji, Gayatri. *Awara*. New Delhi: Wiley Eastern, 1993.

Comolli, Jean-Louis. 'Technology and Ideology'. Bill Nichols (ed.). *Movies and Methods*. Vol.2. Calcutta: Seagull, 1993.

Cook, David A. *A History of Narrative Film*. 2nd edn. New York: W.W. Norton, 1990.

Cook, Pam. 'Melodrama and the Women's Picture'. Marcia Landy (ed.). *Imitations of Life: A Reader on Film and Television Melodrama*. Detroit: Wayne State University Press, 1991.

Dale, Stephen F. 'The Poetry and Autobiography of the *Babur-nama*'. *Journal of Asian Studies* 55.3 (August 1996): 635–64.

Dasgupta, Biplab. *The Naxalite Movement*. Bombay: Allied Publishers, 1974.

Dasgupta, Chidananda. *Talking about Films*. New Delhi: Orient Longman, 1981.

———. *The Painted Face: Studies in India's Popular Cinema*. New Delhi: Roli Books, 1991.

Deshpande, Satish. 'Imagined Economies: Styles of Nation-Building in 20th Century India'. *Journal of Arts and Ideas.* 25–6 (December 1993): 5–36.

Dhareshwar, Vivek. 'Our Time': History, Sovereignty and Politics'. *Economic and Political Weekly* (11 February 1995): 317–24.

———— 'The Postcolonial in the Postmodern; or, the Political after Modernity ' *Economic and Political Weekly* 30. 30 (29 July 1995).

Dhareshwar, Vivek and Tejaswini Niranjana. '*Kaadalan* and the Politics of Resignification: Fashion, Violence and the Body.' *Journal of Arts and Ideas* 29 (January 1996): 5–26.

Dickey, Sara. *Cinema and the Urban Poor in South India.* Cambridge: Cambridge University Press, 1993.

Dickinson, Margaret and Sarah Street. *Cinema and State: The Film Industry and the British Government, 1927–84.* London: British Film Institute, 1985.

Dissanayake, Wimal ed. *Melodrama and Asian Cinema.* Cambridge: Cambridge University Press, 1993.

Dissanayake, Wimal and Malti Sahai. *Sholay: A Cultural Reading.* New Delhi: Wiley Eastern, 1992.

Doane, Mary Ann. *The Desire to Desire: The Woman's Film of the 1940s.* Bloomington: Indiana University Press, 1987.

Dobb, Maurice. *Papers on Capitalism, Development and Planning.* London: Routledge and Kegan Paul, 1967.

Donzelot, Jacques. *The Policing of Families.* London: Hutchinson, 1980.

Doraiswamy, Rashmi. 'Les Genres dans le Cinema Indien'. CinemAction 68 (1993): 70–9.

Doty, Alexander. 'Music Sells Movies: (Re)new(ed) Conservatism in Film Marketing'. *Wide Angle* 10.2: 70–9.

Dyer, Richards. *Stars.* London: British Film Institute, 1987.

————'Charisma.' Christine Gledhill (ed.) *Stardom: Industry of Desire.* London: Routledge, 1991: 57–9.

Eck, Diana. *Darsan: Seeing the Divine Image in India.* Chambersburg: Anima Books, 1981.

Ellis, John. 'Stars as a Cinematic Phenomenon'. Gerald Mast et al. (eds) *Film Theory and Criticism.* New York: Oxford University Press, 1992.

Elsaesser, Thomas. 'Tales of Sound and Fury'. In Marcia Landy (ed.) *Imitations of Life: A Reader on Film and Television Melodrama.* Detroit, Wayne State University Press, 1991.

Ermarth, Elizabeth Deeds. *Realism and Consensus in the English Novel.* Princeton: Princeton University Press, 1983.

Fanon, Frantz. *A Dying Colonialism*. New York: Grove Press, 1965.

Fazalbhoy, Y.A. *The Indian Film: A Review*. Bombay: Bombay Radio Press, nd.

Feuer, Jane. *The Hollywood Musical*. Bloomington: Indiana University Press, 1982.

Foucault, Michel. 'The Subject and Power'. In Hubert L. Dreyfus and Paul Rabinow, *Michel Foucault: Beyond Structuralism and Hermeneutics*. Brighton: Harvester Press,1982.

————. *The History of Sexuality: An Introduction*. London: Penguin, 1987.

Frankel, Francine R. *India's Political Economy, 1947–77: The Gradual Revolution*. Princeton, Princeton University Press, 1978.

Gallieni. *Gallieni Pacificateur*. Paris: Presses Universitaires de France, 1949.

Gandhy, Behroze and Rosie Thomas. 'Three Indian Film Stars'. Christine Gledhill ed. *Stardom: Industry and Desire*. London: Routledge, 1991.

Gargi, Balwant. *Theatre in India*. New York: Theatre Arts Books, 1962.

Ghatak, Ritwick. *Cinema and I*. Calcutta: Rupa, 1987.

Gledhill, Christine ed. *Home is Where the Heart Is: Studies in Melodrama and the Woman's Film*. London: British Film Institute, 1987.

Gopal, Sarvepalli. *Jawaharlal Nehru: A Biography* 1956–64. Vol. 3. Delhi: Oxford University Press, 1984.

Gramsci, Antonio. *Selections from Prison Notebooks*. Quintin Hoare and Geoffrey Nowell Smith (eds). London: Lawrence and Wishart, 1971.

————. *Selections from Cultural Writings*. David Forgacs and Geoffrey Nowell Smith (eds). London: Lawrence and Wishart, 1985.

Grant, Barry Keith. *Film Genre Reader*. Austin: University of Texas Press, 1986.

Grimsted, David. *Melodrama Unveiled: American Theatre and Culture 1800–50*. Chicago: University of Chicago Press, 1968.

Grosrichard, Alain. *Structure du Serail: La Fiction du Despotisme Asiatique dans l'Occident Classique*. Paris: Editions du Seuil, 1979.

Guha, Ranajit. 'Dominance Without Hegemony and Its Historiography' Ranajit Guha ed. *Subaltern Studies* Vol.6. Delhi: Oxford University Press, 1989.

Hegel, G.W.F. *The Philosophy of Right*. Trans. T.M. Knox. London: Oxford University Press, 1967.

Higson, Andrew. 'The Concept of National Cinema'. *Screen*, 30.4 (1989): 36–46.

Horkheimer, Max and Theodor W. Adorno. *Dialectic of Enlightenment*. New York: Continuum, 1988.

Huyssen, Andreas. *After the Great Divide*. Bloomington: Indiana University Press, 1986.

Hyslop, Gabrielle. 'Pixerecourt and the French Melodrama Debate: Instructing Boulevard Theatre Audiences.' *Melodrama*. Cambridge: Cambridge University Press, 1992.

Jain, Rikhab Dass. *The Economic Aspects of the Film Industry in India*. Delhi: Atma Ram, 1960.

Jameson, Fredric. *The Political Unconscious: Narrative as a Socially Symbolic Act*. Ithaca: Cornell University Press, 1981.

————. 'World Literature in the Age of Multinational Capitalism'. Koelb and Lokke (eds). *The Current in Criticism*. West Lafayette, Indiana: Purdue University Press, 1987.

————. 'Cognitive Mapping'. Cary Nelson and Larry Grosberg (eds). *Marxism and the Interpretation of Culture*. Urbana: University of Illinois Press, 1988.

Johnson, Richard. 'What is Cultural Studies Anyway?' *Social Text* 6 (Winter 1986/87): 38–80.

Kak, Siddharta. 'Commercial Cinema: Breezes of Change?' *Cinema Vision India* 1.3 (July 1980): 25–7.

Kakar, Sudhir. 'The Ties that Bind: Family Relationships in the Mythology of Hindi Cinema'. *India International Centre Quarterly*. 8.1 (March 1980): 11–21.

————. *Intimate Relations: Exploring Indian Sexuality*. New Delhi: Penguin, 1989.

Kant, Immanuel. *Perpetual Peace and Other Essays*. Trans. Ted Humphrey. Indianapolis: Hackett, 1983.

Kaplan, E. Ann. *Motherhood and Representation: The Mother in Popular Culture and Melodrama*. New York: Routledge, 1992.

————. 'Melodrama/Subjectivity/Ideology: Western Melodrama Theories and Their Relevance to Recent Chinese Cinema'. Wimal Dissanayake ed. *Melodrama and Asian Cinema*. Cambridge: Cambridge University Press, 1993.

Kapur, Anuradha. 'The Representation of Gods and Heroes: Parsi Mythological Drama of the Early Twentieth Century'. *Journal of Arts and Ideas* 23/24 (January 1993): 85–107.

Kapur, Geeta. 'Mythic Material in Indian Cinema'. *Journal of Arts and Ideas* 14/15 (1987): 79–108.

Karanjia, B.K. 'The State's Responsibility to Cinema'. *Cinema in India* (July–September 1987): 38–41.

Karnad, Girish. 'Natakakara Girish Karnadaru: Ondu Sahitya Charche'. *Rujuvathu* 37 (October 1994): 37–58.

Kaviraj, Sudipta. 'Indira Gandhi and Indian Politics'. *Economic and Political Weekly*. 21.38/39 (September 20–7: 1986): 1697–708.

———. 'A Critique of the Passive Revolution'. *Economic and Political Weekly*. Special Number (November 1988): 2429–43.

Kilgarriff, Michael ed. *The Golden Age of Melodrama: Twelve 19th Century Melodramas*. London: Wolfe Publishing Ltd., 1974.

Kuhn, Annette. 'Women's Genres: Melodrama, Soap Opera and Theory'. Christine Gledhill ed. *Home is Where the Heart Is*. London: British Film Institute, 1987.

Landy, Marcia. *British Genres: Cinema and Society, 1930–60*. Princeton: Princeton University Press, 1991.

Landy, Marcia ed. *Imitations of Life: A Reader on Film and Television Melodrama*. Detroit: Wayne State University Press, 1991.

Larsen, Neil. *Modernism and Hegemony: A Materialist Critique of Aesthetic Agencies*. Minneapolis: University of Minnesota Press, 1990.

Levin, Harry. 'What is Realism?' *Contexts of Criticism*. New York: Atheneum, 1963.

MacCabe, Colin. *Theoretical Essays: Film, Linguistics, Literature*. Manchester: Manchester University Press, 1985.

Marx, Karl. *Capital*. Vol.1. trans. Ben Fowkes. New York: Vintage, 1977.

———. *The German Ideology*. New York: International, 1986.

Mast, Gerald et al. (eds). *Film Theory and Criticism*. New York: Oxford University Press, 1992.

Mayne, Judith. *Cinema and Spectatorship*. London: Routledge, 1993.

McKeon, Michael. *The Origins of the English Novel 1400–1700*. Baltimore: Johns Hopkins, 1987.

Metz, Christian. 'The Imaginary Signifer'. Philip Rosen ed. *Narrative Apparatus Ideology*. New York: Columbia University Press, 1986: 244–78.

Mirza, Saeed. 'How Far Can a Film-maker Go?' *Cinema Vision India* 1.3 (July 1980): 72.

Misra, Vijay. 'Towards a Theoretical Critique of Bombay Cinema'. *Screen* 26.3/4 (May–August 1985): 133–46.

———. 'Filmic Narrative: Text and Transformation in Bombay Cinema'. *Continuum* 2.1 (1988–9): 9–43.

Mulvey, Laura. 'Visual Pleasure and Narrative Cinema'. *Screen* 16.3 (1975): 6–18.

Nandy, Ashish. 'An Intelligent Critic's Guide to Indian Cinema'. In three parts. *Deep Focus* 1988–9: 1.1. pp. 68–72; 1.2, pp. 53–60; 1.3 pp. 58–61.

Neale, Steve. *Genre.* London: British Film Institute, 1980.

Nehru, Jawaharlal. 'The Basic Approach'. In S.Gopal ed. *Jawaharlal Nehru: An Anthology.* Delhi: Oxford University Press, 1983.

Nichols, Bill ed. *Movies and Methods.* 2 Vols. Calcutta: Seagull, 1993.

Niranjana, Tejaswini. 'Integrating whose Nation? Tourists and Terrorists in *Roja'. Economic and Political Weekly* 15 (January 1994): 79–82.

O'Flaherty, Wendy Doniger. 'The Mythological in Disguise: An Analysis of *Karz'. India International Centre Quarterly* 8.1 (March 1980): 23–9.

Oommen, M.A. and K.V. Joseph. *Economics of Indian Cinema.* New Delhi: Oxford and IBH Publishing Co., 1991.

Pandian, M.S.S. *The Image Trap.* Delhi: Sage, 1992.

Pateman, Carol. *The Sexual Contract.* Stanford: Stanford University Press, 1988.

Pathak, Zakia and Rajeswari Sundar Rajan. 'Shahbano', *Signs: Journal of Women in Culture and Society* 14.3 (Spring 1989): 558–82.

Pendakur, Manjunath. 'The Indian Film Industry'. In John A. Lent, *The Asian Film Industry.* London: Christopher Helm, 1990.

Pfleiderer, Beatrix and Lothar Lutze, *The Hindi Film: Agent and Re-agent of Cultural Change.* New Delhi: Manohar, 1985.

Phalke, D.G. 'Swadeshi Moving Pictures'. Research and Trans. Narmada S. Shahane. *Continuum* 2.1 (1988/89); 51–73. Previously published in N. Shahane and Satish Bahadur (eds). *Phalke Centenary Volume,* 1971.

Poulantzas, Nicos. *Classes in Contemporary Capitalism.* London: Verso, 1978.

Rajadhyaksha, Ashish. 'The Phalke Era: Conflict of Traditional Form and Modern Technology'. *Journal of Arts and Ideas* 14/15 (1987): 47–78.

―――. 'Neo–traditionalism: Film as Popular Art in India'. *Framework* 32/33 (1987): 20–67.

―――. 'The Epic Melodrama: Themes of Nationality in Indian Cinema'. *Journal of Arts and Ideas* 25/26 (December 1993): 55–70.

Rajadhyaksha, Ashish and Paul Willemen (eds). *Encyclopaedia of Indian Cinema.* New Delhi, Oxford University Press, 1995.

Ranga Rao, V.A.K. 'Cultural Dissemination Through Cinema'. *Indian Cinema 1990.* New Delhi: Directorate of Film Festivals, 1991.

Ravichandran K. 'Karma Yoga and the Middle Class: Recasting Identities in *Thevar Magan'.* Paper presented at Cultural Studies Workshop, Gwalior

1–5 February 1997, organized by the Centre for Studies in Social Sciences, Calcutta.

Ray, Satyajit. *Our Films Their Films*. Hyderabad: Orient Longman, 1992.

Report of the Enquiry Committee on Film Censorship. New Delhi: Government of India, 1969.

Report of the Film Enquiry Committee. New Delhi: Government of India Press, 1951.

Report of the Indian Cinematograph Committee 1927–28. Madras: Government Press, 1928.

Report of the Indian Film Industry's Mission to Europe and America. Bombay: Avanti Prakashan, nd.

Report of the Working Group on National Film Policy. New Delhi: Government of India, 1980.

Rhode, Eric. *A History of the Cinema from its Origins to 1970*. London: Penguin, 1978.

Rizvi, Ahmed and Parag R. Amlad. 'Is There a New Cinema Movement?' *Cinema Vision India* 1.3 (July 1980).

Rosen, Philip. *Narrative Apparatus Ideology*. New York: Columbia University Press, 1986.

Rossellini, Roberto. 'Ten Years of Cinema'. David Overbey (ed.). *Springtime in Italy: A Reader on Neo-realism*. Hamden: Conn.: Archon Books, 1979.

Rulfo, Juan. *The Burning Plain and Other Stories*. Trans. George D. Schade. Austin: University of Texas Press, 1967.

Sen, Mrinal. *Views on Cinema*. Calcutta: Ishan, 1977.

Shah, Panna. *The Indian Film* (1950). Westport, Conn.: Greenwood Press, 1981 (reprint).

Shahani, Kumar. 'The Media Police'. *Framework* 30/31, pp. 87–90.

Singer, Irving. *The Nature of Love*. Vol.2: *Courtly and Romantic*. Chicago: University of Chicago Press, 1984.

Spivak, Gayatri Chakravorty. 'Subaltern Studies: Deconstructing Historiography'. *In Other Worlds*. New York: Routledge, 1988.

Srinivas, S.V. 'Devotion and Difference in Fan Activity'. *Journal of Arts and Ideas* 29 (January 1996): 66–83.

Staiger, Janet. 'The Hollywood Mode of Production to 1930' and 'The Hollywood Mode of Production, 1930–60'. Bordwell et al. *The Classical Hollywood Cinema: Film Style and Mode of Production to 1960*. New York: Columbia University Press, 1985.

Studlar, Gaylyn. 'Masochism and the Perverse Pleasures of the Cinema '

Gerald Mast et al. (eds). *Film Theory and Criticism*. New York: Oxford University Press, 1992.

Thomas, Rosie. 'Indian Cinema: Pleasures and Popularity'. *Screen* 26.3/4 (May–August 1985): 116–31.

———. 'Mythologies and Modern India'. William Luhr (ed.). *World Cinema Since 1945*. New York: Ungar, 1987.

Turim, Maureen. 'Psyches, Ideologies and Melodrama: The United States and Japan'. Wimal Dissanayake ed. *Melodrama and Asian Cinema*. Cambridge: Cambridge University Press, 1993.

Valicha, Kishore. *The Moving Image*. Bombay: Orient Longman, 1988.

Vanaik, Achin. *The Painful Transition*. London: Verso, 1990.

Vasudev, Aruna. *The New Indian Cinema*. Delhi: Macmillan, 1986.

Vasudevan, Ravi. 'The Melodramatic Mode and the Commercial Hindi Cinema: Notes on Film History, Narrative and Performance in the 1950s'. *Screen* 30.3 (Summer 1989): 29–50.

———. 'The Cultural Space of a Film Narrative: Interpreting *Kismet* (Bombay Talkies, 1943)', *Indian Economic and Social History Review* 28.2 (April–June 1991): 171–85.

———. 'Shifting Codes, Dissolving Identities: The Hindi Social Film of the 1950s as Popular Culture'. *Journal of Arts and Ideas* 23/24 (January 1993): 51–84.

———. 'Other Voices: *Roja* Against the Grain'. *Seminar* 423 (November 1994): 43–7.

Willemen, Paul. 'Negotiating the Transition to Capitalism: The Case of *Andaz*'. Wimal Dissanayake ed. *Melodrama and Asian Cinema*. Cambridge: Cambridge University Press, 1993.

Williams, Christopher ed. *Realism and the Cinema*. London: Routledge and Kegan Paul, 1980.

Wolfe, Charles ed. *Meet John Doe*. New Brunswick: Rutgers University Press, 1989.

Zizek, Slavoj. *The Sublime Object of Ideology*. London: Verso, 1989.

———. *Looking Awry: An Introduction to Jacques Lacan Through Popular Culture*. Cambridge: MIT Press, 1991.

———. *For They Know Not What They Do: Enjoyment as a Political Factor*. London: Verso, 1991.

Index